The Structure of
American Economy
1919-1939

The Structure of American Economy 1919-1939

AN EMPIRICAL APPLICATION OF
EQUILIBRIUM ANALYSIS

SECOND EDITION ENLARGED

Wassily W. Leontief

 International Arts and Sciences Press, Inc., White Plains, N.Y.

To

MY FATHER AND MOTHER

PREFACE

THE FIRST EDITION of this book appeared—under the title *The Structure of American Economy, 1919–1929*—in 1941, and the second enlarged edition—of which this is a reprint—in 1951. Its first two chapters, presenting the first input-output tables of the U.S. economy and their interpretation in terms of a system of linear equations, were originally published in the *Review of Economics and Statistics* in 1937–38.

The first input-output table—that of the USA—was compiled in terms of 42 sectors, but for purposes of analytical computations the size of the system had to be reduced, through aggregation, to only ten sectors. Twenty years had to pass before the introduction of the first large-scale electronic computer removed, for all practical purposes, limits on the size of systems that can be handled computationally. The first multiregional worldwide input-output system, to be published simultaneously with this volume, contains some 2,600 equations.

Growth, naturally, was accompanied by progressive differentiation: The productive apparatus of advanced industrial economies is now often described in terms of as many as 600 distinct sectors and at the same time the spatial distribution of economic activities is being refined by the introduction of multiregional input-output structures. Still more significant is the gradual widening and deepening both of the data base and of the analytical structure that expands the application of the same methodological approach beyond the circumscribed limits of the modern market economy. Through inclusion of the primary resources base, on the one hand, and pollution generation and abatement, on the other, as well as such activities as health care and education, the framework of some of the recently designed input-output systems comprises not only narrowly defined economic processes but the entire natural and social environment in which all human activities in both the simple and the advanced industrialized societies must necessarily be embedded.

Some of the theoretical themes that have been taken up

with renewed vigor in recent years—such as technological change or the treatment of households not as an external focus but as an integral part of the economic system—are articulated in the pages of this volume more incisively than in most of the later writing devoted to practical short-run applications of the input-output methodology.

W.W.L.

NEW YORK, N.Y.
MAY 1976

ACKNOWLEDGMENTS

PRELIMINARY RESEARCH for this investigation was concluded in 1931 while I was holding the position of Research Associate in the National Bureau of Economic Research. The actual statistical analysis was begun the next year and with the generous support from the Harvard Committee on Research in the Social Sciences was conducted without interruption till 1939. The Committee also made possible the original publication of this volume.

Maynard Heins, Orville McDiarmid, and Louis Weiner were to a large extent responsible for the difficult task of gathering and organizing the basic statistical material. Whatever deficiencies may be discovered in this part of the work—and doubtless there are many—they certainly are not due to any lack of workmanship or technical ingenuity on the part of these skilled statisticians.

Elizabeth W. Gilboy, Secretary of the Committee on Research in the Social Sciences, as well as other members of its staff, have given me most valuable help through all the stages of the work up to the reading of the last proof sheets of the first edition.

The text of the original 1941 edition of *The Structure of American Economy 1919–1929* is reproduced in Parts I, II, and III of this volume without any changes.

Part IV comprises the four additional chapters. Three of them were first published in 1944 and 1946 in the *Quarterly Journal of Economics*. The last chapter was first published in the 1949 Proceedings volume of the *American Economic Review*.

W.W.L.

NEW YORK, N.Y.
MAY 1976

CONTENTS

PART III

PART IV

TABLES

In addition to the tables listed above, fourteen basic tables will be found in Appendix III.

CHARTS

FIGURES

THE STRUCTURE OF AMERICAN ECONOMY

1919–1939

Les sciences qui admettent le calcul ont donc la même base de certitude que les autres. Cette certitude, il est vrai, peut s'étendre par le calcul sur les quantités qui ne peuvent être supputées que par le calcul, et dans ce cas il est toujours en lui-même essentiellement infaillible, c'est-à-dire qu'il présente toujours infailliblement et conséquemment ou des erreurs ou des réalités, selon qu'on l'applique à des réalités ou a des erreurs. D'où suit que, dans la recherche de la vérité par le calcul, toute la certitude est dans l'évidence des données.

FRANÇOIS QUESNAY, *Premier problème économique*

INTRODUCTION

THIS MODEST VOLUME describes an attempt to apply the economic theory of general equilibrium — or better, general interdependence — to an empirical study of interrelations among the different parts of a national economy as revealed through covariations of prices, outputs, investments, and incomes.

The ultimate aim of such study needs no special justification. Layman and professional economist alike, practical planner and the subjects of his regulative activities, all are equally aware of the existence of some kind of interconnection between even the remotest parts of a national economy. The presence of these invisible but nevertheless very real ties can be observed whenever expanded automobile sales in New York City increase the demand for groceries in Detroit; it is dramatically demonstrated when the sudden shutdown of the Pennsylvania coal mines paralyzes the textile mills in New England, and it reasserts itself with relentless regularity in alternative ups and downs of business cycles.

To interpret the nature of these highly involved interrelationships, economists have developed many abstract schemes. Some of these theories are so simple that even the man on the street is expected to follow the argument and accept the conclusions; others are so complicated that even among professional economists few can appreciate their technical intricacies.

But, complicated or simple, most of these schemes are tentative maps of unexplored areas. Whatever empirical material they contain is gathered mostly by common observations, i.e., on hearsay. Infrequently, the supposedly simple factual statement of this' kind becomes the subject of heated statistical controversies, with the responsible theorist keeping himself modestly on the sidelines.

While theorists were improving their blueprints, empiricists approached the problem of general interdependence from the other end — by statistical analysis of detailed factual observations. Their analysis usually begins with the study of simple correlations between a few prices and quantities. It is gradually expanded by the inclusion of additional variables in each correlation group and at the same time by an increase in the number of the separate samples.

Few of these statistical studies are entirely devoid of theoretical background. But the underlying conceptual schemes are for the most part elementary, and, what is more important, many statistical economists still seem to believe that a string of partial correlations, if spun sufficiently long, can in some way represent a system of general interdependence. They ignore the fact that no stable analytical structure can possibly be built piecemeal without a predesigned plan and sturdy theoretical scaffolding.

This present inquiry like any other attempt at realistic analysis, carries the marks of a compromise between unrestricted generalities of purely theoretical reasoning and the practical limitations of empirical fact finding. A pure theorist may find the statistical part of this study unnecessarily elaborate, the economic statistician will have good reason to complain of the abstract intricacies of its theoretical groundwork.

The whole investigation is subdivided into three distinct, although closely interrelated, tasks: gathering and arrangement of the necessary statistical material; formulation of an appropriate theoretical scheme; the application of the previously developed theoretical devices to analysis of empirical data.

Part I of this inquiry presents a factual statistical description of the structure of the American economy. The two basic statistical tables, 5 and 6, show the actual flow of commodities and services from one industry to another, from industries to households, and from households to industries.

The principle of this method of statistical description is rather simple. Each "industry" (including households) is treated as a single accounting entity — comparable to a "country" in official foreign-trade statistics — with sales entered on one side of its trading account and purchases on the other. As in the trade between countries, the sales of one industry are the purchases of another. Entering the sales and purchase accounts of all the separate industries in one large table we get a comprehensive view of the structure of the national economy as a whole.

Sections 7–10 are devoted to the explanation and interpretation of these statistical tables. Special problems of industrial classification and definitions of the national income, of saving and investment, are discussed here in detail. Some of the more controversial questions — such as the treatment of undistributed corporate surpluses, imputation of the transportation costs, etc. — are also taken up in connection with the general discussion of the fundamental accounting scheme.

The information thus gathered is designed to supply the factual background for subsequent analysis of a rather specialized kind. The quantitative data contained in the two main tables can easily, however, be utilized for economic inquiries of quite different types. The general requirements of such alternative uses were kept in mind in the preparation and presentation of this statistical material.

Part II gives a concise formulation of the economic theory of general interdependence (general equilibrium). The discussion is limited to statements of the fundamental assumptions and derivation of important quantitative relationships. Controversy is avoided. The theoretical picture of the economic system presented in these chapters is admittedly simplified. No abstract discussion, however, can possibly prove or disprove our contention that the approximation is accurate enough to be of empirical significance.

In Part III, the analytical tools developed in the course of the previous theoretical inquiry are put to work. Empirical data summarized in the statistical tables of Part I are used as raw material. We show how the outputs of various industries and the prices of their products would have reacted to different types of primary changes, i.e., changes in the technical productivity of one or another industry, variations in the willingness to invest capital into one or another branch of production, or shifts in the willingness to save by the income receivers.

These price and output reactions are empirical insofar as they are computed from actual statistical data; they are also theoretical insofar as the computation formulae are deduced (in Part II) from abstract theoretical assumptions. In this respect the numerical results obtained are comparable to elasticities derived by methods of conventional statistical supply and demand analysis. These latter are also derived from actual (price and quantity) data, their significance, however, is also conditioned by the validity of a particular theory; in this case it is the Marshallian or neo-classical theory of supply and demand.

Both our computed price and output reactions and the usual statistical supply and demand curves answer hypothetical questions. A statistical demand curve for wheat shows for example how the price and the quantity of this commodity would vary had its supply been changed with the demand conditions remaining the same as before. Similarly the output reaction of the metal industry to an increase in the technical productivity of coal mining — as presented in Part III, Section 6 — shows what would happen to the output of metals in response to a shift in the productivity of the coal industry, provided the technical conditions of production in all other industries remained the same as before. From such partial reactions it is possible to determine also the combined effect of two or more simultaneous primary changes.

It is hardly necessary to say that the similarity between our price and quantity reactions and the conventional statistical supply and demand curves does not extend beyond this purely formal analogy.

The direction of the inquiry is reversed in Sections 7 and 8. If price and quantity changes can be predicted from primary structural shifts, is it not possible to compute these latter from the known combined price and quantity variations?

The answer to this question is more complex than might be expected; with some additional theoretical qualifications, however, it can be given in the affirmative. Thus we obtain a series of indices showing the structural changes which marked the development of the American economic system in the crucial decade of 1919–29. For purposes of a final cross check these indices are used for an indirect roundabout computation of the corresponding price and output indices. A comparison of the resulting figures with the actual price and output statistics for the same years 1919 and 1929 reveals a satisfactory agreement.

Of the last two sections, one deals with the question of industrial classification and the other with the general repercussion of changes in the consumption pattern.

In an introductory summary of this kind it is customary to present a set of general conclusions. The main findings of the following inquiry do not lend themselves to such a brief description. They are essentially concrete, not abstract, and because of this, particular and not general.[1]

---

[1] The theoretical Part II and a few chapters of Part III contain a certain amount of mathematical analysis. A reader acquainted with partial differentiation and with elementary theory of determinants and linear equations will have no difficulty in following the argument in detail. *Mathematical Analysis for Economists* by R. G. D. Allen (Macmillan, 1939), ch. XIII, sections 1–6, and ch. XVIII, sections 1–6, could supply all the mathematical background required. But even omitting a few of the more intricate steps of mathematical deduction, the reader will be able to discern the main outlines of the general discussion.

PART I

PART I

QUANTITATIVE INPUT AND OUTPUT RELATIONS IN THE ECONOMIC SYSTEM OF THE UNITED STATES IN 1919 AND 1929

THE STATISTICAL STUDY presented in the following pages may be best defined as an attempt to construct, on the basis of available statistical materials, a *Tableau Économique* of the United States for 1919 and 1929.

One hundred and fifty years ago, when Quesnay first published his famous schema, his contemporaries and disciples acclaimed it as the greatest discovery since Newton's laws. The idea of general interdependence among the various parts of the economic system has become by now the very foundation of economic analysis. Yet, when it comes to the practical application of this theoretical tool, modern economists must rely exactly as Quesnay did upon fictitious numerical examples. What would be the present state of the theory and policy of international trade if, instead of actual balances of foreign trade, the economist had to base his analysis upon assumed numerical setups, supplemented by scattered items of actual statistical information? This is the situation in which the student of economics finds himself at present when he faces a problem of national production, consumption, and distribution. Despite the remarkable increase in primary statistical data, the proverbial boxes of theoretical assumptions are in this respect as empty as ever. Considerable progress has been achieved in the field of national income statistics. The economic balance of some of the most important branches of the national economy, particularly agriculture, has been studied with much success. Thus the ground has been prepared, at least in part, for a more complete analysis of the interrelations of the whole economic system. Nevertheless, the difficulty of the task still remaining can hardly be exaggerated.

Governmental publications constitute the main source of primary statistical information used in this study. Additional data were gathered from trade publications, and in some instances the results of special investigations have been utilized.

In many cases, use was made of the work of the National Bureau of Economic Research on national income.

The general business conditions prevailing in the United States during 1919 and 1929, covered by our statistical investigation, were described in the following terms:

Recession followed by revival, 1919. — The post-war reaction ended early in the year; and brisk revival followed, despite severe

CHART 1

SERIES INDICATIVE OF BUSINESS CONDITIONS, 1919–1939

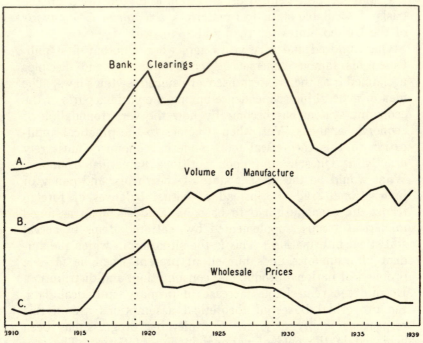

A. Bank clearings outside New York City.   B. For 1910–25, E. E. Day's Index of the Volume of Manufactures; for 1924–39, Federal Reserve Board Index. C. U.S. Bureau of Labor Statistics Index of Wholesale Prices.

coal and steel strikes in the autumn. Our government made large loans abroad, and export trade expanded vigorously. Gold exports became large; and rediscount rates, which had been held low by the federal reserve banks during the period of government financing, were advanced in November. Credit strain then developed; and stock prices, which had been irregular since early summer, declined.

Prosperity, recession, panic, 1929. — Active business continued, and boom conditions existed early in the year, although some re-ductions — as in construction activity — were already evident; but recession had begun before midsummer and became severe after the speculative panic of October-November. Spectacular advances oc-curred in stocks through August, and security loans, especially by non-banking lenders, reached huge proportions. New security issues, especially of stocks of investment trusts, were enormous and absorp-tion of credit for speculation produced a strain which intensified the crash of October. The export of capital was reduced to a minimum, and gold imports were very large. Rediscount rates and open-market money rates rose sharply, and then declined swiftly after the panic. The Washington conferences sought with slight success to minimize the effect of the panic upon business.[1]

The position of 1919 and 1929 within the framework of cyclical fluctuations of adjacent decades is fairly well indicated by the three basic economic series presented in Chart 1.

A. Fundamental Concepts

1. Individual Revenue and Cost Accounts

The conceptual basis of the subsequent statistical analysis is rather simple. The economic activity of the whole country is visualized as if covered by one huge accounting system. Not only all branches of industry, agriculture, and transportation, but also the individual budgets of all private persons are sup-posed to be included within this system. Each business enter-prise as well as each individual household is treated as a separate accounting unit. A complete bookkeeping system consists of a large number of different types of accounts. For our particu-lar purpose, however, only one is important: the expenditure and revenue account. It registers on its credit side the outflow of goods and services from the enterprise or household (which corresponds to total receipts or sales) and on the debit side the acquisition of goods or services by the particular enter-prise or household (corresponding to its total outlays). In other words, such an account describes the flow of commodi-ties and services as it enters the given enterprise (or household) at one end and leaves it at the other. In contrast to a balance sheet, this type of account is related not to a single instant but rather to a period of time, say a year, a month, or a week. It

---

[1] International Abstract of Economic Statistics 1919–1930, published by the International Conference of Economic Services (London, 1934), pp. 201–202.

differs from the usual profit and loss account so far as it includes *all* receipts and *all* disbursements. In the case of purchases, it includes not only those representing expenses in the accounting sense, but also capital outlays, etc. Our expenditure and revenue account covers, in other words, the entire balance of trade of the individual enterprise (or household).

Profits paid out to the owners, as well as expenditures connected with additional investment (in plant, etc.), are supposed to be debited, together with payments for all the current operating expenses, purchases, replacements of machinery, etc. Purchases made on credit or paid for with borrowed money are also entered, along with all other expenditures, on the debit side; while sales, even if made on credit, are credited in the same way as cash sales.

An expenditure and revenue account of this kind may show over a period a negative balance (sales smaller than purchases) only to the extent that a given household or enterprise disburses its previously accumulated cash, bank balances, or other negotiable titles, or spends funds obtained by additional borrowings. A positive balance (sales greater than expenditures), on the other hand, can result from an accumulation of cash, repayment of debts, or an increase in bank deposits or security holdings. The structure of the expenditure and revenue account thus described is very similar to that of the balance of trade of a country; it covers explicitly all the commodity and service transactions, but not the so-called capital items.

2. THE NATIONAL REVENUE AND COST ACCOUNTS

It follows from the obvious nature of economic transactions that each revenue item (as defined above) of an enterprise or household must reappear as an outlay item in the account of some other enterprise or household. This consideration makes it possible to present the whole system of interconnected accounts in a single two-way table (Table 1).

Every business and household unit is identified by a number: 1, 2, 3, 4, or 5. Each row contains the revenue (output) items of one separate business (or household), subdivided according to the origin of revenue, or, what amounts to the same thing, the destination of its products. The figures in row 1, for example, show that the product of firm 1 was distributed during some specified period in the following way: the amount v_{21} was bought by firm 2, the amount v_{31} by firm 3, and the amounts

v_{41} and v_{51} were sold to firms 4 and 5, respectively. The last item, $\sum_{i=1}^{i=5} v_{i1}$, represents the sum total of these separate entries and shows the total revenue or production of firm 1. In a similar manner, the subsequent rows show the production-revenue distribution of firms 2, 3, 4, and 5.

TABLE 1

ACCOUNTING SCHEME FOR DESCRIPTION OF INTERINDUSTRIAL TRANSACTIONS

DISTRIBUTION OF OUTLAYS (INPUT)	DISTRIBUTION OF OUTPUT (REVENUE)					Total
	1	2	3	4	5	
1	...	v_{21}	v_{31}	v_{41}	v_{51}	$\sum_{i=1}^{i=5} v_{i1}$
2	v_{12}	...	v_{32}	v_{42}	v_{52}	$\sum_{i=1}^{i=5} v_{i2}$
3	v_{13}	v_{23}	...	v_{43}	v_{53}	$\sum_{i=1}^{i=5} v_{i3}$
4	v_{14}	v_{24}	v_{34}	...	v_{54}	$\sum_{i=1}^{i=5} v_{i4}$
5	v_{15}	v_{25}	v_{35}	v_{45}	...	$\sum_{i=1}^{i=5} v_{i5}$
Total	$\sum_{k=1}^{k=5} v_{1k}$	$\sum_{k=1}^{k=5} v_{2k}$	$\sum_{k=1}^{k=5} v_{3k}$	$\sum_{k=1}^{k=5} v_{4k}$	$\sum_{k=1}^{k=5} v_{5k}$	S

Read vertically, column by column, the table shows the expenditure sides of the successive accounts. The last item of the first column, $\sum_{k=1}^{k=5} v_{1k}$, shows, for example, the total expenditures of firm 1; the entries above it in the same column indicate the distribution of these expenditures among all the different sources of supply; v_{12} was obtained from 2, v_{13} from 3, etc. The succeeding columns reveal the cost distribution of firms 2, 3, 4, and 5.

If it contained empirical data, Table 1 would naturally have several empty squares. Those lying along the main diagonal are necessarily left open because our accounting principle does not allow for registration of any transaction within the same firm. Actually, no firm or household exists which sells its products or supplies its services to *all* the other households or firms, and which makes its purchases also from every one of them. This means that not only the diagonal but also many other boxes of our revenue-expenditure table will remain blank.

The grand total of all transactions, S, in the lower right-hand corner, may be obtained by adding up the revenues of all the firms, as shown in the last column, or the expenditures, as listed in the last row. Although, as pointed out above, the credit and the debit side of the account for each particular enterprise or household will not necessarily balance, the total expenditures of all the firms and households must, for obvious reasons, equal the sum total of their combined revenues.

3. PRINCIPLE OF CONSOLIDATION

Even if the construction of an exhaustive table describing all the transactions between the independent economic units within a national economy were possible, the very size of such a table would constitute a serious impediment to any profitable use of the information contained in it. Obviously, considerable simplification of the original scheme is essential. The first step toward such simplification is the grouping of accounts. The majority of theoretical and practical economic problems for the solution of which the *Tableau Économique* may be used are not formulated in terms of individual business enterprises and households but relate rather to whole classes of such independent units. The grouping can be based on many different principles. The business enterprises can be classified, for example, according to the type of their products and segregated into separate *industries*, or, if location differences are to be brought out, a regional grouping must be applied. Whatever the principle of classification, the actual technique of consolidating the accounts is fundamentally always the same. If, for example, firms 2 and 3 of Table 1 had to be combined into one industry, a new accounting unit $(2 + 3)$ must be formed (Table 2). The new row $(2 + 3)$ is obtained by adding (vertically) the corresponding items of rows 2 and 3 of Table 1. An addition (horizontally) of the corresponding items of columns 2 and 3 produces the new group column $(2 + 3)$.

One difference between Table 1 and Table 2 is that the latter contains fewer separate accounts. The grand total, S, remains the same. The consolidated account $(2 + 3)$ differs, however, from any of the original primary accounts: the box which lies on the main diagonal is not necessarily empty. If firms 1 and 2 buy commodities or services from each other, as well as from other concerns, the new consolidated account will show purchases or sales from $2 + 3$ to $2 + 3$. This kind of registered internal turnover gives rise to a distinction between gross and net accounts. The former registers *all* the value transfers between the original simple accounting units, irre-

TABLE 2

CONSOLIDATED SCHEME OF INTERINDUSTRIAL ACCOUNTS

DISTRIBUTION OF OUTLAYS (INPUT)	DISTRIBUTION OF OUTPUT (REVENUE)				
	I	$2 + 3$	4	5	Total
I	...	$v_{21} + v_{31}$	v_{41}	v_{51}	$\sum_{i=1}^{i=5} v_{i1}$
$2 + 3$	$v_{12} + v_{13}$	$v_{23} + v_{32}$	$v_{42} + v_{43}$	$v_{52} + v_{53}$	$\sum_{i=1}^{i=5} (v_{i2} + v_{i3})$
4	v_{14}	$v_{24} + v_{34}$	...	v_{54}	$\sum_{i=1}^{i=5} v_{i4}$
5	v_{15}	$v_{25} + v_{35}$	v_{45}	...	$\sum_{i=1}^{i=5} v_{i5}$
Total	$\sum_{k=1}^{k=5} v_{1k}$	$\sum_{k=1}^{k=5} (v_{2k} + v_{3k})$	$\sum_{k=1}^{k=5} v_{4k}$	$\sum_{k=1}^{k=5} v_{5k}$	S

spective of any further grouping. The latter suppresses all the transactions among the members of the consolidated accounting group; in other words, it reveals only the external relations and treats the newly formed groups as if they were the original firms and households.

Table 2 is constructed on the principle of gross accounting. In order to convert it to a net transaction basis, the entry $v_{23} + v_{32}$ has to be suppressed. The total revenue sum at the right end of row $2 + 3$ and the total outlays sum at the bottom of column $2 + 3$ must be diminished by the same amount.

The result is shown in Table 3. The notation of Table 2 is now somewhat modified. The consolidated items are defined not as sums of the originally independent accounting elements, but simply as homogeneous transactions between the new *composite* groups. For example, the content of the box at the crosspoint of row $2 + 3$ and column 1, described in Table 2 as $v_{12} + v_{13}$, is now defined as $v_{1(2+3)}$ (the product of the firm $2 + 3$ going to the firm 1); similarly we write $v_{(2+3)\,4}$ instead of $v_{24} + v_{34}$. The grand total $(S - v_{32} - v_{23})$ of the consolidated Table 3 is smaller than that of Table 2, the difference being due to the exclusion of the internal transactions $v_{23} + v_{32}$.

TABLE 3

CONSOLIDATED SCHEME OF INTERINDUSTRIAL ACCOUNTS REDUCED TO A
NET BASIS

DISTRIBUTION OF OUTLAYS (INPUT)	DISTRIBUTION OF OUTPUT (REVENUE)				
	I	2+3	4	5	Total
I	...	$v_{(2+3)1}$	v_{41}	v_{51}	$\sum\limits_{i=1}^{i=5} v_{i1}$
2 + 3	$v_{1(2+3)}$	...	$v_{4(2+3)}$	$v_{5(2+3)}$	$\sum\limits_{i=1}^{i=5} (v_{i2} + v_{i3})$
4	v_{14}	$v_{(2+3)4}$	...	v_{54}	$\sum\limits_{i=1}^{i=5} v_{i4}$
5	v_{15}	$v_{(2+3)5}$	v_{45}	...	$\sum\limits_{i=1}^{i=5} v_{i5}$
Total	$\sum\limits_{k=1}^{k=5} v_{1k}$	$\sum\limits_{k=1}^{k=5} v_{(2+3)k}$	$\sum\limits_{k=1}^{k=5} v_{4k}$	$\sum\limits_{k=1}^{k=5} v_{5k}$	$S - v_{32} - v_{23}$

The process of consolidation, i.e., the reduction in the number of independent accounts, may proceed up to the point where the whole table is reduced to a single box. The *net* content of these completely unified accounts equals zero.

It hardly need be said that such integration of accounts reduces the scope of information conveyed. The statement that the total amount of transactions between firms 2 and 3 equals $v_{23} + v_{32}$ (Table 2) is considerably less informative than a separate listing of sales from 2 to 3 and from 3 to 2.

As already mentioned, even the most detailed economic study would hardly require an individual treatment of all the actually independent households and firms. On the other hand, many modern business enterprises combine such a conglomeration of heterogeneous economic activities that a distribution of all their transactions among several smaller, more homogeneous, quasi-independent accounting units seems highly desirable.

4. THE UNDISTRIBUTED ACCOUNT

Up to this point, the discussion has been based on the assumption that the primary statistical material, consisting of the expenditure and revenue accounts of all the separate firms and households, is absolutely complete. In view of the practical difficulties which make such a thorough coverage of all economic transactions actually impossible, the question arises what effect the inevitable gaps in the primary accounts have on the form and content of the final table. The absence of a single account would not in any way impair the completeness of the picture. As every transaction is always credited to one firm or household and debited to another, the missing item can always be found in the corresponding opposite account. In case of a larger gap, only partial reconstruction is possible. All transactions among the firms whose accounts are missing in our records are definitely irreplaceable. Only those revenue and outlay items which originate in sales to or purchases from the reporting firms can be picked out indirectly from the opposite entries. This means that the final result of the completed tabulation will be the same as that we would get if the accounts of the unreported firms were consolidated into a single group and reduced to a net basis. For instance, taking our previous example, if the reports of firms 2 and 3 were missing, the revenue and outlay table would be identical with Table 3, which presents the net accounts.

5. VALUE ADDED AND THE NATIONAL INCOME

The meaning and economic nature of a national revenue and outlay table may be further elucidated by relating it to some of the basic concepts of national income statistics such as value added and social product. This relation would be particularly simple in a static economy. By dividing all the accounts into two large groups, one containing the household accounts, the other all the rest, which might be called business, and consolidating each group into a single item (H and B, respectively, of Table 4), we can reduce the total number of boxes to four. Since, under static conditions, the corresponding row and column sums are necessarily equal, we find that the sum of the values transferred from business to households is equal to the total value movement in the opposite direction. The sum total of the household expenditures (column H) represents national income; it is equal to the total value of services credited to households (row H). The value added in business is equal in its magnitude to v_{bh} (i.e., the services contributed to business by households), and this is equal, under static conditions, to the value of goods and services supplied by business to households (v_{hh}). The total product of industry $v_{hb} + v_{bb}$ equals $v_{bh} + v_{bb}$.

The item v_{bb} represents the payments from business to business. Its inclusion is often defined as double counting and it

TABLE 4

INTERRELATIONS BETWEEN BUSINESS AND HOUSEHOLD ACCOUNTS

Distribution of outlays (input)	Distribution of output (revenue)		
	H (Households)	B (Business)	Total
H (Households)	v_{hh}	v_{bh}	$v_{hh} + v_{bh}$
B (Business)	v_{hb}	v_{bb}	$v_{hb} + v_{bb}$
Total	$v_{hh} + v_{hb}$	$v_{bh} + v_{bb}$	S

is very often struck from the final accounts. The item v_{hb} ($= v_{bh}$) is defined as the net product of industry. The household accounts can also be reduced to a net basis by disregarding the services furnished and paid for from household to household (v_{hh}). On such a net basis national income is v_{hb}, which equals the value added, v_{bh}.

Under dynamic conditions the relations are less symmetric. The value added, v_{bh}, is not necessarily equal to the household expenditures, v_{hb}. In an expanding economy the second item will often be somewhat smaller than the first. The difference, measuring the active balance of trade between household and business, would indicate the transfer of purchasing power from household to business (see Section 10). Such transfer will also be revealed in a corresponding surplus of total industrial expenditures (input), column B, over the aggregate industrial sales (output), row B.

The foregoing analysis is based on the assumption that the saving and investment accounts are strictly separable. In some instances, as in farming, strict separation of household and business units is not only practically but also theoretically impossible. A combined unit of this kind can increase its capital assets by the full amount of its revenue; buying capital goods, for example, yet keeping its expenditure and revenue account as balanced as ever.

The same is true of an industrial enterprise which is incurring capital losses, or accumulating undistributed surplus. Its current expenditures may still be equal to its total revenue (see Section 10). In order to discover the deficit or surplus it is necessary to examine the status of its fixed assets account. But capital accounting in this sense leads to an entirely new range of economic problems, such as depreciation and valuation of assets. The straightforward methods of registering the actual value of all commodities and services as they cross the border lines of separate accounting units cannot contribute anything to the solution of these problems.

6. DOUBLE COUNTING

In the statistical literature dealing with methods of calculating national income, much attention has been given to the concept of double counting. It is hardly an exaggeration to say that the principle of double entry constitutes the very foundation of a rational accounting system. Statistical double counting emerges from a process of consolidation of accounts. If two interrelated accounts are added, the same item may appear simultaneously on the credit and on the debit side of the new account. If the purpose of such an addition happens to be the elimination of all traces of the interrelation of the two accounts, this item can be suppressed on both sides.

Whether some particular transaction appears on both sides of the same (consolidated) account depends upon the method of grouping the accounting units for the purpose of consolidation. If, instead of segregating the household accounts in one group and all the others in a second, as is done in Table 4, we separated all agricultural from all non-agricultural items, an entirely different picture would emerge. A grouping of the latter kind reveals, for example, the balance of trade between industry and agriculture. Many value items, which according to the first arrangement might have been excluded because of double counting, would have to be retained in the second, while some of the original income items of the first table would have to be eliminated after the subsequent regrouping.

In its actual application, the elimination of the doubly

counted items means the suppression from our record of all those statistical data which describe the mechanism of inter-industrial relations. But it is exactly this mechanism which determines the size of the net income flow and its variations.

For the understanding of the economic structure of a business enterprise and evaluation of the prospects of its future development, even an approximate knowledge of the itemized expenditure and revenue account is more important than the most accurate information concerning the single figure given for its net revenue or deficit. The same is true regarding empirical analysis of the structure of the whole national economy. It is true that, from the viewpoint of welfare economics, the part of the annual flow of values which is more or less arbitrarily defined as the national income deserves particular attention. To a more detached observer, however, it may appear to be a mere by-product of the whole highly complex process of production and distribution of economic values.[1]

B. STATISTICAL APPLICATION

7. CLASSIFICATION OF INDUSTRIES

The classification of accounts in the following statistical study is a compromise between a theoretical ideal and practical necessity. According to the abstract theoretical scheme, all production enterprises should be segregated into several homogeneous industrial groups, homogeneity being defined in terms of (a) identity of products and (b) qualitative and quantitative similarity of the cost structure of the firms within each group (see also Part II, Section 2). Further, all the households should be subdivided into separate classes according to the kind of services they supply, i.e., the type of income received. Actually, neither of these desiderata can be achieved.

To begin with, a definite departure from the basic functional classification and grouping of industries has been made in dealing with international transactions. The consolidation of all foreign economic units into a single foreign-countries (imports and exports) account is obviously based upon a geographic, i.e., locational principle.

---

[1] In this connection it may be interesting to note the extreme variability of the theoretical concept of national income. Ricardo, for example, definitely treated all wages as a doubly counted item and identified the net income of society with the sum total of rents and profits.

Even more important is the fact that the very nature of the actual process of production and consumption precludes a clean-cut differentiation of industries. In agriculture, even the fundamental distinction between enterprise and household is impossible. On the other hand, the primary statistical information for industry as a whole is fragmentary and incomplete. Practically none of it could be used directly; a large part of the entries in our final tables (Tables 5 and 6, in pocket at end of book) represents more or less indirect estimates. Among the lines of economic activity completely ignored in our analysis, the most important are the entire fields of (a) distribution, wholesale and retail, (b) banking and finance, and (c) all non-rail transportation. Not less serious is the omission of (d) the income-expenditure accounts of all public bodies, including the budgets of federal, state, and local governments. It would be erroneous, however, to conclude that these omissions, significant as they are, destroy the basic coherence of Tables 5 and 6. The relation of all the unaccounted economic units to the rest of the system is implicitly reflected in the anonymous undistributed account.

The methods of computation and all statistical sources are described in detail in Appendix II. The purpose of this analysis is to show the meaning of Tables 5 and 6 if the numerical data contained therein are accepted at their face value.

The major part of the 44 accounts of Tables 5 and 6 consists of 41 production accounts: of these, 1 represents agriculture; 34 represent various industrial groups; 4, mining; 1, transportation (railroads); and 1, electric utilities. Agriculture is represented by a combination of production and household items. The household expenditures and receipts are consolidated in the total services row and the consumption column. Foreign commodity trade is entered in the export column and the import row.

The tables can be examined systematically from three angles. If the distribution of products of different industries is to be selected as the starting point, the analysis must proceed row by row; on the other hand, if the cost aspect is put in the foreground, the table should be studied column by column. Finally, the question of industrial balance will lead to a comparison of each column with the corresponding row.

8. DISTRIBUTION OF INDUSTRIAL OUTPUTS

A typical industrial distribution is exemplified by row 32, yarn and cloth, in Table 5. The gross total of 5578 million dollars represents the value of the output of this industrial group in 1919, appraised at factory. Exports amounted to 318 million dollars; 41 millions were used in agricultural production; 8 millions in automobile manufacturing; 31 millions in other wood industries (furniture). Nine hundred eleven millions were traded among the different stages of the yarn and cloth manufacturing industry itself, while 1208 millions were absorbed by the clothing industry, and 290 millions by other textile products. The leather-shoe industry took in 6 millions; the other leather industries, 1 million; and 189 millions went to the rubber industry. One million can be traced to the heterogeneous group of industries under the single heading "industries n.e.s." (not elsewhere specified), and 1812 millions went to consumption.

Thus 4816 millions of yarn and cloth products are allocated to definite accounts; subtracting this from the sum total, 5578 millions, we obtain a residue of 762 millions. This balancing item is entered into the special undistributed column. This column includes both those products the use of which is entirely unknown and those the classification of which (as derived from available statistical data) is not determinate enough to assign them to one of the other accounts. This means that the undistributed column, on one hand, contains the net debits of the unreported accounts as defined above, and on the other hand, includes the aggregated errors in the allocation of the respective products among the 43 reported accounts. It is quite likely that a certain portion of the undistributed product may actually have been absorbed by industries which, according to the present distribution, are not credited with any takings of yarn and cloth products. The underestimation of some of the distributed amounts represents another source of the undistributed surplus.

The 9102 millions of its own product, absorbed by agriculture, include both feed and other intermediate products as well as those consumption goods which were. according to available statistical information, retained on the farm. There is little doubt, however, that a considerable amount of agricultural products consumed by the farmer is obtained through the medium of the usual distributary channels. This means that some part of the 2209 millions of agricultural products assigned in our table to consumption was, in fact, used on the farm.

The distribution of transportation services (steam railroads) raises a new problem: in whose cost schedule should the transportation costs of commodities moved by rail be included? Even if it were practically possible to distinguish between the cases in which the producer sells at factory and those in which he delivers his goods free at the purchaser's door, such a twofold system of entry would hardly be advisable. One of the principal aims of our statistical analysis is to reveal the typical productive and distributive interrelations which determine the structure of the national economy. This requires such a classification and grouping of the different elements of the system as will reveal the most stable aspect of these interrelations. Differentiation between f.o.b. and c.i.f. transactions, as well as any other classification by mode of payment, scarcely meets this criterion. Thus a systematic presentation of all transactions on a uniform (f.o.b. or c.i.f.) basis seems theoretically preferable. In Tables 5 and 6 the transportation costs of each class of goods are charged to the industry which produces them, i.e., the value of every product includes the sum total of revenue obtained by the railroads for transportation of this particular kind of commodity. In distributing the products of an industry, however, the available statistical information does not enable us to identify the value (quantity $\times$ price, including transportation costs) of the finished commodity according to the location of the buyers. The freight costs allocated to the product of an industry are, therefore, spread in our table in an equal ratio over all units, which would be correct only under the obviously unrealistic assumption that the actual freight charges constitute a fixed proportion of the total price paid by each and every buyer.

Application of our method to imports makes it necessary to augment the import values of foreign commodities by a proportional amount of domestic transportation costs. An equivalent of the sum total of these transportation costs is charged — in the distribution row of railway services — to exports. This item must not be confused with that part of transportation services which is charged directly to the cost accounts of the particular industries and thereby increases the at factory value of American export goods.

It will be seen that 4161 million dollars of the railroad product are allocated to definite accounts in 1919. The undistributed 1464 millions contain less than 1000 millions of transportation costs still unaccounted for; the rest represents the so-called non-operating revenues.

In allocating imports we meet in part the difficulty discussed in connection with the distribution of transportation services. One portion of wares obtained from abroad consists of goods which, like rubber, silk, or diamonds, cannot possibly come from domestic sources. The data revealing the consumption of these particular kinds of commodities by different industries indicate at the same time the distribution of the imports of these goods. This simple solution cannot be applied, however, to imports directly competing with domestic products of the same kind. In this case, consumption data still leave open the question what part of the total amount absorbed by any single industry was of foreign origin. In this, as in the instance of freight costs, proportional distribution has been used throughout as the only practicable solution. The ratio between total domestic production and foreign imports of each particular kind of goods was applied as a fixed distribution key to all the different categories of users of this commodity. Import duties are included in the value of commodities obtained from abroad.

9. DISTRIBUTION OF HOUSEHOLD SERVICES (INCOMES)

The service row (43) is, for the sake of convenience, divided into two parts. Distribution of labor services (row 43a) is rather simple: each industry is debited with total wages and salaries disbursed. As the figures in this row include only payments to hired labor, agriculture is credited only with the money wages of hired farm workers.

The definition and evaluation of capital and entrepreneurial services (row 43b) raise an extremely difficult theoretical and statistical problem. Capital services are clearly discernible only so far as an enterprise is working with borrowed funds and makes contractual interest payments. But even in this case, ever changing economic conditions regularly produce a situation in which the contractual rate differs considerably from the current. The remuneration of that part of the capital investment which belongs to the owners of the enterprise is hardly distinguishable from entrepreneurial returns, monopolistic revenue, windfall profits resulting from appreciation of commodity stocks on hand, etc. So far as monopolistic and speculative profits are concerned, it is highly doubtful whether they could and should be considered as remuneration for some specific kind of service.

The theoretical difficulty and practical impossibility of distinguishing these different kinds of remuneration made it necessary to lump all into one single group, loosely defined as capital and entrepreneurial services. It corresponds rather closely to the bookkeeping concept of net revenue (minus taxes) augmented by the sum total of all interest payments on borrowed capital, and it includes three elements of a typical corporate revenue and expenditure account: (a) interest paid, (b) dividends paid, (c) undistributed profits. According to this setup, the undistributed surplus plays, so to speak, a double role in the cost account of an enterprise. On the one hand, it represents the value of materials, additional payrolls, and other cost elements on which it usually is spent in the process of new investment; on the other hand, it measures (in addition to the two other items mentioned above) the productive services of capital and entrepreneurship. This twofold function would be more apparent if each enterprise were to pay out its total net revenue to the stockholders and other owners and subsequently would obtain from them, in the form of a loan or in exchange for a new stock issue, an equal sum to be spent on new investment. The formal difference between this and the usual method of retaining undistributed surplus lies only in the fact that the former operation involves two additional monetary transactions; the immediate material consequences are in both cases identical. The identity of the material consequences in this case holds even to the extent that, should the valuation of services obtained be arbitrarily changed, it would make no difference so long as it were offset by a corresponding write-up (or reduction) of the loan value (if profits were distributed and then immediately borrowed). From a certain viewpoint, therefore, it may be said that the surplus values in the table are fictitious. Their meaning is entirely dependent upon the interpretation of the actual valuation and accounting practices of the industry.[1]

---

[1] Without embarking upon a fundamental discussion of the valuation problem, it is important to indicate that the explanation of actual economic forces should be clearly distinguished from any attempt to improve existing

According to our definition, therefore, the value of capital services will be nil, if no interest or dividend payment is forthcoming and no additional surplus has been accumulated during the period under consideration. Every payment on interest and dividend account is debited as a capital service, even if accompanied by a deficit.

The fundamental setup of our tables necessitates a radical departure from the conventional accounting practices so far as the treatment of deficits is concerned. The existence of a deficit indicates that the given enterprise either (a) purchased more goods and services (including dividend and interest payments) than it sold, or (b) failed to maintain its fixed investment, inventories, etc. In the first case, the enterprise must spend some of its previously accumulated cash balances or, if this proves to be impossible or impracticable, the loss is financed out of additional investment. In either situation, we have a surplus of expenditures over sales which influences the balance of trade of this enterprise in exactly the same way as a new additional investment. In the second case, the deficit is confined to so-called book losses. It is indeed accompanied by the revaluation of some assets but does not affect in any direct way the equilibrium of external payments and receipts. The balance of payments as well as the balance of trade of an enterprise remains entirely unaffected by internal revaluations of this kind. This leads to the conclusion that, unless financed by reduction of cash holdings or additional investment, deficits in our setup should be disregarded; negative surpluses (deficits) can be left entirely out of the picture (see Appendix II).

Official financial statistics do not for obvious reasons follow this line of reasoning. The revenue data computed for any industrial group on the basis of usual accounting practices show only the net difference between the aggregate positive net revenue of all enterprises showing net income and the net losses sustained by the rest of the industry. The income statistics published by the Bureau of Internal Revenue, however, give separately incomes of Corporations Reporting Net Income as well as for the aggregate deficits of Corporations Reporting

financial practices. Thus it would be as inadmissible to contest the validity of corporate surplus data on the ground of inadequacy of existing accounting systems as it would be wrong, for example, to dismiss our wage statistics with the remark that the existing wage rate cannot provide an adequate standard of living for the working class.

No Net Income. The former figure can be used in the calculation of the services of capital as defined for our special purpose.

In using official net income data we still introduce a systematic underestimation of entrepreneurial and capital services. The sum total of dividend payments and other capital services actually exceeds by a certain amount the aggregate net income of industry because many business concerns pay dividends in excess of actual earnings. The exact extent of these over-payments cannot be ascertained readily; in 1919 for the manufacturing and mining industries alone they appear not to have exceeded 100 million dollars.[1]

The situation of an industry which is suffering losses is, in certain respects, identical with that which arises in the case of additional investment (which might be financed by undistributed profits, security sales, or out of already available cash resources). From the viewpoint of our analysis, it is of no import that in one case the surplus of expenses over receipts is accompanied by a decrease in the value of capital assets, while in the other this value is increasing. The whole approach is based on registration of the current *stream* of goods and services; the appreciation and depreciation of capital *assets* are explicitly not taken into account. These considerations lead to a corresponding interpretation of the total expenditures row.

The theoretical and statistical difficulties in dealing with agricultural labor and capital services are essentially the same as in the case of the corresponding industrial cost schedules, but they are enhanced by the impossibility of falling back on objective accounting figures. Any attempt to split the gross expenditures of agricultural accounting units into the standard components of wages, entrepreneurial and capital income, and other production costs is bound to lead back to arbitrary principles of imputation.

The most radical method of solving the problem would be to include the farm purchases of consumer goods among all the other outlays and place in the service row only the amounts of wages, interest, etc., actually paid out. This type of reasoning has been applied in the general table to the distribution of

[1] The aggregate net income (minus income tax) of Manufacturing and Mining Corporations Reporting Net Income in 1919 amounted to 4217 million dollars, according to *Statistics of Income* (Bureau of Internal Revenue), while total dividend payments and corporate savings as estimated by W. I. King (*National Income and its Purchasing Power*, National Bureau of Economic Research, 1930) amounted to 4276 million dollars.

that part of agricultural production which was consumed directly on the farm (see Appendix II). Obvious statistical difficulties make the consistent use of this procedure impracticable. Furthermore, a good theoretical reason exists for keeping, so far as possible, the distribution of marketable consumption goods separate from that of other kinds of commodities.

A simple non-controversial solution of our difficulty is to relegate all agricultural outlays other than those which are already allocated among other industries to the undistributed row. This device is essentially that used in Tables 5 and 6. The residual amount (except taxes) is shifted, however, from the undistributed to the service row. This allocation is justified by the fact that most of these monetary expenditures are analogous in their economic nature to the industrial incomes entered in the adjacent boxes of the service row. Strictly speaking, the value of agricultural service expenses obtained in this indirect way represents an overestimate. They include a certain amount of trade services absorbed in connection with the purchase of agricultural cost goods; if the exact figure for this item were known, it would go in the undistributed row. On the other hand, in using this figure, one has to keep in mind that, as indicated above, one part (approximately 1900–2000 million dollars in 1919 and 1700–1800 millions in 1929) of the sum total of the commodities charged from agriculture to agriculture consist of consumption goods.

The 5382 millions of capital and entrepreneurial services charged in 1919 to consumption include rental payments for hired houses and apartments, as well as the contribution of these factors to the so-called service industries, liberal professions, etc.

10. COST STRUCTURES; SAVINGS AND INVESTMENTS

Each vertical column of Tables 5 and 6 shows the structure of expenditures of the corresponding industrial (or household) account. It lists the commodities and services which were absorbed by each particular branch of economic activity during the period under consideration. In an entirely static system this distribution could be defined as the cost structure. Under the actual dynamic conditions prevailing, however, a large part of the total outlay represents not only current production costs but also additional investment. No attempt is made in this investigation to split the expenditures of an enterprise into two parts corresponding to these two types of outlay.

The primary statistical data do not contain direct information concerning the total expenditures of the different industries similar to that which the census data on total value of product give for total receipts. The magnitude of the total outlays can be determined, however, indirectly through augmenting the total value of product by the value of additional new capital investment and the reduction of cash holdings. The difficulties involved in the capital accounting problem, so far as they reflect the difficulty of distinguishing current costs from new capital expenditures, do not impair the validity of the sum totals thus obtained — so long as we are interested in aggregate expenditures and not in their two parts (current and additional expenditures as defined above). The evaluation practices in current use affect, however, the magnitude of the total outlay so far as they determine that part of the value of capital and entrepreneurial services which is reflected in the surplus accounts.

The general principle for treating corporate surpluses as service items has been laid down in the preceding discussion of capital and entrepreneurial services. The total outlays of an enterprise can be defined accordingly as value of sales (product) plus additional capital investment, and borrowing plus increment of positive surplus minus net changes in the cash balance (which might be positive or negative). The available statistical information does not give any clue for an evaluation of the last item. There is good reason to believe, however, that the financing of new investment through disbursement of previously accumulated cash balances was in 1919 and 1929 a relatively minor item. Much more serious is the omission of short term bank credits obtained by the various industries between the beginning and the end of the accounting years 1919 and 1929. A very rough estimate indicates that approximately one billion dollars was added in this way to total industrial expenditures in 1919.[1] The absolute lack of any statistical

---

[1] According to the *Report of the Comptroller of the Currency* for 1920 (vol. 1, p. 31), 23 per cent of the total loans and discounts made by national banks during this year were absorbed by industrial enterprises, including railroads and public utilities. Applying this percentage to the average annual increase in total loans and discounts by all reporting banks between June 1918 and June 1920, we find that the proportional share of industry for 1919 would be approximately one billion dollars.

evidence concerning distribution of the sum total among the separate industries precludes any attempt to use such an estimate in our study.

The total outlay items at the bottom of columns 1–45 represent the total values of product, including imputed transportation costs augmented by additional positive surpluses and long term capital investments, of the respective individual industries.

The undistributed-outlays figure (row 44c) is a balancing item which fills the gap between the total outlay for each industry and the sum total of the individual outgo items distributed among the other rows. Taxes are segregated for 1919 (Table 5) in a special subdivision of the undistributed account in order to show to what extent the expenditure accounts of industries and households were linked to the revenue accounts of the government (for 1929 — see Table 6 — no comparable data are available). The total of expenditures for consumption (column 43) is taken from the careful estimate by Arthur R. Gainsborough.[1]

The elementary structural characteristics of the economic system represented in Tables 5 and 6 can be seen more clearly when all entries are expressed as percentages of the *net* sum totals of the corresponding rows and columns rather than in dollars. Each box contains such figures. One figure shows the value of the particular item in its relation to the total *net output* of the industry or service group from which it originates; the other gives the magnitude of the same item in relation to the total *net outlay* of the industrial or household account by which it was absorbed.

The undistributed items in the agricultural and industrial rows and columns (1–41) are relatively much smaller than in the service row and in the consumption column. The explanation seems to be that a large part of total household expenditures are directed toward undistributed non-material production branches, which in their turn absorb a great amount of services but a relatively small quantity of material costs.

[1] As given in W. H. Lough, *High-Level Consumption* (New York, 1935).

PART II

PART II

THE THEORETICAL SCHEME

I. GENERAL INTERDEPENDENCE

IN MAKING the difficult decision concerning the type of theoretical scheme he is to use as a basis of his analysis, a present-day economist faces two pairs of fundamental alternatives: general equilibrium versus partial, and dynamics versus statics. Until recently, the most elementary — partial and static — approach was alone used in empirical statistical investigations. The general, and at the same time dynamic, type of analysis still remains an unwritten chapter of economic theory, the claims of innumerable "model-builders" notwithstanding. Since the successful explanation of the famous hog cycle, the partial but dynamic scheme seems to dominate the field of applied economic theory. The fourth type of theoretical approach, based on the combination of the complexities of a general interdependent system with the simplifying assumptions of static analysis, constitutes the background of this investigation.

The relative merits of the partial but dynamic and general but static type of analysis can hardly be determined on any *a priori* grounds. Only a complete and exhaustive understanding of the actual working of an empirically given economic system would enable us to evaluate conclusively the relative importance of the two aspects of its mechanism — an understanding which, incidentally, would remove the necessity of sacrificing one aspect in favor of the other. The simple test of empirical application, or prediction, of course remains. Unfortunately, it cannot be used in mapping out a program of future research, because its verdict becomes available only after completion of the proposed task. But even without attempting to determine the relative advantages of the different theoretical assumptions, it may be useful to indicate some of the reasons which have prompted the choice of this particular type of approach.

The principal merit of the general equilibrium theory is that it enables us to take account of the highly complex network of interrelationships which transmits the impulses of any local primary change into the remotest corners of the economic system. While in the case of partial analysis, which operates simultaneously with only two or three variables, the interrelation among these few elements can often be perceived directly, such intuitive inference becomes practically impossible as soon as the number of variables increases up to four or five, not to say ten or twenty. A doubtful reader of these lines can ascertain the limitation of his own common-sense intuition by trying to hazard at least an approximate solution of a system of three simple linear equations with three variables; or, after having found the right answers mathematically, by trying to guess out intuitively what effect a change in one of the constants would have on the values of all three unknowns.

No economist would seriously deny the existence of analogous, and even much more complicated, interrelations within the actual economic system he is endeavoring to study. The critics of the theory of general interdependence seldom fail to mention that in its present state and on the basis of existing empirical information, this theory cannot possibly cope with the extreme complexity of actual economic processes. But then, instead of trying to refine the theory or to fortify the shaky base of our factual information, these critics proceed to solve, or at least to interpret, the very same complicated problems, relying upon their own common-sense intuition and shopworn partial-equilibrium conceptions of "shifts," "elasticities of substitution," "relations," etc.

The problem is indeed extremely complex, but if the most powerful theoretical tools applied to the fullest amount of available factual information should prove inadequate for even an approximate solution, it is difficult to see how shrewd common-sense observations backed by approximate short-cut methods of partial analysis could possibly achieve more significant results.

2. BASIC EQUATIONS IN STATIONARY EQUILIBRIUM

The picture of the economic system underlying every general equilibrium theory is that of a large set of data which determine in their totality the magnitudes of all the dependent variables of the system. Variables are the unknowns we try to explain; data are those elements which are used as a basis of explanation. The distinction between the two categories is obviously relative. The data of a partial theory are considered as variables within the framework of a more general analysis. In our scheme all the (relative) quantities of different types of commodities and services, as well as their (relative) prices, are treated as variables; the technical and natural conditions of production and the tastes of consumers, as data.

The term "variable" must not be taken too literally in this connection; these unknowns are as much or as little variable as the conditions which determine their values. If the data are constant, the variables remain unchanged. As soon as the determining conditions are modified, some or all variables react with corresponding changes. The character of such reactions depends upon the initial structural properties of the empirically given system. This particular aspect of the general equilibrium problem constitutes the central issue of this investigation.

Three sets of equations make up the proposed scheme of general interdependence. For the purposes of clear exposition, the fundamental theoretical setup is described first under the assumption of stationary equilibrium — a hypothetical state of simple reproduction which knows neither saving nor investment.

The equations of Set I describe the fact that the total output of each industry (measured in physical terms) equals the sum total of the amounts of its products consumed by all other industries. Thus, if X_i indicates the net output (total output minus the amount of its products consumed within the same industry) of the ith industry, and $x_{1i}, x_{2i}, x_{3i}, \ldots, x_{ni}$ stand for the amounts of its products absorbed by the first, second, third, and so on up to the nth industry, we have for an economic system consisting of n industries the following set of linear equations:

$$
\begin{aligned}
-X_1 + x_{21} + x_{31} + \cdots + x_{i1} + \cdots + x_{k1} + \cdots + x_{n1} &= 0 \\
x_{12} - X_2 + x_{32} + \cdots + x_{i2} + \cdots + x_{k2} + \cdots + x_{n2} &= 0 \\
x_{13} + x_{23} - X_3 + \cdots + x_{i3} + \cdots + x_{k3} + \cdots + x_{n3} &= 0 \\
\cdots\cdots\cdots\cdots\cdots\cdots\cdots\cdots\cdots\cdots\cdots\cdots\cdots \\
x_{1i} + x_{2i} + x_{3i} + \cdots - X_i + \cdots + x_{ki} + \cdots + x_{ni} &= 0 \\
\cdots\cdots\cdots\cdots\cdots\cdots\cdots\cdots\cdots\cdots\cdots\cdots\cdots \\
x_{1k} + x_{2k} + x_{3k} + \cdots + x_{ik} + \cdots - X_k + \cdots + x_{nk} &= 0 \\
\cdots\cdots\cdots\cdots\cdots\cdots\cdots\cdots\cdots\cdots\cdots\cdots\cdots \\
x_{1n} + x_{2n} + x_{3n} + \cdots + x_{in} + \cdots + x_{kn} + \cdots - X_n &= 0
\end{aligned}
$$

(I)

Set II a is equally simple and self-explanatory. It states that under conditions of stationary equilibrium the value (price $\times$ quantity) of the product of each industry is equal to the value of all goods and services absorbed by it.

$$-X_1P_1 + x_{12}P_2 + x_{13}P_3 + \cdots + x_{1i}P_i + \cdots + x_{1k}P_k$$
$$+ \cdots x_{1n}P_n = 0$$

$$x_{21}P_1 - X_2P_2 + x_{23}P_3 + \cdots + x_{2i}P_i + \cdots + x_{2k}P_k$$
$$+ \cdots x_{2n}P_n = 0$$

$$x_{31}P_1 + x_{32}P_2 - X_3P_3 + \cdots + x_{3i}P_i + \cdots + x_{3k}P_k$$
$$+ \cdots x_{3n}P_n = 0$$

$$\cdots\cdots\cdots\cdots\cdots\cdots\cdots\cdots\cdots\cdots\cdots\cdots\cdots\cdots\cdots$$

(II a)
$$x_{i1}P_1 + x_{i2}P_2 + x_{i3}P_3 + \cdots - X_iP_i + \cdots + x_{ik}P_k$$
$$+ \cdots x_{in}P_n = 0$$

$$\cdots\cdots\cdots\cdots\cdots\cdots\cdots\cdots\cdots\cdots\cdots\cdots\cdots\cdots\cdots$$

$$x_{k1}P_1 + x_{k2}P_2 + x_{k3}P_3 + \cdots + x_{ki}P_i + \cdots - X_kP_k$$
$$+ \cdots x_{kn}P_n = 0$$

$$\cdots\cdots\cdots\cdots\cdots\cdots\cdots\cdots\cdots\cdots\cdots\cdots\cdots\cdots\cdots$$

$$x_{n1}P_1 + x_{n2}P_2 + x_{n3}P_3 + \cdots + x_{ni}P_i + \cdots + x_{nk}P_k$$
$$+ \cdots - X_nP_n = 0$$

$P_1, P_2, P_3, \cdots, P_n$ are the prices of the products of the first, second, third, and nth industries.

The third type of equation is conceptually the most complicated. It describes the technical relation between the physical output of an industry and the input of all the different cost elements absorbed in production. In short, it describes the industrial production function. While the form of all equations in Sets I and II a is determined by rather obvious common-sense considerations, the shape of the production functions is supposed to reflect all the natural and technical conditions of industrial processes; and thus it cannot possibly be derived on purely *a priori* grounds.

The most direct way of obtaining the necessary information concerning the form of technical equations would be empirical observation. Detailed studies of this kind have been made, for example, in agricultural research in the form of numerous attempts at empirical verification of the law of diminishing returns. The practical possibility of covering the entire field of agricultural, mineral, and industrial production with this kind of specialized technological investigation is so remote that at present it cannot be discussed seriously.

Theoretical economists deal with production functions in their quite general form. More specific characteristics, if introduced at all, take the form of hypothetical assumption rather than systematically observed and measured facts.

The very nature of our study necessitates the introduction of quite definite assumptions concerning the shape of our production functions; and at the same time it limits considerably the freedom of theoretical choice, because the numerical values of all the parameters must be ascertainable on the basis of available statistical information. Thus, the most rigid type of production function had to be chosen: the amount of each cost element is assumed to be strictly proportional to the quantity of output. Instead of the most frequently used general functions of the type $X_i = f(x_{i1}, x_{i2}, x_{i3}, \cdots, x_{ik}, \cdots, x_{in})$, we describe the technical setup of each industry by a series of as many homogeneous linear equations as there are separate cost factors involved:

$$x_{i1} = a_{i1}X_i, \ x_{i2} = a_{i2}X_i, \cdots, x_{ik} = a_{ik}X_i, \cdots, x_{in} = a_{in}X_i$$

This is the type of relation originally used by Walras in his first formulation of the general equilibrium theory. Following his terminology, the constants $a_{i1}, a_{i2}, \cdots, a_{in}$ from now on will be referred to as the *coefficients of production*.

In the course of the following argument, frequent reference is made to the proportional variation of all coefficients within any given industry. To facilitate the handling of this kind of problem, common proportionality factors can be introduced and instead of $a_{i1}, a_{i2} \cdots$ we write $a_{i1}/A_i, a_{i2}/A_i, a_{i3}/A_i, \cdots$. Henceforth these A's are often referred to as the *productivity coefficients*. If A_i doubles, for example, it means that with the same amounts of all cost elements industry i can turn out twice as large a product as before. The initial values of all productivity coefficients are for the sake of formal simplicity considered equal to 1.

Thus, in general, the technical setup of the whole national economy can be described by the following system of $n(n-1)$ linear equations:

$$x_{12} = \frac{a_{12}X_1}{A_1}, \ x_{13} = \frac{a_{13}X_1}{A_1}, \ \cdots, \ x_{1i} = \frac{a_{1i}X_1}{A_1}, \ \cdots,$$

$$x_{1k} = \frac{a_{1k}X_1}{A_1}, \ \cdots, \ x_{1n} = \frac{a_{1n}X_1}{A_1}$$

$$x_{21} = \frac{a_{21}X_2}{A_2} \quad x_{23} = \frac{a_{23}X_2}{A_2}, \cdots, x_{2i} = \frac{a_{2i}X_2}{A_2}, \cdots,$$

$$x_{2k} = \frac{a_{2k}X_2}{A_2}, \cdots, x_{2n} = \frac{a_{2n}X_2}{A_2}$$

$$x_{31} = \frac{a_{31}X_3}{A_3}, \quad x_{32} = \frac{a_{32}X_3}{A_3}, \cdots, x_{3i} = \frac{a_{3i}X_3}{A_3}, \cdots,$$

$$x_{3k} = \frac{a_{3k}X_3}{A_3}, \cdots, x_{3n} = \frac{a_{3n}X_3}{A_3}$$

. . . .

$$(\text{IIIa}) \quad x_{i1} = \frac{a_{i1}X_i}{A_i}, \quad x_{i2} = \frac{a_{i2}X_i}{A_i}, \quad x_{i3} = \frac{a_{i3}X_i}{A_i}, \cdots, x_{ik} = \frac{a_{ik}X_i}{A_i}, \cdots,$$

$$x_{in} = \frac{a_{in}X_i}{A_i}$$

. . . .

$$x_{k1} = \frac{a_{k1}X_k}{A_k}, \quad x_{k2} = \frac{a_{k2}X_k}{A_k}, \quad x_{k3} = \frac{a_{k3}X_k}{A_k}, \cdots, x_{ki} = \frac{a_{ki}X_k}{A_k}, \cdots,$$

$$x_{kn} = \frac{a_{kn}X_k}{A_k}$$

. : . . . .

$$x_{n1} = \frac{a_{n1}X_n}{A_n}, \quad x_{n2} = \frac{a_{n2}X_n}{A_n}, \quad x_{n3} = \frac{a_{n3}X_n}{A_n}, \cdots,$$

$$x_{nk} = \frac{a_{nk}X_n}{A_n}, \cdots$$

In this set of equations, each pair of lines is devoted to a separate industry, and, within those, one equation to each cost factor.

Far reaching theoretical consequences ensue from our choice of this particular type of production function. It means no less than a formal rejection of the marginal productivity theory; in this setup all factors appear to be strictly complementary or limitational. The marginal productivity of any of them — defined as the ratio resulting from dividing an infinitesimal separate increment of any one factor into the corresponding infinitesimal increment of total output — equals zero: the output would not increase unless the inputs of all the other factors were also augmented according to their respective coefficients of production. The same restriction can be formulated in another way by saying that our production functions exclude technical substitutability of factors within the framework of any given production process. The practical difference between this limited and the usual, more general, set of theoretical assumptions, however, is in this case not so great as might seem at first sight.

A large number of phenomena, which in economic discussion are referred to as instances of factor substitution, prove upon closer examination to be of a quite different nature. The conventional interpretation of the marginal productivity theory is very often linked with the rather broad, not to say undiscriminating use of the term "factor of production." The venerable trinity of "land, labor, and capital" seems still to dominate the field of theoretical discussion. It is closely linked with the traditional approach to the system of national economy as if the latter were a single tremendously complicated production process absorbing the services of land, labor, and capital on one side and throwing out the national product on the other. If further differentiation is introduced at all, it rarely goes beyond a conventional distinction between consumers' and producers' goods industries. Now, if we compare this simplified scheme with the more realistic picture of our economic system, which instead of one, two, or three would include dozens of separate industries, it becomes evident that the concept of technical substitution and the law of variable proportions — if applied to aggregative industries — have in the main no other function than to conceal the non-homogeneous character of the conventional industrial classification. If two heterogeneous subdivisions of the consumption goods industries — for example, foodstuffs as contrasted with the automobile industry — are using land, labor, and capital in fixed but significantly different proportions, any change in their relative size will necessarily be accompanied by a variation in the relative amounts of land, labor, and capital absorbed by the consumption goods industry as a whole. Many an economist will interpret this phenomenon as a change in the factor combination within the consumption goods industry.

This example shows how many cases of so-called factor substitution can be traced back to simple inter-industrial shifts, without any reference to variable factor combinations within separate strictly defined industrial setups.[1]

The preceding argument indicates that in many cases frequent reference to substitutability of factors is made simply to offset a certain blurredness of our aggregative concepts. This does not dispose, however, of the fact that even a most detailed and minute differentiation among various branches of production fails to eliminate the problem of real technical substitutability.

The assumption of fixed coefficients of production necessarily entails the existence of some disparity between our theoretical scheme and the actual industrial setup it is intended to represent. Empirical investigation alone can reveal how significant this disparity actually is.[2]

Once some degree of flexibility is theoretically admitted, its quantitative importance becomes of foremost practical significance. Even if, by employing an additional amount of any one factor, output can be somewhat increased, a proportional allround addition to all the factors involved might bring about so much better results that actually the second mode of procedure will be given preference, to the practical exclusion of the first. In other words, the different factors of production can be substitutable, but at the same time the degree of complementariness might be so high that even a most violent variation in their relative prices could affect the relative amounts of their inputs only slightly.

Paradoxical as it may seem, some instances of extreme substitutability will often be more favorable to our assumption of

[1] The apparent substitution of factors through shifts from one industry to another has been occasionally referred to as product substitution. The term is somewhat misleading. It seems to indicate that such a process implies a real substitution of one product for another, at least within the expenditure setup of the consumer's budget, that it essentially consists in a simple shift of the necessary readjustment process into the next stage. This is not correct. The whole phenomenon can take place without necessitating the slightest variation in the cost structure of *any* industry or household. The economic system can adjust itself, f.ex., to an increase in the productivity of any one industry through appropriate variation in the size of other industries. For further analysis of problems of industrial classification see Part III, Section 10.

[2] Existence of some degree of substitutability can be established on the basis of much more limited factual information than that which would be necessary for an attempt to derive the actual form of non-linear production functions. Some light upon this first, more limited, issue will be thrown by a comparative study of factor combinations in 1919 and 1929.

rigid proportions than even cases of high complementariness. Take the example of two metals which from a technical point of view are equally well adapted to some particular productive use. Obviously one critical price ratio must exist at which the relative costs of using one or the other will be exactly the same. In all other cases, the relatively cheaper material will be used exclusively. The most violent price fluctuation cannot have even the slightest effect on the resulting factor combination so long as it does not swing the balance to the other side of the critical price ratio. In all the numerous cases in which every cost factor has an unlimited range of possible substitutes, the actual price variations are safely removed from such critical points, so that the assumption of constant proportions is for all practical purposes entirely justified.

In those instances in which shifts between two or more substitutes occur frequently, it might be advisable to treat them as a single commodity. The corresponding technical coefficient is likely to be much more stable than the input ratios of the separate components. On the other hand — as shown above — the production function of the composite commodity itself will be less stable than those of its individual elements.

Nothing is further from the author's mind than an attempt to settle a controversial issue by counting the number of pros and cons. The somewhat prolonged discussion of this important and difficult problem has no other purpose than to indicate the kind of considerations which make the acceptance of this particular rigid type of production function practically justifiable.

3. HOUSEHOLDS AS AN INDUSTRY

Households are treated in our theoretical scheme exactly as any other industry. The accounting aspects of this type of approach have been discussed in Part I; but its technological implications require some immediate clarification. The modern theory of consumers' behavior is, in most aspects of its conceptual development, nearly identical with the theory of production. The formal similarity of a system of isoquants and of indifference lines is well established. The analogy can be easily extended by identifying the service output of a household with the production of an enterprise. Certain psychological resistance to this type of approach — due to memories of ill-conceived subsistence cost theories of wages — would disappear as soon as we realize that nothing more is implied by it than the existence of an obvious connection between the expenditures of an individual and the amount of his earnings.

The application of fixed consumption coefficients in our description of consumers' behavior seems even more controversial than the use of constant production coefficients in an empirical study of industrial cost structures. However, factual investigations, which happen to be more numerous and comprehensive in this case than in industrial cost analysis, seem to indicate that the actual substitution among the different types of consumers' expenditures keeps within rather narrow limits.

In considering this question, it is obvious that the degree of substitutability varies with the commodity classification chosen. If a particular distinction were made, for example, between luxuries and necessities, the highest degree of substitutability would be readily expected. Being based on their industrial origin, our classification of consumption goods coincides in many of its subdivisions with the conventional distinction between food, clothing, fuel and power, transportation, etc. The fact that the grouping used in this study is somewhat more technological increases rather than diminishes the stability of the corresponding consumption coefficients.

Throughout the subsequent theoretical discussion, the subscript n is identified with the household industry: X_n stands for the output of services; P_n for their price; and $a_{n1}, a_{n2} \cdots$ indicate the various coefficients of consumption. A proportional change in all these coefficients, as symbolized by a variation in the proportionality coefficient A_n, can easily be identified with a change in the real wage-rates of services supplied by households.

4. SAVING AND INVESTMENT

Up to this point the discussion has been limited by the initially stipulated assumption of a stationary state, i.e., absence of any saving and investment. Now the phenomenon of savings can be introduced in our theoretical scheme. For general discussion of the saving and investment concept, reference must be made again to Part I. There a terminology is developed according to which the difference between the aggregate expenditures of a household or an enterprise (or a group of households or enterprises) and its aggregate revenue is defined as investment when it is positive and as saving when it is negative.

Introduction of savings and investments obviously requires modification of all the cost equations of our second set. The value product of any industry (or household), instead of being simply equal to its aggregate outlays, can now be either larger or smaller. In other words, total cost must now be equated to the total revenue divided by a certain *saving coefficient*, B_i:

$$-\frac{X_i P_i}{B_i} + (x_{i1}P_1 + x_{i2}P_2 + x_{i3}P_3 + \cdots + x_{ik}P_k \cdots + x_{in}P_n) = 0$$

Whenever B_i is greater than 1, the particular industry shows positive savings; it equals 1 if the total revenue of the enterprise or household exactly covers its outlays; and it becomes smaller than 1 in the case of negative savings, i.e., positive investment.

A separate proportionality factor β is furthermore introduced into all saving coefficients for a reason similar to that which made it advisable to use the special proportionality coefficient A_i. Subsequent discussion will disclose the particular significance of β; now it is sufficient to mention that its initial value, β^0, is taken equal to 1. Thus, in its modified and final form this second set of our fundamental equations reads:

$$-\frac{X_1 P_1}{B_1\beta} + x_{12}P_2 + x_{13}P_3 + \cdots + x_{1i}P_i + \cdots + x_{1k}P_k$$
$$+ \cdots + x_{1n}P_n = 0$$

$$x_{21}P_1 - \frac{X_2 P_2}{B_2\beta} + x_{23}P_3 + \cdots + x_{2i}P_i + \cdots + x_{2k}P_k$$
$$+ \cdots + x_{2n}P_n = 0$$

$$x_{31}P_1 + x_{32}P_2 - \frac{X_3 P_3}{B_3\beta} + \cdots + x_{3i}P_i + \cdots + x_{3k}P_k$$
$$+ \cdots + x_{3n}P_n = 0$$

(IIb) . . . .

$$x_{i1}P_1 + x_{i2}P_2 + x_{i3}P_3 + \cdots - \frac{X_i P_i}{B_i\beta} + \cdots + x_{ik}P_k$$
$$+ \cdots + x_{in}P_n = 0$$

. . . .

$$x_{k1}P_1 + x_{k2}P_2 + x_{k3}P_3 + \cdots + x_{ki}P_i + \cdots - \frac{X_k P_k}{B_k\beta}$$
$$+ \cdots + x_{kn}P_n = 0$$

. . . .

$$x_{n1}P_1 + x_{n2}P_2 + x_{n3}P_3 + \cdots + x_{ni}P_i + \cdots + x_{nk}P_k$$
$$+ \cdots - \frac{X_n P_n}{B_n\beta} = 0$$

For the purpose of terminological convenience, the notion of a saving ratio and the capital letter $\mathcal{B}_i$ is used to denote the product $B_i\beta$. For its initial value, $\mathcal{B}_i{}^0$, the saving ratio equals the corresponding saving coefficient $B_i{}^0$, but as soon a β varies and becomes smaller than or larger than 1, $\mathcal{B}_i$ also deviates from B_i.

The phenomenon of savings and investment not only affects the revenue-outlay relations; it also requires a corresponding adjustment in the form of our production functions. When comparing an enterprise which finds itself in a state of complete equilibrium with another which is absorbing additional investment, we see that not only does the money outlay of the latter exceed its current revenue but also that the physical amount of the currently absorbed cost factors are necessarily greater than the normal requirements of its current production. In other words, the technical proportion between its input and output will be distorted in favor of the former. As a matter of fact, it is this real distortion which causes the aforementioned financial discrepancy between current costs and receipts. In accordance with this argument, the production coefficients of each industry in the third set of our fundamental equations are supplemented by the introduction of the investment coefficient which has been inserted into the corresponding cost equations of the second set.

$$x_{12} = \frac{a_{12}X_1}{A_1 B_1 \beta}, \; x_{13} = \frac{a_{13}X_1}{A_1 B_1 \beta}, \; \cdots, \; x_{1i} = \frac{a_{1i}X_1}{A_1 B_1 \beta}, \; \cdots,$$

$$x_{1k} = \frac{a_{1k}X_1}{A_1 B_1 \beta}, \; \cdots, \; x_{1n} = \frac{a_{1n}X_1}{A_1 B_1 \beta}$$

$$x_{21} = \frac{a_{21}X_2}{A_2 B_2 \beta}, \; x_{23} = \frac{a_{23}X_2}{A_2 B_2 \beta}, \; \cdots, \; x_{2i} = \frac{a_{2i}X_2}{A_2 B_2 \beta}, \; \cdots,$$

$$x_{2k} = \frac{a_{2k}X_2}{A_2 B_2 \beta}, \; \cdots, \; x_{2n} = \frac{a_{2n}X_2}{A_2 B_2 \beta}$$

$$x_{31} = \frac{a_{31}X_3}{A_3 B_3 \beta}, \; x_{32} = \frac{a_{32}X_3}{A_3 B_3 \beta}, \; \cdots, \; x_{3i} = \frac{a_{3i}X_3}{A_3 B_3 \beta},$$

$$x_{3k} = \frac{a_{3k}X_3}{A_3 B_3 \beta}, \; \cdots, \; x_{3n} = \frac{a_{3n}X_3}{A_3 B_3 \beta}$$

(IIIb)   . . . .

$$x_{i1} = \frac{a_{i1}X_i}{A_iB_i\beta}, \quad x_{i2} = \frac{a_{i2}X_i}{A_iB_i\beta}, \quad x_{i3} = \frac{a_{i3}X_i}{A_iB_i\beta}, \quad \cdots, \cdots,$$

$$x_{ik} = \frac{a_{ik}X_i}{A_iB_i\beta}, \quad \cdots, x_{in} = \frac{a_{in}X_i}{A_iB_i\beta}$$

$$x_{k1} = \frac{a_{k1}X_k}{A_kB_k\beta}, \quad x_{k2} = \frac{a_{k2}X_k}{A_kB_k\beta}, \quad x_{k3} = \frac{a_{k3}X_k}{A_kB_k\beta}, \quad \cdots,$$

$$x_{ki} = \frac{a_{ki}X_k}{A_kB_k\beta}, \quad \cdots, \cdots, x_{kn} = \frac{a_{kn}X_k}{A_kB_k\beta}$$

$$x_{n1} = \frac{a_{n1}X_n}{A_nB_n\beta}, \quad x_{n2} = \frac{a_{n2}X_n}{A_nB_n\beta} \quad x_{n3} = \frac{a_{n3}X_n}{A_nB_n\beta}, \quad \cdots,$$

$$x_{ni} = \frac{a_{ni}X_n}{A_nB_n\beta}, \quad \cdots, x_{nk} = \frac{a_{nk}X_n}{A_nB_n\beta}, \quad \cdots$$

Application of an identical investment coefficient to all cost elements of any given industry introduces a hardly warranted assumption, namely, that the investment process affects the input of all the factors in the same degree. Lack of sufficient empirical information, enhanced by certain mathematical difficulties, makes it impossible to treat this aspect of the problem more in conformity to facts.

However, in the tables of inputs and outputs (see Part I), which supply the statistical background of our empirical analysis, the production coefficients of different industries are computed on the basis of actual statistical figures, which are obviously affected by existing saving and investment conditions. Without minimizing the fundamental weakness of the questionable assumption, this circumstance is likely to reduce the size of the errors which would ensue were the empirical input data adjusted to a hypothetical non-investment basis.

Some further important aspects of the investment-savings theory will be developed later in connection with the analysis of the entire system of equations as a whole.

5. PRICES AS DEPENDENT VARIABLES

Combination of the second and third sets of equations makes it possible to express all the prices in terms of the various coefficients. Each small x with the double subscript can be substituted in IIb on the basis of the corresponding equation in IIIb, i.e., the input quantity of each cost element can be expressed in terms of the total output of the particular industry.

Substitution of the first-row equations of IIIb in the first row of IIb gives, for example:

$$-\frac{X_1P_1}{B_1\beta} + \frac{a_{12}X_1P_2}{A_1B_1\beta} + \frac{a_{13}X_1P_3}{A_1B_1\beta} + \cdots + \frac{a_{1i}X_1P_i}{A_1B_1\beta} + \frac{a_{1k}X_1P_k}{A_1B_1\beta}$$
$$+ \cdots + \frac{a_{1n}X_1P_n}{A_1B_1\beta} = 0$$

Cancellation eliminates $\dfrac{X_1}{B_1\beta}$. Thus, clearing the denominator, we obtain a new system of linear equations with the prices, $P_1, P_2, \ldots$ as the only unknowns.

$$-A_1P_1 + a_{12}P_2 + a_{13}P_3 + \cdots + a_{1i}P_i + \cdots + a_{1k}P_k + \cdots$$
$$+ a_{1n}P_n = 0$$

$$a_{21}P_1 - A_2P_2 + a_{23}P_3 + \cdots + a_{2i}P_i + \cdots + a_{2k}P_k + \cdots$$
$$+ a_{2n}P_n = 0$$

$$a_{31}P_1 + a_{32}P_2 - A_3P_3 + \cdots + a_{3i}P_i + \cdots + a_{3k}P_k + \cdots$$
$$+ a_{3n}P_n = 0$$

(IV) ....

$$a_{i1}P_1 + a_{i2}P_2 + a_{i3}P_3 + \cdots - A_iP_i + \cdots + a_{ik}P_k + \cdots$$
$$+ a_{in}P_n = 0$$

....

$$a_{k1}P_1 + a_{k2}P_2 + a_{k3}P_3 + \cdots + a_{ki}P_i + \cdots - A_kP_k + \cdots$$
$$+ a_{kn}P_n = 0$$

....

$$a_{n1}P_1 + a_{n2}P_2 + a_{n3}P_3 + \cdots + a_{ni}P_i + \cdots + a_{nk}P_k + \cdots$$
$$- A_nP_n = 0$$

The system is homogeneous: if satisfied by some given set of prices, it will be equally well satisfied by any other set obtained from the first by multiplying it by any given number. The proposition that the material structure of our economic system determines only the *relative,* not the absolute, prices of all the commodities is so familiar that it hardly deserves further discussion.[1]

The homogeneity of a linear system leads, however, to another, additional condition. Our n equations can be consistent (i.e. compatible with each other) only if the determinant Δ of such a system (see below) equals zero. Unless it is assumed that the values of all the coefficients are subject to some un-

[1] See "The Fundamental Assumption of Mr. Keynes' Monetary Theory of Unemployment," *Quarterly Journal of Economics,* LI, pp. 192–97 (November 1936).

known law of prestabilized harmony, this requirement indicates that at least one of them is not a genuine independent datum but rather a variable which adjusts itself to the values of all the other parameters so as to satisfy the aforementioned consistency condition.

$$(A_1{}^0 = A_2{}^0 = \cdots = 1)$$

$$\begin{vmatrix}
-A_1 & a_{12} & a_{13} \cdots & a_{1i} \cdots & a_{1k} \cdots & a_{1n} \\
a_{21} & -A_2 & a_{23} \cdots & a_{2i} \cdots & a_{2k} \cdots & a_{2n} \\
a_{31} & a_{32} & -A_3 \cdots & a_{3i} \cdots & a_{3k} \cdots & a_{3n} \\
 & & & & & \\
a_{i1} & a_{i2} & a_{i3} \cdots -A_i & \cdots & a_{ik} \cdots & a_{in} \\
 & & & & & \\
a_{k1} & a_{k2} & a_{k3} \cdots & a_{ki} \cdots -A_k & \cdots & a_{kn} \\
 & & & & & \\
a_{n1} & a_{n2} & a_{n3} \cdots & a_{ni} \cdots & a_{nk} \cdots & -A_n
\end{vmatrix} \equiv \Delta$$

Turning to its economic interpretation, we see that this formal requirement finds complete material justification. No economic system could possibly exist in which all the technical and consumption coefficients were independent of one another. On the contrary, the relation between the amount of services supplied by households and the rate of their remuneration (as measured by the value of the coefficients $\dfrac{a_{n1}}{A_n}, \dfrac{a_{n2}}{A_n}, \ldots$) is necessarily limited by the productivity of the system as reflected in the numerical values of all production coefficients. Whenever the productivity of the system falls or rises, the magnitudes of the consumption coefficients are stepped up or down automatically.

Assuming that the described adjustment affects the total consumption level without disturbing the relative distribution of expenditures, we make the proportionality factor A_n responsible for the maintenance of equilibrium. The equilibrium condition itself can now be expressed by the equation:

(v) $$\Delta(A_n) = 0$$

which implicitly determines the value of variable coefficient A_n as a function of all the other independent parameters.

This condition being satisfied, one of the n equations in IV becomes redundant. Accordingly, we strike out the first equation and solve the system for all the other prices according to the general formula:

(VI a) $$P_{i1} = \frac{\Delta_{1i}}{\Delta_{11}}$$

where P_{i1} is the price of commodity i expressed in terms of commodity 1 while Δ_{1i} and Δ_{11} represent algebraic complements (co-factors) of the elements a_{1i} and A_1 in Δ obtained by striking out the 1st row and the ith column and the 1st row and the 1st column respectively and multiplying the resulting minors with $(-1)^{1+1}$ and $(-1)^{1+i}$.

6. PHYSICAL OUTPUTS AS DEPENDENT VARIABLES

Determination of equilibrium quantities is similar to that of equilibrium prices. Substitution of the values from Set IIIb for the corresponding unknowns (x's with double subscripts) of Set I results in the following system of n equations:

$$-X_1 + \frac{a_{21}X_2}{A_2B_2\beta} + \frac{a_{31}X_3}{A_3B_3\beta} + \cdots + \frac{a_{i1}X_i}{A_iB_i\beta}$$
$$+ \cdots + \frac{a_{k1}X_k}{A_kB_k\beta} + \cdots + \frac{a_{n1}X_n}{A_nB_n\beta} = 0$$

$$\frac{a_{12}X_1}{A_1B_1\beta} - X_2 + \frac{a_{32}X_3}{A_3B_3\beta} + \cdots + \frac{a_{i2}X_i}{A_iB_i\beta}$$
$$+ \cdots + \frac{a_{k2}X_k}{A_kB_k\beta} + \cdots + \frac{a_{n2}X_n}{A_nB_n\beta} = 0$$

$$\frac{a_{13}X_1}{A_1B_1\beta} + \frac{a_{23}X_2}{A_2B_2\beta} - X_3 + \cdots + \frac{a_{i3}X_i}{A_iB_i\beta}$$
$$+ \cdots + \frac{a_{k3}X_k}{A_kB_k\beta} + \cdots + \frac{a_{n3}X_n}{A_nB_n\beta} = 0$$

....

$$\text{(VII)} \quad \frac{a_{1i}X_1}{A_1B_1\beta} + \frac{a_{2i}X_2}{A_2B_2\beta} + \frac{a_{3i}X_3}{A_3B_3\beta} + \cdots - X_i + \cdots$$
$$+ \frac{a_{ki}X_k}{A_kB_k\beta} + \cdots + \frac{a_{ni}X_n}{A_nB_n\beta} = 0$$

....

$$\frac{a_{1k}X_1}{A_1B_1\beta} + \frac{a_{2k}X_2}{A_2B_2\beta} + \frac{a_{3k}X_3}{A_3B_3\beta} + \cdots + \frac{a_{ik}X_i}{A_iB_i\beta}$$
$$+ \cdots - X_k + \cdots + \frac{a_{nk}X_n}{A_nB_n\beta} = 0$$

....

$$\frac{a_{1n}X_1}{A_1B_1\beta} + \frac{a_{2n}X_2}{A_2B_2\beta} + \frac{a_{3n}X_3}{A_3B_3\beta} + \cdots + \frac{a_{in}X_i}{A_iB_i\beta}$$
$$+ \cdots + \frac{a_{kn}X_k}{A_kB_k\beta} + \cdots - X_n = 0$$

Like Set IV, this system is homogeneous and can be solved only for the relative values of the unknown quantities X_1, $X_2 \cdots$.

While the concept of relative prices occurs often in theoretical discussion, an analogous use of *relative quantities* seems to be less familiar. As long as it is assumed (a) that all production and consumption functions are homogeneous, i.e. there is no "economy of scale" (even if they are not linear as in the present setup) and, at the same time, (b) that the amounts of all the services and commodities are variable, their absolute equilibrium values must remain entirely undetermined. Only by abandoning at least one of these two conditions can the determination of the absolute production level (analogous to the absolute price level) be made possible.

There can be little doubt that neither is actually fulfilled. On the other hand, there is good reason to believe that the lumpiness of certain cost factors which explains the non-homogeneity of many production functions of single plants has a much smaller significance when considered from the viewpoint of the total output of an industry as a whole. The classical idea of an absolutely fixed supply of the primary factors of production is by now considerably shaken.

Thus, although not exactly homogeneous, the actual structure of our economic system might be analogous to that of a large set of linear equations with a single non-homogeneous member. While the relative values of all the unknowns can be quite stable, their absolute level might depend almost entirely upon the size of one single coefficient, so that the slightest variation in this particular datum might produce a very violent, although nearly proportional, change in the absolute values of all the unknowns. In a case of pronounced instability of this kind, the study of the system might well be undertaken in terms of the relative values of its unknowns. The necessity of expressing the quantities of outputs in relative rather than absolute terms seems from this viewpoint to be a strong feature of our theoretical scheme rather than a drawback.

The consistency of Set VII requires that its determinant D (see p. 50) equal zero. As in Set IV, this requirement shows that at least one of our coefficients is not an independent datum but rather a variable which satisfies the consistency condition formulated above.

Since all the production coefficients are considered as given, and since the value of the variable consumption coefficient A_n is already fixed on the basis of the first consistency requirement (v), only the investment (or saving) ratios can be made responsible for realization of the second consistency requirement.

$$(A_1{}^0 = A_2{}^0 = \cdots = 1)$$
$$(\beta^0 = 1)$$

$$
\begin{vmatrix}
-A_1 B_1 \beta & a_{21} & a_{31} & \cdots & a_{i1} & \cdots & a_{k1} & \cdots & a_{n1} \\
a_{12} & -A_2 B_2 \beta & a_{32} & \cdots & a_{i2} & \cdots & a_{k2} & \cdots & a_{n2} \\
a_{13} & a_{23} & -A_3 B_3 \beta & \cdots & a_{i3} & \cdots & a_{k3} & \cdots & a_{n3} \\
\cdots \\
a_{1i} & a_{2i} & a_{3i} & \cdots & -A_i B_i \beta & \cdots & a_{ki} & \cdots & a_{ni} \\
\cdots \\
a_{1k} & a_{2k} & a_{3k} & \cdots & a_{ik} & \cdots & -A_k B_k \beta & \cdots & a_{nk} \\
\cdots \\
a_{1n} & a_{2n} & a_{3n} & \cdots & a_{in} & \cdots & a_{kn} & \cdots & -A_n B_n \beta
\end{vmatrix}
$$

$$\frac{1}{A_1 \cdot A_2 \cdot A_3 \cdots A_i \cdots A_k \cdots A_n \cdot B_1 \cdot B_2 \cdot B_3 \cdots B_i \cdots B_k \cdots B_n \cdot \beta^n}$$

$$\equiv D \cdot \frac{1}{A_1 \cdot A_2 \cdot A_3 \cdots A_i \cdots A_k \cdots A_n \cdot B_1 \cdot B_2 \cdot B_3 \cdots B_i \cdots B_k \cdots B_n \cdot \beta^n}$$

The saving ratio $\mathcal{B}_n$, which is the ratio between the total revenue and the total purchases of the consolidated household account, could adjust itself, for example, so as to make the value of the determinant D equal zero. On the basis of our knowledge of the functioning of the actual economic system, it seems, however, more realistic to assume that the burden of adjustment of this kind is more or less equally distributed between all savings and investments, i.e., that whenever the former increase the latter tend to do the same and vice versa.

Among the many factors determining the size of the investment coefficient of any given industry, we can distinguish, on one hand, those which are explained by the special situation of that particular industry, and, on the other, forces of a more general character which influence all savings and investments simultaneously. The first type is well exemplified by the particular savings habits of income receivers or the specific profitability conditions of individual industries; the second is closely identified with general conditions of the capital market, the interest-rate level being one of the most conspicuous factors.

Without being able to apply empirically any more refined theoretical construction, we are constrained to choose *ad hoc* a more or less plausible, simple algebraic relation, and to identify it with the foregoing distinction: the specific part B_i of an investment ratio $\mathcal{B}_i$ ($\equiv B_i\beta$) is supposed to represent the effect of all the specific investment — or saving — conditions of every particular industry, while the proportionality factor β stands for the second set of general influences common to all industries, for example, the interest rate.

If a particular $B_i\beta$ is smaller than 1 (negative values are obviously excluded), an increase of β will indicate a diminishing, and a decrease, an advancing, investment ratio. On the other hand, with $B_1\beta$ larger than 1, an increase of β will mean a higher saving ratio and vice versa. An increased β signifies increased saving ratios and reduced investment ratios; a reduced β, smaller saving ratios and greater investment ratios. Thus, the coefficient β in our theoretical scheme is made responsible for the realization of the second consistency condition, which can now be put in the form of the following equation:

(VIII) $$D(\beta) = 0$$

In the singular situation where all $\mathcal{B}_i$'s equal 1, each row of the determinant D becomes identical with the corresponding column of the determinant Δ, which means that $D = \Delta$. In this special case, satisfaction of condition (v) makes D also equal zero, which obviates the necessity of formulating a separate consistency condition for system VII.

In order to obtain the relative sizes of the unknown outputs (with output of industry 1 used as numéraire, i.e., standard of value), we set $X_1 = 1$, drop the first equation (as redundant), and solve the system of the remaining $n - 1$ equations for values of the unknown total outputs $X_{21}, X_{31}, \cdots$, according to the formula

(IX a) $$X_{i1} = \frac{D_{1i}}{D_{11}} \cdot \frac{A_i}{A_1} \cdot \frac{B_i}{B_1}$$

X_{i1} is the output of commodity i, measured in terms of commodity 1; D_{1i} and D_{11} are algebraic complements (co-factors) of elements $a_{i1} - A_1 B_1 \beta$ of the determinant D.

7. PRICE AND OUTPUT REACTIONS TO PRIMARY TECHNICAL CHANGES

Completion of the general theoretical scheme leads directly to the central problem of our inquiry. Equations VI a and IX a show explicitly the dependence of every (relative) price and (relative) quantity on the values of all the coefficients of our system. A change in the magnitude of any of these coefficients will obviously have a definite effect upon the prices and quantities of all the commodities and services. What is the actual numerical measure of this effect?

The most direct answer to this question could be obtained if we knew the actual shape of equations VI a and IX a as functions of two variables — the price or quantity of commodity i, on the one hand, and some particular parameter, say A_k or B_k, whose influence we intend to investigate, on the other. Technical difficulties militate against the practical use of this direct approach. Instead, the first derivatives of all such functions can be computed, i.e., the ratios between infinitesimal changes in our dependent and independent variables. Knowing the numerical values of such derivatives, it will be possible to estimate the effect of finite changes in any independent variable, provided they are small enough to enable us to neglect the influence of higher derivatives.[1]

The number of separate parameters, even in the relatively simple empirical setup as used in Part III exceeds one hundred. Thus, our practical task had to be restricted by the selection of a few representative cases; the variation of the system was studied only in respect of changes in the technical proportionality factors, $A_1, A_2, A_3, \cdots$, and the specific investment coefficients, $B_1, B_2, B_3 \cdots$.[2]

The actual computation of the theoretical formulae of the corresponding derivatives requires nothing but routine application of elementary rules of differential calculus. The setup of these computations might as well be adjusted at once to the practical requirements of subsequent numerical applications. Thus, as mentioned above, the *initial* values of all the proportionality coefficients are considered equal to 1;

$$A_1^0 = A_2^0 = A_3^0 = \cdots = A_n^0 = \beta^0 = 1$$

Similarly, each of the *initial* total outputs, $X_1^0, X_2^0 \cdots X_n^0$, is expressed in appropriately chosen physical units of measurement, so that

$$P_1^0 = P_2^0 = \cdots = P_n^0 = 1$$

[1] Although not actually calculated, the values of higher derivatives can easily be computed. Theoretically it can be shown that the number of such derivatives is, in general, infinite.

[2] Separate variation of the individual consumption coefficients $a_{n1}, a_{n2}, \cdots$ is discussed on page 132 ff.

The previously discussed decision to take the price and quantity of commodity 1 as a common reference point, or *numéraire*, gives two additional equations:

(x) $\qquad\qquad X_{11} = 1$ $\qquad\qquad$ (xi) $\quad P_{11} = 1$

It is convenient to begin the analysis with the computation of the derivative $\dfrac{dP_{i1}}{dA_k}$ where i and k are identified with any subscript from 2 to n (P_1 is constant), and from 1 to $n - 1$ (A_n does not represent an independent variable), respectively.

From vi we have:

(xii) $\quad \dfrac{dP_{i1}}{dA_k} =$

$$\frac{\left(\dfrac{d\Delta_{1i}}{dA_k}\cdot\Delta_{11} - \dfrac{d\Delta_{11}}{dA_k}\cdot\Delta_{1i}\right)}{(\Delta_{11})^2} = P_{i1}\left[\frac{d\Delta_{1i}}{dA_k}\cdot\frac{1}{\Delta_{1i}} - \frac{d\Delta_{11}}{dA_k}\cdot\frac{1}{\Delta_{11}}\right]$$

(xiii) $$\frac{d\Delta_{1i}}{dA_k} = -\,\Delta_{1i\,\cdot\,kk} - \Delta_{1i\,\cdot\,nn}\,\frac{dA_n}{dA_k}$$

(xiv) $$\frac{d\Delta_{11}}{dA_k} = -\,\Delta_{11\,\cdot\,kk} - \Delta_{11\,\cdot\,nn}\,\frac{dA_n}{dA_k}$$

With A_k as the independent variable, v can be rewritten:

(xv) $\qquad\qquad \Delta(A_n, A_k) = 0$

Consequently

(xvi) $$\frac{dA_n}{dA_k} = -\,\frac{\partial\Delta}{\partial A_k} \div \frac{\partial\Delta}{\partial A_n} = -\,\frac{\Delta_{kk}}{\Delta_{nn}}$$

substituting xiii, xiv, and xvi in xii:

(xvii a) $$\frac{dP_{i1}}{dA_k} = P_{i1}\left[\frac{\Delta_{kk}}{\Delta_{nn}}\left(\frac{\Delta_{1i\,\cdot\,nn}}{\Delta_{1i}} - \frac{\Delta_{11\,\cdot\,nn}}{\Delta_{11}}\right)\right.$$
$$\left. + \frac{\Delta_{11\,\cdot\,kk}}{\Delta_{11}} - \frac{\Delta_{1i\,\cdot\,kk}}{\Delta_{1i}}\right]$$

Computation of the quantity derivative $\dfrac{dX_{i1}}{dA_k}$ is based on ix a.

(xviii)

$$\frac{dX_{i1}}{dA_k} = \frac{\frac{dD_{1i}}{dA_k}D_{11} - \frac{dD_{11}}{dA_k}D_{1i}}{(D_{11})^2} \cdot \frac{B_i A_i}{B_1 A_1} + \frac{B_i}{B_1} \cdot \frac{D_{1i}}{D_{11}} \cdot \frac{d}{dA_k}\left(\frac{A_i}{A_1}\right)$$

$$= X_{i1}\left[\frac{dD_{1i}}{dA_k} \cdot \frac{1}{D_{1i}} - \frac{dD_{11}}{dA_k} \cdot \frac{1}{D_{11}} + \frac{d}{dA_k}\left(\frac{A_i}{A_1}\right)\right]$$

(xix) $$\frac{dD_{1i}}{dA_k} = -(B_2\,D_{1i\,.\,22} + B_3\,D_{1i\,.\,33} + \cdots + 0 + \cdots$$

$$+ B_k\,D_{1i\,.\,kk} + \cdots + B_n\,D_{1i\,.\,nn})\frac{d\beta}{dA_k} - B_k\,D_{1i\,.\,kk}$$

$$- B_n\,D_{1i\,.\,nn}\frac{dA_n}{dA_k}$$

(xx) $$\frac{dD_{11}}{dA_k} = -(B_2\,D_{11\,.\,22} + B_3\,D_{11\,.\,33} + \cdots + B_i\,D_{11\,.\,ii}$$

$$+ \cdots + B_k D_{11\,.\,kk} + \cdots + B_n D_{11\,.\,nn})\frac{d\beta}{dA_k}$$

$$- B_k\,D_{11\,.\,kk} - B_n\,D_{11\,.\,nn}\frac{dA_n}{dA_k}$$

Substitution of xix and xx in xviii gives:

(xxia) $$\frac{dX_{i1}}{dA_k} = X_{i1}\left[\ \left\{\ B_2\left(\frac{D_{11\,.\,22}}{D_{11}} - \frac{D_{1i\,.\,22}}{D_{1i}}\right)\right.\right.$$

$$+ B_3\left(\frac{D_{11\,.\,33}}{D_{11}} - \frac{D_{1i\,.\,33}}{D_{1i}}\right)$$

$$+ \cdots B_i\left(\frac{D_{11\,.\,ii}}{D_{11}} - 0\right)$$

$$+ \cdots B_n\left(\frac{D_{11\,.\,nn}}{D_{11}} - \frac{D_{1i\,.\,nn}}{D_{1i}}\right)\right\}\frac{d\beta}{dA_k}$$

$$+ B_k\left(\frac{D_{11\,.\,kk}}{D_{11}} - \frac{D_{1i\,.\,kk}}{D_{1i}}\right) + B_n\left(\frac{D_{11\,.\,nn}}{D_{11}}\right.$$

$$\left.\left.- \frac{D_{1i\,.\,nn}}{D_{1i}}\right)\frac{dA_n}{dA_k} + \frac{d}{dA_k}\left(\frac{A_i}{A_1}\right)\right]$$

Equation viii can now be rewritten:

(xxii) $$D(\beta,\ A_n(A_k),\ A_k) = 0$$

From that we obtain:

$$(\text{XXIII}) \quad \frac{d\beta}{dA_k} = -\frac{\left(\dfrac{\partial D}{\partial A_k}\right)_\beta}{\left(\dfrac{\partial D}{\partial \beta}\right)_{A_k}}$$

$$= -\frac{\left(\dfrac{\partial D}{\partial A_k}\right)_{\beta,A_n} + \left(\dfrac{\partial D}{\partial A_n}\right)_{\beta,A_k} \cdot \left(\dfrac{dA_n}{dA_k}\right)}{\left(\dfrac{\partial D}{\partial \beta}\right)_{A_k}}$$

Rearrangement of terms and substitution from XVI gives:

$$(\text{XXIV}) \quad \frac{d\beta}{dA_k} =$$

$$-\frac{\dfrac{D_{kk}}{D_{nn}}B_k + B_n \dfrac{dA_n}{dA_k}}{(D_{11}B_1 + D_{22}B_2 + D_{33}B_3 + \cdots + D_{ii}B_i + \cdots D_{kk}B_k + \cdots D_{nn}B_n) \div D_{nn}}$$

Excluding for obvious reasons all cases in which $i = n$ or $k = n$,

$$(\text{XXV}) \quad \frac{d}{dA_k}\left(\frac{A_i}{A_1}\right) \begin{cases} = \dfrac{\Delta_{kk}}{\Delta_{nn}} & \text{if } n = 1,\ k \neq i \\[2mm] = 1 + \dfrac{\Delta_{kk}}{\Delta_{nn}} & \text{if } n = 1,\ k = i \\[2mm] = 1 & \text{if } n \neq 1,\ i = k \\[2mm] = -1 & \text{if } n \neq 1,\ k = 1 \\[2mm] = 0 & \text{in all other cases.} \end{cases}$$

A similar procedure gives us the quantity-derivative in respect of savings, $\dfrac{dX_i}{dB_k}$, where k indicates any subscript from 1 to n. Starting again with IX a:

$$(\text{XXVI}) \quad \frac{dX_{i1}}{dB_k} = \left[\frac{\dfrac{dD_{1i}}{dB_k} \cdot D_{11} - \dfrac{dD_{11}}{dB_k}D_{1i}}{(D_{11})^2} \cdot \frac{B_i}{B_1} \cdot \frac{A_i}{A_1}\right.$$

$$\left. + \frac{A_i}{A_1} \cdot \frac{D_{1i}}{D_{11}} \cdot \frac{d}{dB_k}\left(\frac{B_i}{B_1}\right)\right]$$

$$= X_{i1}\left[\frac{dD_{1i}}{dB_k} \cdot \frac{1}{D_{1i}} - \frac{dD_{11}}{dB_k} \cdot \frac{1}{D_{11}} + \frac{B_1}{B_i} \cdot \frac{d}{dB_k}\left(\frac{B_i}{B_1}\right)\right]$$

Developing $\dfrac{dD_{1i}}{dB_k}$ and $\dfrac{dD_{11}}{dB_k}$ and collecting terms:

$$\text{(xxvii)} \quad \frac{dX_{i1}}{dB_k} = X_{i1}\Bigg[\left\{\ B_2\left(\frac{D_{11\cdot22}}{D_{11}} - \frac{D_{1i\cdot22}}{D_{1i}}\right)\right.$$

$$+ B_3\left(\frac{D_{11\cdot33}}{D_{11}} - \frac{D_{1i\cdot33}}{D_{1i}}\right) + \cdots B_i\left(\frac{D_{11\cdot ii}}{D_{11}} - 0\right)$$

$$+ \cdots + B_k\left(\frac{D_{11\cdot kk}}{D_{11}} - \frac{D_{1i\cdot kk}}{D_{1i}}\right)$$

$$+ \cdots B_n\left(\frac{D_{11\cdot nn}}{D_{11}} - \frac{D_{1i\cdot nn}}{D_{1i}}\right)\Bigg\}\frac{d\beta}{dB_k}$$

$$+ \left.\left(\frac{D_{11\cdot kk}}{D_{11}} - \frac{D_{1i\cdot kk}}{D_{1i}}\right) + \frac{B_1}{B_i}\cdot\frac{d}{dB_k}\left(\frac{B_i}{B_1}\right)\right]$$

With B_k being now the independent variable, equation viii acquires a new form:

$$\text{(xxviii)} \qquad\qquad D(\beta,\ B_k) = 0$$

Thus,

$$\text{(xxix)} \quad \frac{d\beta}{dB_k} = -\frac{\left(\dfrac{\partial D}{\partial B_k}\right)_\beta}{\left(\dfrac{\partial D}{\partial \beta}\right)_{B_k}}$$

$$= -\frac{D_{kk} \div D_{nn}}{(D_{11}B_1 + D_{22}B_2 + D_{33}B_3 + \cdots + D_{ii}B_i + \cdots + D_{kk}B_k + \cdots + D_{nn}B_n) \div D_{nn}}$$

Furthermore, while the case of $i = 1$ is in general excluded from this discussion because X_1 serves as *numéraire*,

$$\text{(xxx a)} \quad \frac{B_1}{B_i}\cdot\frac{d}{dB_k}\left(\frac{B_i}{B_1}\right)\quad \begin{cases} = -\dfrac{1}{B_1} & \text{if } k = 1 \\[2mm] = \dfrac{1}{B_i} & \text{if } k = i \\[2mm] = 0 & \text{in all other cases.} \end{cases}$$

8. ELASTICITY CONCEPTS, VALUE AND COST REACTIONS, ETC.

The results of this theoretical analysis can be approached and interpreted from nearly as many angles as the observations of actual economic processes themselves. Special computation formulae can be worked out as necessity arises.

The subsequent interpretation of empirical conclusions will be facilitated, however, if some basic interrelations are considered before they are applied statistically.

(*a*) In studying the reaction of all the different prices and quantities, it is particularly interesting to compare the *relative* strength of such simultaneous changes. The magnitude of heterogeneous price and quantity dimensions must be reduced to some common unit. All derivatives can be expressed for this purpose in relative terms by dividing them by the absolute magnitudes of the respective independent variables. Thus, we can compare $\dfrac{dP_{i1}}{dA_k} \cdot \dfrac{1}{P_{i1}}$, $\dfrac{dX_{i1}}{dA_k} \cdot \dfrac{1}{X_{i1}}$, and $\dfrac{dX_{i1}}{dB_k} \cdot \dfrac{1}{X_{i1}}$, instead of $\dfrac{dP_{i1}}{dA_k}$, $\dfrac{dX_{i1}}{dA_k}$, or $\dfrac{dX_{i1}}{dB_k}$.

(*b*) In measurements of relative prices and quantities of all the other commodities, the output of industry 1 and its price were used as *numéraires*. The formulae for shifting the base of reference from the first to any other, say *j*th, industry, can easily be derived. For example,

$$(\text{xxxi}) \qquad X_{ij} = \frac{X_i}{X_j} = \frac{X_i}{X_1} \div \frac{X_j}{X_1}$$

Consequently,

$$(\text{xxxii})$$

$$\frac{d}{dA_k}\left(\frac{X_i}{X_j}\right) = \left[\frac{d}{dA_k}\left(\frac{X_i}{X_1}\right) \cdot \frac{X_j}{X_1} - \frac{d}{dA_k}\left(\frac{X_j}{X_1}\right) \cdot \frac{X_i}{X_1}\right] \div \left(\frac{X_j}{X_1}\right)^2$$

and finally

$$(\text{xxxiii}) \qquad \frac{d}{dA_k}\left(\frac{X_i}{X_j}\right) \div \frac{X_i}{X_j} = \frac{d}{dA_k}\left(\frac{X_i}{X_1}\right) \div \frac{X_i}{X_1} - \frac{d}{dA_k}\left(\frac{X_i}{X_1}\right) \div \frac{X_j}{X_1}$$

Similarly, for shift of the price base, we have

$$(\text{xxxiv}) \qquad \frac{d}{dA_k}\left(\frac{P_i}{P_j}\right) \div \frac{P_i}{P_j} = \frac{d}{dA_k}\left(\frac{P_i}{P_1}\right) \div \frac{P_i}{P_1} - \frac{d}{dA_k}\left(\frac{P_j}{P_1}\right) \div \frac{P_j}{P_1}$$

Analogous relations hold naturally also between the derivatives in respect of B_k.

(*c*) From output and price derivatives, corresponding value ($v_i = X_i P_i$) changes can be computed. For example:

$$(\text{xxxv}) \qquad \frac{dv_i}{dA_k} = \frac{dX_i}{dA_k} \; P_i + \frac{dP_i}{dA_k} \cdot X_i$$

or in relative terms:

(XXXVI)
$$\frac{dv_i}{dA_k} \cdot \frac{1}{v_i} = \frac{dX_i}{dA_k} \cdot \frac{1}{X_i} + \frac{dP_i}{dA_k} \cdot \frac{1}{P_i}$$

(d) A combined effect of a simultaneous variation in two or more parameters, say A_k and B_e, can be derived provided we know the relative magnitude, $\dfrac{dB_e}{dA_k}$, of both primary changes. So, for example, if B_e is considered to depend upon A_k,

(XXXVII)
$$\frac{dX_i}{dA_k} = \frac{\partial X_i}{\partial A_k} + \frac{\partial X_i}{\partial B_e}\left(\frac{dB_e}{dA_k}\right)$$

$\dfrac{dX_i}{dA_k}$ is the total derivative of X_i in respect of A_k, provided B_e varies with A_k according to $\dfrac{dB_e}{dA_k}$.

(e) The saving or investment of an industry is defined [1] as the difference between its total revenue, v_i, and total expenditures, $\dfrac{v_i}{B_i\beta}$. Thus $\left(1 - \dfrac{1}{B_i\beta}\right)$ represents the *proportion* of total revenue which is being saved (or invested). The variation of this proportion in response to a change of some primary datum, say A_k, can be expressed by the formula:

(XXXVIII)
$$\frac{d}{dA_k}\left(1 - \frac{1}{B_i\beta}\right) = \frac{1}{B_i} \cdot \frac{d\beta}{dA_k} \qquad (\beta^0 = 1)$$

For the variation of the *total saving* or investment, we have

(XXXIX)
$$\frac{d}{dA_k}\left(v_i - \frac{v_i}{B_i\beta}\right) = \frac{dv_i}{dA_k}\left(1 - \frac{1}{B_i}\right)$$
$$- \frac{d}{dA_k}\left(1 - \frac{1}{B_i\beta}\right)v_i \qquad (\beta^0 = 1)$$

Total *cost variations* taken separately can be computed from

(XL)
$$\frac{d}{dA_k}\left(\frac{v_i}{B_i\beta}\right) = \frac{dv_i}{dA_k} \cdot \frac{1}{B_i} - \frac{v_i}{B_i} \cdot \frac{d\beta}{dA_k} \qquad (\beta^0 = 1)$$

(f) Instead of considering any of the dependent variables of our system in its direct relation to the variation in a basic datum, we might compare it with a simultaneous change in

[1] See formula II b.

some other independent variable caused by the same primary disturbance. Thus, the relative change in the quantity and the price of commodity i as induced by a variation in some productivity coefficient A_k requires parametric presentation.

(XLI)
$$\frac{dX_i(A_k)}{dP_i(A_k)} = \frac{dX_i(A_k)}{dA_k} \div \frac{dP_i(A_k)}{dA_k}.$$

The necessity of specifying the nature of the ultimate independent variable — in this case, A_k — must be particularly emphasized, in view of the common error of asking such questions as "What will happen to the price P_i with a change in the quantity X_i?" The correct answer to such a general question would be "Anything, depending upon the nature of the common cause of both variations."

9. SIMPLIFIED FORMULAE WITH HOUSEHOLD SERVICES USED AS NUMÉRAIRE

The final formulae become much simpler if the total output and the price of household services are chosen to serve as *numéraire*, i.e., if X_n and P_n are used as a base for the measurement of all the physical quantities and prices respectively Formulae VI a and IX a are transformed into

(VI b) $\quad P_{in} = \dfrac{\Delta_{ni}}{\Delta_{nn}}$, and $\qquad$ (IX b) $\quad X_{in} = \dfrac{D_{ni}}{D_{nn}} \cdot \dfrac{B_i}{B_n}$

A number of terms in XVII, XXI, and XXVII vanish and the new formulae are:

(XVII b) $\quad \dfrac{dP_{in}}{dA_k} = P_{in} \left[\dfrac{\Delta_{nn \cdot kk}}{\Delta_{nn}} - \dfrac{\Delta_{ni \cdot kk}}{\Delta_{ni}} \right]$

(XXI b)
$$\frac{dX_{in}}{dA_k} = X_{in} \left[\left\{ B_1 \left(\frac{D_{nn \cdot 11}}{D_{nn}} - \frac{D_{ni \cdot 11}}{D_{ni}} \right) \right. \right.$$
$$+ B_2 \left(\frac{D_{nn \cdot 22}}{D_{nn}} - \frac{D_{ni \cdot 22}}{D_{ni}} \right) + \cdots$$
$$+ B_i \left(\frac{D_{nn \cdot ii}}{D_{nn}} - 0 \right) + \cdots$$
$$+ B_k \left(\frac{D_{nn \cdot kk}}{D_{nn}} - \frac{D_{ni \cdot ii}}{D_{ni}} \right) + \cdots$$

$$+ B_{n-1} \left(\frac{D_{nn \cdot (n-1)(n-1)}}{D_{nn}} - \frac{D_{ni \cdot (n-1)(n-1)}}{D_{ni}} \right) \Bigg\} \frac{d\beta}{dA_k}$$

$$+ B_k \left(\frac{D_{nn \cdot kk}}{D_{nn}} - \frac{D_{ni \cdot kk}}{D_{ni}} \right) + \frac{d}{dA_k} \left(\frac{A_i}{A_n} \right) \Bigg]$$

$\dfrac{d\beta}{dA_k}$ is the same as in XXIII and with $i = n$ and $k = n$ excluded from consideration.

(xxv a) $\quad \dfrac{d}{dA_k} \left(\dfrac{A_i}{A_n} \right) \begin{cases} = 1 + \dfrac{\Delta_{kk}}{\Delta_{nn}} & \text{if } i = k \\[2ex] = \dfrac{\Delta_{kk}}{\Delta_{nn}} & \text{in all other cases} \end{cases}$

(xxvii a)

$$\frac{dX_{in}}{dB_k} = X_{in} \left[\left\{ B_1 \left(\frac{D_{nn \cdot 11}}{D_{nn}} - \frac{D_{ni \cdot 11}}{D_{ni}} \right) \right. \right.$$

$$+ B_2 \left(\frac{D_{nn \cdot 22}}{D_{nn}} - \frac{D_{ni \cdot 22}}{D_{ni}} \right) + \cdots$$

$$+ B_i \left(\frac{D_{nn \cdot ii}}{D_{nn}} - 0 \right) + \cdots$$

$$+ B_k \left(\frac{D_{nn \cdot kk}}{D_{nn}} - \frac{D_{ni \cdot ii}}{D_{ni}} \right) + \cdots$$

$$+ B_{n-1} \left(\frac{D_{nn \cdot (n-1)(n-1)}}{D_{nn}} - \frac{D_{ni \cdot (n-1)(n-1)}}{D_{ni}} \right) \Bigg\} \frac{d\beta}{dB_k}$$

$$+ \left(\frac{D_{nn \cdot kk}}{D_{nn}} - \frac{D_{ni \cdot kk}}{D_{ni}} \right) + \frac{B_n}{B_i} \cdot \frac{d}{dB_k} \left(\frac{B_i}{B_n} \right) \Bigg]$$

$\dfrac{d\beta}{dB_k}$ is the same as in XXIX and

(xxx b) $\quad \dfrac{B_n}{B_i} \cdot \dfrac{d}{dB_k} \left(\dfrac{B_i}{B_n} \right) = \begin{cases} = -\dfrac{1}{B_n} & \text{if } k = n \\[2ex] = \dfrac{1}{B_i} & \text{if } k = i \\[2ex] = 0 & \text{in all other cases.} \end{cases}$

These are the formulae actually used in all subsequent numerical computation.

10. PRODUCTIVITY OF AN INDUSTRY AND THE PRODUCTIVITY OF A COMMODITY

The type of analysis used above to determine the effects of a primary variation in some technical coefficient A_k, i.e., the effects of a proportional change in the productivity of all the cost factors employed in industry k, makes it possible to describe also the repercussions of any other kind of technical changes.

In connection with the subsequent empirical application of these general theoretical formulae, one particular type of technical variation deserves special attention: The proportional increase in the production coefficients a_{1i}, a_{2i}, $\cdots$, a_{ni}, i.e., *a proportional change in the productivity of a given commodity i in all its many uses as a cost factor* of other industries.

The problem can be put in a manageable form by introducing into the system of basic technical production functions III b a new set of proportionality coefficients A'_1, A'_2, $\cdots$, A'_n. Substitution of $\dfrac{a_{12}}{A'_2}$ for a_{12}, $\dfrac{a_{13}}{A'_3}$ for a_{13}, and $\dfrac{a_{ik}}{A'_k}$ for a_{ik} transforms the first equation in the first row of III b into $x_{12} = \dfrac{a_{12}X_1}{B_1\beta A_1 A'_2}$, the second into $x_{13} = \dfrac{a_{13}X_1}{B_1\beta A_1 A'_3}$, and the general element of the whole system into

$$(\text{III c}) \qquad x_{ik} = \frac{a_{ik}X_i}{B_i\beta A_i A'_k}$$

An increase or decrease in A'_k, with all other magnitudes on the right side of the corresponding equation remaining constant, would reduce or raise proportionally inputs x_{1k}, x_{2k}, x_{3k} $\cdots$ of commodity k in various industries. In short, the new proportionality coefficient A'_k can be called the *productivity coefficient of commodity k* (in contrast to A_k, which is the productivity coefficient of *industry k*).

For the purpose of the following argument, the old productivity coefficients, A_1, A_2, A_3, etc. (with the exception of A_n), can be conveniently dropped from all the basic equations.

Carried through, all along the line, the modification of the former theoretical setup leads to a new description of the equilibrium prices and quantities:

(VIc) $\quad P_{in} = \dfrac{\Delta'_{ni}}{\Delta'_{nn}} \cdot \dfrac{A'_i}{A'_n}$ $\qquad$ (IXc) $\quad X_{in} = \dfrac{D'_{in}}{D'_{nn}} \cdot \dfrac{B_i}{B_n} \cdot \dfrac{1}{A_n}$

Δ'_{ni} and Δ'_{nn} are co-factors of a new determinant Δ', which differs from the previously defined determinant Δ only so far as the new coefficients A'_1, A'_2, A'_3, $\cdots$, and $A'_n A_n$ stand in its main diagonal instead of A_1, A_2, A_3, $\cdots$, and A_n. In their numerical values, the new determinant and its minors, as used in the following equations, are identical with the old: the initial magnitudes of the new proportionality coefficients $(A'_1)^0$, $(A'_2)^0$, $(A'_3)^0$ all equal 1. D'_{in} and D'_{nn} are minors of D', which can be obtained from D by replacing A_1, A_2, A_3, $\cdots$, and A_n through A'_1, A'_2, A'_3, $\cdots$, $A'_1 A_n$ respectively. The numerical values of the two sets of corresponding minors are also identical.

The derivatives $\dfrac{dP_{in}}{dA'_k}$ and $\dfrac{dX_{in}}{dA'_k}$, computed in analogy to XVII and XXI and expressed in terms of $\dfrac{dP_{in}}{dA_k} \cdot \dfrac{1}{P_{in}}$ and $\dfrac{dX_{in}}{dA_k} \cdot \dfrac{1}{X_{in}}$, are:

(XLII) $\qquad \dfrac{dP_{in}}{dA'_k} \cdot \dfrac{1}{P_{in}} = \dfrac{dP_{in}}{dA_k} \cdot \dfrac{1}{P_{in}} + \dfrac{d}{dA'_k}\left(\dfrac{A'_i}{A'_n}\right)$

(XLIII) $\qquad \dfrac{dX_{in}}{dA'_k} \cdot \dfrac{1}{X_{in}} = \dfrac{dX_{in}}{dA_k} \cdot \dfrac{1}{X_{in}} - \dfrac{dA'_i}{dA'_k}$

where

(XLIV) $\quad \dfrac{d}{dA'_k}\left(\dfrac{A'_i}{A'_k}\right) \begin{cases} = 1 & \text{if } k = i \\ = -1 & \text{if } k = n \\ = 0 & \text{in all other cases.} \end{cases}$

and

$\qquad -\dfrac{dA'_i}{dA'_k} \begin{cases} = -1 & \text{if } k = .i \\ = 0 & \text{in all other cases.} \end{cases}$

These formulae show that a change in the productivity A'_k of any commodity k affects the prices and outputs of all *other commodities* $(i \neq k)$ exactly in the same way as a proportionally equal increase or decrease in the productivity A_k of industry k in which the commodity k is being manufactured.

The *direct* effect of the first type of technical change upon the price of commodity k itself $(i = k)$ exceeds by 1 the corresponding repercussion of the second type of technical variation in industry k. Direct output reactions show the opposite relationship. It follows that in their effect on the *total values* of various outputs, both types of technical variations are perfectly equivalent.

(XLV)
$$\frac{dv_{in}}{dA_k} = \frac{dv_{in}}{dA'_k}$$

The productivity of household services can vary as spontaneously as the productivity of any other cost factor, i.e., A'_n, in contrast to A_n, must be considered to be an independent variable similar to any other technical coefficient. Simple computation shows, however, that a change in A'_n will have an idencal effect on all other prices and outputs:

(XLVI)
$$\frac{dP_{in}}{dA'_n} \cdot \frac{1}{P_{in}} = +1 \qquad \frac{dX_{in}}{dA'_n} \cdot \frac{1}{X_{in}} = -1$$

The total value figures will obviously remain invariant.

The productivity of the household A_n would necessarily change in the opposite direction: from $\Delta(A_n, A'_n) = 0$ (see formula XVI), it follows:

(XLVII)
$$\frac{dA_n}{dA'_n} = -\frac{\Delta_{nn}}{\Delta_{kk}} = -1$$

That means that (*ceteris paribus*) the standard of living rises and falls as the productivity of the household services increases or decreases.

11. PRODUCTIVITIES, EFFICIENCIES, PRICES, AND OUTPUTS

The observed similarity between the repercussions of the two types of productivity changes is rooted in the nature of the economic system in general and the position of any single commodity within it in particular. This position is now defined by two sets of technical relationships: on the one hand, those in which the particular commodity is described as a product with the other commodities and services appearing as elements of cost; on the other hand, there are numerous other relationships in which the same commodity constitutes one of the cost elements used in the production of other goods. The position of the commodity coal within the American national economy is determined, for example, by the technical conditions of coal mining, and at the same time by the technical structures of all the coal-using industries. From the viewpoint of all the other commodities, coal is simply an intermediate link which connects these two sets of relationships.

The equivalence of the two types of technical changes is a logical consequence of this situation. From the viewpoint of all other industries, an increase in the productivity of coal mining, i.e., in the productivity of all factors involved in coal mining, has exactly the same significance as a proportionally equal increase in the productivity of the commodity coal itself in its various uses as a cost factor of other industries.

For the purpose of later discussion, it is useful to introduce a new concept — the *efficiency of a given commodity*. In precise terms the efficiency coefficient of commodity k can be defined as the product $A_k A'_k$ of its two components — the productivity coefficient A_k of industry k and the productivity coefficient A'_k of commodity k. If A_k and A'_k were to change proportionally but in opposite directions, $A_k A'_k$ would remain the same. If the productivity of the coal mining industry had fallen to one-half its original level, but the combustion technique at the time had improved so as to reduce proportionally the amount of coal required in the production of any other commodity, the efficiency of the commodity coal considered from the viewpoint of the economic system as a whole would remain unchanged. The prices and quantities of all the other commodities would be the same, but the price of coal would be raised 100 per cent and its output fall to one-half its previous level. If coal happens to be used as *numéraire*, its own price and output must always be equal to 1, irrespective of any other change. But the relative prices and output of all other commodities would fall and rise in this case to one-half and the double of their original levels respectively. The total values of all the inputs and outputs (including the input and output of coal) would remain unchanged.

12. SIGNIFICANCE OF THE VALUE PATTERN

The nature of mutually compensated technological transformations can be interpreted also in quite different terms. Let it be assumed that no actual material changes have taken place at all, but instead new and different physical units were introduced to measure the quantity and state the prices of coal. Let, for example, long tons replace the previously used short tons; and let it be assumed that one long ton is equal to two short tons. All the numerical characteristics of the given economic system must then be revised accordingly: the production coefficients describing inputs of various cost factors used per one physical unit of the coal output have to be raised 100 per cent, while the other coefficients which describe coal inputs per unit of output in other commodities must be cut to 50 per cent of their former magnitudes. In short, the productivity coefficient of the coal industry expressed in terms of the new physical units will be twice as large and the productivity coefficient of the commodity coal half as large as it was before. This nominal dimensional transformation will affect the numerical picture of the economic system precisely in the same way as the previously described mutually compensated technical variations.

By appropriate substitutions in the basic set III, and in all the subsequent equations, it can be demonstrated that the numerical magnitudes of all the relative price and quantity derivatives, such as $\dfrac{dP_{in}}{dA_k} \cdot \dfrac{1}{P_{in}}, \dfrac{dX_{in}}{dA_k} \cdot \dfrac{1}{X_{in}}, \dfrac{dX_{in}}{dB_k} \cdot \dfrac{1}{X_{in}}$, are invariant toward any changes of this dimensional type, whether real or nominal.

This observation leads to an important conclusion: the basic properties of an economic system are uniquely determined by the (relative) *value figures* of all the different kinds of outputs and inputs. Two systems with identical value patterns will have also the same price and output reactions. Even if the prices and quantities taken separately were quite different (because of real or nominal differences), the identity of the value figures shows that each of the two setups could be transformed into the other by changes of purely dimensional kind. But as indicated before, none of the basic properties of an economic system could be affected by this type of transformation. This means that they are the same in both setups.

For the subsequent empirical analysis, this invariance is of cardinal importance. It makes it possible to determine the most significant properties of the actual economic system on the basis of its value pattern alone. Separate price and quantity figures can, in large part, be dispensed with.

PART III

PART III

DATA AND VARIABLES IN THE AMERICAN ECONOMIC SYSTEM, 1919–1929

A. Price and Output Reactions

I. THE BASIC PRICE AND OUTPUT DETERMINANTS STATISTICALLY DERIVED

TABLES 5 and 6 [1] supply statistical information required for the numerical solution of equations derived in Part II. They are based on a rather detailed classification of industries which distributed all economic activities of this country over 44 separate schedules (including households, international trade, and the undistributed account).

Technical reasons make it necessary to reduce the number of separate industries to ten for purposes of our analysis. The original detailed distribution table is accordingly consolidated.[2]

Tables 7 and 8 present the factual background of these computations in the form in which they are actually used. The figures not in parentheses in each horizontal row represent the distribution of the product of one single industry. If read in a vertical direction, they indicate the cost distribution of the industry listed at the head of each column. The numbers affixed to all the separate industries will henceforth be identified with the subscripts of our theoretical formulae; X_2 will indicate, for example, the output of the minerals industry; P_{10}, the price of household services, etc. Detailed contents of each of the ten industrial schedules are listed below.

1. *Agriculture and Foods*
   Agriculture
   Flour and grist-mill products
   Canning, preserving
   Bread and bakery products
   Sugar, glucose, starch
   Liquors, beverages
   Tobacco manufactures
   Slaughtering, meat packing
   Butter, cheese, etc.
   Other food industries

2. *Minerals Industry*
   Iron mining
   Blast furnaces
   Non-ferrous metals
   Smelting, refining
   Non-metal minerals

---

[1] Tables 5 and 6 are placed in a pocket on the back cover.
[2] See Section 9 below.

TABLE 7.—QUANTITATIVE INPUT AND OUTPUT RELATIONS IN THE ECONOMIC SYSTEM OF THE UNITED STATES, 1919 (CONSOLIDATED) *

DISTRIBUTION OF OUTLAYS (INPUT) OF CLASSES LISTED AT TOP OF TABLE	Class number	DISTRIBUTION OF OUTPUT OF CLASSES LISTED AT LEFT OF TABLE										Net output
		Agriculture and foods	Minerals industry	Metals and their products	Fuel and power	Textiles and leather	Transportation (steam railroads)	Foreign trade (exports)	Industries n.e.s.	Undistributed	Households (consumption)	
Class number		1	2	3	4	5	6	7	8	9	10	
Agriculture and foods	1	(—0.9377)	(0) 0	(0) 0	(0) 0	(0.1361) 1420	(0) 0	(0.5150) 4063	(0.0296) 391	(0.0354) 1364	(0.2739) 11920	19158
Minerals industry	2	(0.0023) 48	(—0.8595)	(0.0724) 1157	(0.0022) 16	(0.0001) 1	(0.0025) 15	(0.0271) 214	(0.0558) 734	(0.0159) 612	(0.0045) 194	2991
Metals and their products	3	(0.0381) 778	(0.0241) 84	(—0.9199)	(0.0830) 614	(0.0162) 169	(0.2581) 1529	(0.1809) 1427	(0.0813) 1073	(0.1690) 6513	(0.0539) 2520	14707
Fuel and power	4	(0.0065) 133	(0.1284) 447	(0.0249) 398	(—0.8317)	(0.0121) 126	(0.0871) 516	(0.0638) 503	(0.0173) 228	(0.0326) 1257	(0.0585) 2545	6153
Textiles and leather	5	(0.0060) 122	(0) 0	(0.0113) 181	(0) 0	(—0.9294)	(0) 0	(0.0973) 768	(0.0068) 90	(0.0400) 1541	(0.1607) 6993	9695
Transportation (steam railroads)	6	(0.0460) 940	(0.0940) 327	(0.0164) 262	(0.1208) 894	(0.1519) 1584	(—0.9488)	(0.0179) 141	(0.0262) 346	(0.0380) 1464	(0.0286) 1246	5620
Foreign trade (imports)	7	(0.0558) 1140	(0.0428) 149	(0.0056) 89	(0.0035) 26	(0.0149) 155	(0.0002) 1	(—0.5324)	(0.0293) 387	(0.0067) 257	(0.0132) 572	4205
Industries n.e.s.	8	(0.0395) 807	(0.0092) 32	(0.0108) 174	(0.0157) 116	(0.2958) 3085	(0.0211) 125	(0.0918) 724	(—0.9515)	(0.1620) 6240	(0.0963) 4191	12564
Undistributed	9	(0.1752) 3580	(0.3583) 1247	(0.4100) 6554	(0.3777) 2794	(0.3730) 3891	(0.1172) 694	(0.0063) 50	(0.3724) 4918	(—0.9409)	(0.3064) 13335	36257
Households (services)	10	(0.6506) 12883	(0.3431) 1194	(0.4486) 7172	(0.3971) 2938	(0) 0	(0.5138) 3043	(0) 0	(0.3815) 5038	(0.5005) 19288	(—1.2742)	55447
Net outlays (input)		20431	3480	15987	7398	10431	5923	7890	13205	38536	43516	

* The unit for figures not in parentheses is one million dollars; figures in parentheses represent production, consumption, and investment coefficients.

TABLE 8.—QUANTITATIVE INPUT AND OUTPUT RELATIONS IN THE ECONOMIC SYSTEM OF THE UNITED STATES, 1929 (CONSOLIDATED)*

DISTRIBUTION OF OUTPUT OF CLASSES LISTED AT TOP OF TABLE

DISTRIBUTION OF OUTLAYS (INPUT) OF CLASSES LISTED AT LEFT OF TABLE	Class number	Agriculture and foods	Minerals industry	Metals and their products	Fuel and power	Textiles and leather	Transportation (steam railroads)	Foreign trade (exports)	Industries n.e.s.	Undistributed	Households (consumption)	Net output
Class number		1	2	3	4	5	6	7	8	9	10	
Agriculture and foods	1	(−0.9960)	(0)	(0)	(0) 0	(0.08074) 764	(0)	(0.32141) 1681	(0.01639) 329	(0.01087) 588	(0.22229) 13669	17031
Minerals industry	2	(0.00404) 69	(−0.9562)	(0.08234) 1484	(0.00139) 16	(0.00106) 10	(0.00385) 28	(0.04551) 238	(0.06720) 1349	(0.00967) 523	(0.00242) 149	3866
Metals and their products	3	(0.03959) 677	(0.01830) 74	(−0.9283)	(0.09144) 1055	(0.01786) 169	(0.24340) 1770	(0.30019) 1570	(0.09146) 1836	(0.09953) 5382	(0.06824) 4196	16729
Fuel and power	4	(0.00977) 167	(0.10784) 436	(0.02613) 471	(−0.8880)	(0.01628) 154	(0.05528) 402	(0.13040) 682	(0.01853) 372	(0.05398) 2919	(0.07550) 4643	10246
Textiles and leather	5	(0.00316) 54	(0)	(0.01703) 307	(0)	(−0.9659)	(0)	(0.06635) 347	(0.00692) 139	(0.02112) 1142	(0.11627) 7150	9139
Transportation (steam railroads)	6	(0.06029) 1031	(0.10339) 418	(0.02885) 520	(0.12307) 1420	(0.00264) 25	(−0.9167)	(0.01396) 73	(0.02496) 501	(0.03196) 1728	(0.01545) 950	6666
Foreign trade (imports)	7	(0.05924) 1013	(0.04823) 195	(0.01060) 191	(0.00867) 100	(0.15546) 1471	(0.00014) 1	(−0.9554)	(0.03895) 782	(0.00743) 402	(0.01369) 842	4997
Industries n.e.s.	8	(0.05999) 872	(0.02028) 82	(0.02896) 522	(0.04151) 479	(0.03213) 304	(0.03328) 242	(0.01822) 566	(−0.9466)	(0.17361) 9388	(0.10648) 6548	19003
Undistributed	9	(0.25883) 4426	(0.31635) 1279	(0.34380) 6196	(0.26356) 2041	(0.32107) 3038	(0.14343) 1043	(0.01396) 73	(0.31851) 6394	(−0.9031)	(0.37965) 23346	48836
Households (services)	10	(0.51409) 8791	(0.38560) 1559	(0.46227) 8331	(0.47036) 5427	(0.37275) 3527	(0.52063) 3786	(0) 0	(0.41709) 8373	(0.59183) 32003	(−1.1676)	71797
Net outlays (input)		17100	4043	18022	11538	9462	7272	5230	20075	54075	61493	

* The unit for figures not in parentheses is one million dollars; figures in parentheses represent production, consumption, and investment coefficients.

3. *Metals and Their Products*
   Steel works, rolling mills
   Other iron and steel and
     electric manufactures
   Automobiles
   Brass, bronze, copper man-
     ufactures
4. *Fuel and Power*
   Petroleum, natural gas
   Refined petroleum
   Coal
   Coke
   Manufactured gas
   Electric utilities
5. *Textiles and Leather*
   Yarn and cloth
   Clothing
   Other textile products
   Leather tanning
   Leather shoes
   Other leather products
   Rubber manufactures
6. *Steam Railroads*

7. *International Trade*
   (with imports as its output
     and exports as its costs)
8. *Industries n. e. s.*
   Chemicals
   Lumber and timber prod-
     ucts
   Other wood products
   Paper and wood pulp
   Other paper products
   Printing, publishing
   Industries, n. e. s.
   Construction
9. *Undistributed*
   (A predominant part of
     this division consists of
     distributive trade serv-
     ices and direct profes-
     sional services.)
10. *Households*
    (with services as their out-
      put and consumption as
      their costs)

The titles selected for each of the ten schedules do not indicate adequately the nature of all included subgroups. More accurate, long descriptions would be too cumbersome for practical use. To facilitate the reading of various tables and graphs, the number of an industry always accompanies its name. Some of the separate items are described more comprehensively in Appendix II. All figures not in parentheses indicate millions of dollars.

In order to obtain the corresponding physical amounts of all commodities and services, we simply define the unit of physical measurement of every particular type of product so as to make it equal to that amount of the commodity which can be purchased for one dollar at prevailing prices. Thus the physical quantity of agricultural and food (1) output equals the net dollar value of this type of commodity produced in 1919, which was 19,158 million dollars; the total quantity of mineral production (2) is the dollar value of the net output of the minerals industry, which in 1919 was 2991 million dollars, etc. Thus the last column in Tables 7 and 8 can be considered also as representing the net physical outputs for 1919 and 1929 respectively.

Accordingly, 398 million dollars of fuels absorbed by the metals industry represents 398 physical units; similarly, 3891 million dollars' worth of services absorbed in textile and leather production constitutes 3891 physical units, etc.

The price of a commodity being equal to the number of dollars paid for one unit, all prices are one dollar per unit.

Using household services (10) as a *numéraire*, we finally divide all other physical quantities by the physical output of this industry and obtain the series of relative physical outputs as presented in Table 9.

TABLE 9

RELATIVE PHYSICAL NET OUTPUTS, 1919–1929

	$X_{1\,10}$	$X_{2\,10}$	$X_{3\,10}$	$X_{4\,10}$	$X_{5\,10}$	$X_{6\,10}$	$X_{7\,10}$	$X_{8\,10}$	$X_{9\,10}$	$X_{10\,10}$
1919	0.346	0.054	0.265	0.111	0.175	0.101	0.076	0.227	0.654	1.000
1929	0.237	0.054	0.233	0.143	0.127	0.093	0.070	0.265	0.680	1.000

According to Set IIb of our theoretical equations, an investment coefficient B_i of industry i is equal to the value of its total output (X_iP_i) divided by the corresponding aggregate outlay $X_{i1}P_1 + X_{i2}P_2 + \cdots$. For example, the numerical value of B_{10} (1.274) for 1919 is obtained by dividing the total value of the household output (55,447 million dollars) by the aggregate household expenditures (43,516 million dollars). The initial value of $B_{10}\beta$ equals B_{10} because $\beta^0 = 1$.

The investment coefficient B_3 of the metals industry (0.920) is similarly given by the ratio between the value of the net output of this industry (14,707 millions) and its aggregate outlays (15,987 millions).

From equations of Set IIb

$$a_{ik} = \frac{x_{ik}A_i^0 B_i^0 \beta^0}{X_i^0} = \frac{x_{ik}B_i^0}{X_i^0}$$

where

$$A_i^0 = \beta^0 = 1$$

Since the magnitudes of all the elements on the right side of this equation are now given, the numerical value of a technical coefficient a_{ik} can readily be computed. For example: the coefficient a_{34} describing the use of fuel and power ($k = 4$) in the metals industry ($i = 3$) for 1919 equals

$$\left(\frac{398}{14707} \right) 0.920 = 0.0249$$

The figures in parentheses in Tables 7 and 8 reproduce the matrix of determinant D. They were computed from the statistical data not in parentheses; i.e., except for the diagonal elements they are percentage distributions of the column totals. The diagonal elements are the ratios of the total for each row to the total of the corresponding column, with a minus sign affixed. The matrix of Δ is easily obtained from it by interchanging all rows and columns, and replacing each of the ten investment coefficients (in parentheses in the main diagonal) by 1 (the minus signs remain unchanged).

2. INTERPRETATION OF GRAPHS

Once the two matrices D and Δ are given, the computation of all the derivatives on the basis of our theoretical formulae is a matter of simple arithmetic. The word simple can be used in this connection, however, merely to indicate the absence of any conceptual difficulties; technically, the task is anything but simple. For one year alone, 99 minors of each of the two basic determinants had to be computed, the majority of these minors being determinants of the eighth and some of them of the ninth order. The total number of multiplications involved in the practical solution of our problem exceeds 450,000. This task alone would mean a two-year job, at 120 multiplications per hour. Fortunately, the recent invention of the Simultaneous Calculator by Professor Wilbur of the Massachusetts Institute of Technology has made it possible to perform all the necessary computations in a small fraction of the time they otherwise would have required.[1] This apparatus solves nearly automatically a system of nine simultaneous linear equations, i.e., it calculates the ratio of two determinants interrelated in a certain way. For purposes of its application, all our final formulae were expressed in terms of this particular type of quotient.

The numerical magnitudes of all the basic elements used in

[1] See John B. Wilbur, "The Mechanical Solution of Simultaneous Equations," *Journal of the Franklin Institute*, vol. 222, no. 6 (December 1936), pp. 715–24.

subsequent calculations are given in Appendix III, Tables 1, 2, 3 and 4; the price and quantity derivatives, computed on the basis of the general theoretical formulae, are also listed in Appendix III.

Two-way tables, each containing nearly one hundred figures, are quite convenient for dead storage of statistical figures. A detailed analysis of complex quantitative interrelationships requires, however, the use of some open, preferably graphic, method of presentation. Scatter diagrams are very helpful in the description of a few fundamental interrelations, each represented by a relatively large group of figures. In dealing with problems requiring comparison of a great many separate relationships, each comprising only a few individual items, this familiar device becomes wasteful in space and bulky in handling. Thus, on the following pages, a less conventional but much more compact method of diagrammatic presentation is used. Chart 2, for example, gives a comparative picture of the (relative) price reactions, $\dfrac{dP_{in}}{dA_k} \cdot \dfrac{1}{P_{in}}$, in 1919 and 1929.

The graph is based on Tables 5 and 6, App. III. All derivatives are grouped according to the location of the primary change, i.e., each column of Table 5 is directly compared with the corresponding column of Table 6. The first pair of vertical lines on the left side of Chart 2 depicts the price reactions of various commodity groups which would result from a given (hypothetical) increase in the productivity coefficient A_1 of the agriculture and foods industry ($k = 1$). The figures for 1919 are plotted along the first and those for 1929 along the second vertical scale. Corresponding points showing the magnitude of the price reaction of the same commodity in two years are connected by straight lines and marked with price numbers. The graph shows, for example, that the magnitude of the price reaction of railroad transport (point 6) to a hypothetical increase in agricultural ($k = 1$) productivity rose from -0.027 in 1919 to -0.012 in 1929. Similarly, the influence of increased productivity of the fuel and power industry (4) upon the price of metal products (3) can be traced above $k = 4$: point 3 fell from -0.068 in 1919 to -0.072 in 1929.

In examining all charts and tables which describe the various price and quantity derivatives, it is important to keep in mind that the choice of the *numéraire*, i.e., of the common price and

CHART 2

PRICE REACTIONS $\dfrac{dP_{in}}{dA_k} \cdot \dfrac{1}{P_{in}}$ TO PRIMARY PRODUCTIVITY CHANGES, 1919–1929

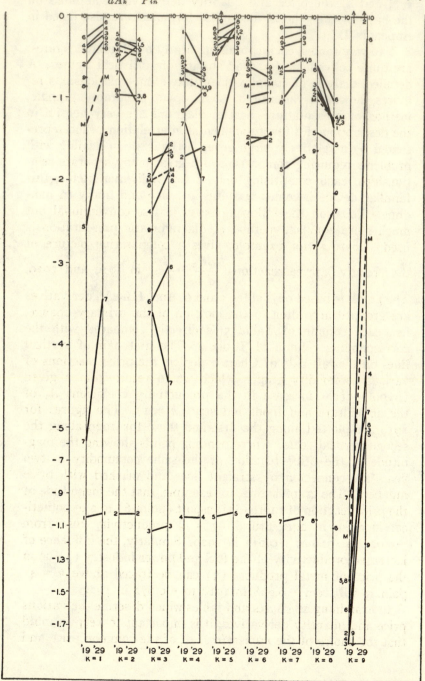

Basic classification of industries.　　　Data in Appendix III, Tables 5 and 6.

quantity base to which all the prices and quantities are being related, affects the numerical results of our computation. The price of household services (10) and their total output is used as a base throughout. The price and the output of the *numéraire* itself obviously must remain constant; it is invariant by definition. This is why the price and quantity derivatives of industry 10 in all the diagrams are invariably on the zero line.

Were a different industry chosen as a base for our price and output measurements, all charts would have to be redrawn so as to place all price and quantity derivatives of this new *numéraire* on the zero line. All other price and output derivatives would have to be adjusted accordingly. Formula XXXIII indicates that the necessary transformation would simply require a parallel shift of all the points along the respective vertical scales. If, for example, in the analysis of output reactions $\left(\dfrac{dX_{in}}{dA_k} \cdot \dfrac{1}{X_{in}} \right)$ to primary productivity changes (see Chart 3), the output of industry 6, railroad transport were used as the new quantity base, point 6 on the 1919 scale for $k = 1$ (primary change in agriculture and foods) would have to be moved from its present position, +0.089, down to the zero line and with it all the other points on the same vertical scale would have to be shifted downward by the same amount.[1] Point 7, international trade, incidentally, would have changed its present position above the zero line to one below it. Point 10, households, at the same time would be transferred to −0.089. On some other scales, $k = 2$, 1919 for example, a transition to the same new base would require an upward instead of a downward shift of all points.

In an analysis based on concepts of relative prices and quantities, it is the relative magnitude of various price and quantity reactions which counts; this relative magnitude is graphically depicted by the distances between the corresponding points on the vertical scales of our charts and obviously cannot be affected by any change in the *numéraire*. The fact that a point is below or above the zero line simply indicates that, under the influence of the particular primary change, the absolute price or output of the corresponding commodity decreases or increases in comparison with the absolute price or quantity of the *numéraire*.

[1] Insofar as the vertical scales on all our charts are somewhat distorted an additional adjustment had to-be made for the variable size of the units.

CHART 3

OUTPUT REACTIONS $\dfrac{dX_{in}}{dA_k} \cdot \dfrac{1}{X_{in}}$ TO PRIMARY PRODUCTIVITY CHANGES, 1919–1929

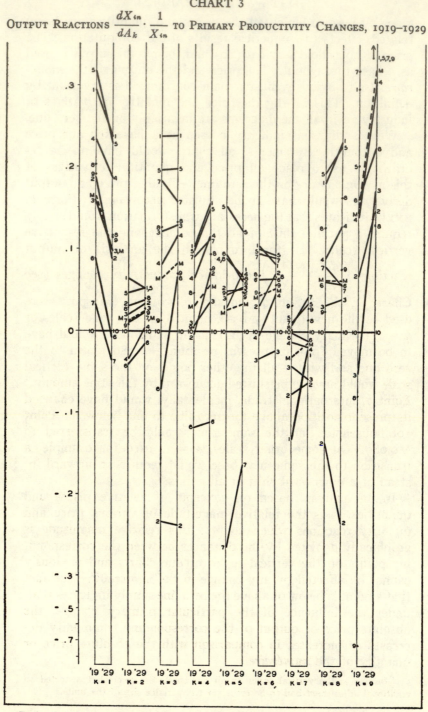

Basic classification of industries.   Data in Appendix III, Tables 7 and 8.

The detailed analysis and interpretations of all the various price and output reactions can be conveniently divided into two parts: (*a*) a general survey of the types of price and quantity reaction, and (*b*) a comparative study of the typical reaction patterns by separate industries. The second task of necessity involves repetition of observations made in the course of the general survey. Some of these observations will furthermore lead back to the fundamental theoretical scheme which lies at the basis of the whole investigation. Rather than being developed in a purely abstract vein, these essentially theoretical considerations are brought up in connection with the interpretation of the tangible, numerical results.

3. INVARIANCE OF REACTION PATTERNS

Before attempting any discussion of the various patterns of price and quantity reactions, it is appropriate to ask whether any such typical pattern actually exists. That at any given moment a particular economic system will react to any given primary change in a definite, uniquely determined fashion is implied in the very concept of an economic system. As a purely methodological presumption, this contention lies beyond empirical verification. If *controlled* experimentation with a national economy were feasible, it could demonstrate at least the insufficiency of any particular set of empirical data or the deficiency of any particular type of theoretical setup. Uncontrolled observation can show, however, whether the reactions of any particular economic system actually reveal a certain degree of invariance over time. The significance of our factual analysis would be considerably enhanced if the empirically derived reaction patterns showed this kind of persistence.[1]

Cursory inspection of Charts 2, 3, and 4 reveals a quite pronounced similarity between the corresponding reaction patterns as computed for 1919 and 1929. The relative position of analogous points on the neighboring vertical scales has for the

---

[1] The prevailing belief in the inherent instability of economic phenomena seems in large part to be the result of a singular optical — or rather, psychological — illusion. As a moving object, however small, is likely to distract the attention of a casual observer from all the static features of a vast landscape, so the changing elements of the economic scene attract very often the attention of investigators to the exclusion of the other, less dynamic elements of the picture. The impersonal, quasi-mechanical methods of statistical analysis often help to dispel this distortion and enable him to perceive the facts more objectively.

CHART 4

OUTPUT REACTIONS $\dfrac{dX_{in}}{dB_k} \cdot \dfrac{1}{X_{in}}$ TO PRIMARY CHANGES OF THE INVESTMENT AND

SAVING COEFFICIENTS, 1919–1929

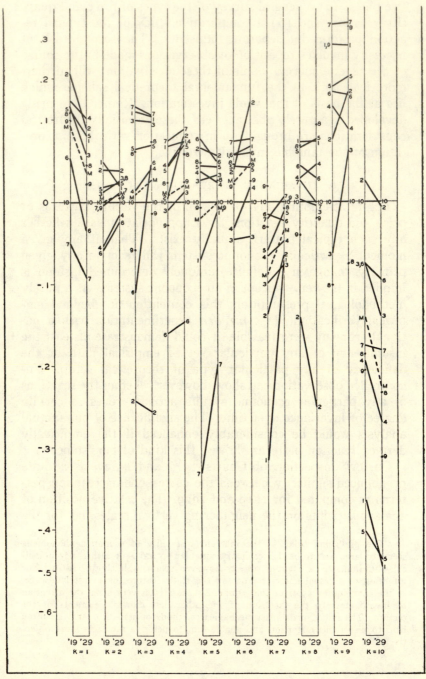

Basic classification of industries.   Data in Appendix III, Tables 9 and 10.

most part remained substantially the same: the interconnecting lines cross each other only in relatively few cases and only
few of those indicate violent displacements. The least systematic behavior is displayed by industries 8 and 9, especially the
latter. But one of these two classes — the undistributed (9)
— represents an accidental combination of various balancing
items, while the other — industries n. e. s. (8) — comprises
such heterogeneous elements as chemicals, lumber and timber
products, printing and publishing, etc. Thus, these two instances of irregular behavior seem to constitute the kind of
exceptions which tend to justify the rule. Introduced in our
numerical computations for reasons of practical expediency,
these two industrial groups, if taken separately, are of very
little interest. Thus, unless specifically mentioned, they will
be entirely omitted from further consideration. Points 8 and
9 can be found on all the diagrams, but they are not marked
with interconnecting lines.

For an explanation of the characteristic invariance of the
reaction patterns, one must turn back to the fundamental data
which constitute the factual basis of all these findings. Chart 5
gives a comparative picture of the cost structures of all ten
industrial divisions. The formal setup of this diagram is the
same as of the previously explained charts. Two vertical scales
are devoted to the product of each particular industry — one
for 1919, the other for 1929. Each point represents the magnitude of the technical coefficient a_{ik} (see p. 73) as listed in
Tables 7 or 8. Point numbers indicate the nature of the particular industry in which the product k is used. Chart 5 represents, in other words, the primary data which enter into the
basic price determinant Δ (see p. 47). The last two vertical
scales describe the net outlay of each separate industry i as a
proportion of the sum total of the net outlay (sum total of
all outputs) of all 10 industrial divisions:

$$\frac{v_i}{B_i} \cdot \frac{1}{\displaystyle\sum_{k=1}^{k=10} v_k}$$

Chart 6 describes in somewhat modified form the elements
of the quantity determinant D (see p. 50). Each vertical distribution shows the values v_{ki} of the separate cost elements of
an industry k as percentages of their respective total outputs

CHART 5

Technical Coefficients $a_{ik} = \left(\dfrac{v_{ik}}{v_i} \cdot B_i \right)$ Describing the Use of Each

Product, k, in Various Industries,* 1919–1929

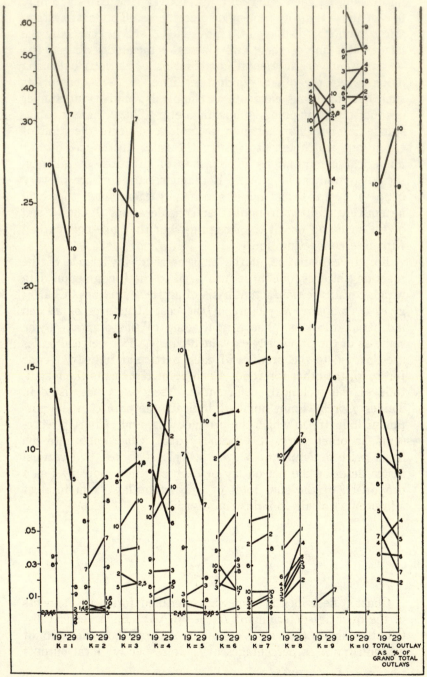

*Marked by their numbers along the vertical scales.   Basic classification of industries.   Data in text, Tables 7 and 8.

CHART 6

INPUT VALUES OF SEPARATE COST ELEMENTS * OF EACH INDUSTRY, k, EXPRESSED
AS PERCENTAGES $\dfrac{v_{ki}}{v_i} = \left(\dfrac{a_{ki}}{B_k} \cdot \dfrac{v_k}{v_i} \right)$ OF THEIR RESPECTIVE TOTAL OUTPUTS, v_i

1919–1929

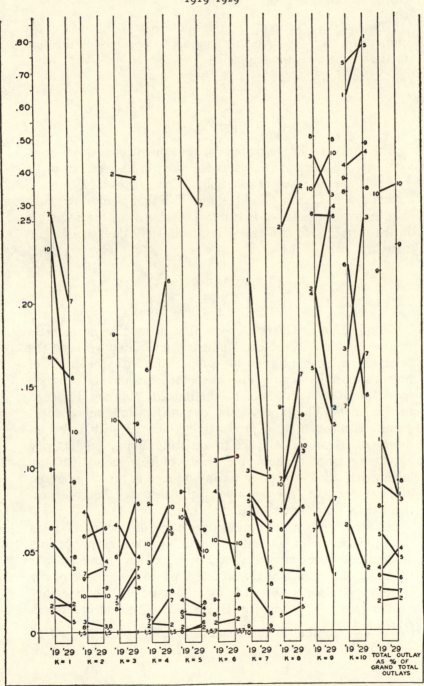

* Marked by their numbers along the vertical scales.   Basic classification of
industries.   Data not reproduced here.

v_i. According to our formula used in computing the technical coefficients of production (see p. 73) $\dfrac{v_{ki}}{v_i}$ equals $\dfrac{a_{ki}}{B_k} \cdot \dfrac{v_k}{v_i}$.

The last two vertical scatters on Chart 6 show the net outputs of each separate industry as proportions of the sum total of the entire net output, i.e.,

$$\frac{v_i}{\sum\limits_{k=1}^{k=10} v_k}$$

The similarity in the pattern of the American national economy in 1919 and 1929 explains the observed invariance of its typical price and output reactions. Comparison of Charts 2, 3, and 4 with Charts 5 and 6 shows also that whatever change took place in the latter is commensurable with the variation in the former; the two are of approximately the same magnitude.

4. PRICE REACTIONS

i. Primary Price Reactions

Examination of Chart 2 shows first of all that an increase in the productivity of any industry invariably reduces the prices of all commodities in comparison with the price of household services (10). This phenomenon is obviously rooted in the peculiar reactions of the households industry discussed in Section 6. The price of the commodity falls most whenever it is affected by a productivity increase within the industry of its origin. Change in agricultural (1) productivity affects the price of farm and food products more than any other price. Similarly, point 2 can be found at the very bottom of the second pair ($k = 2$) of vertical scales, etc. This observation hardly needs any special explanation.

In connection with the previously made distinction between the productivity of an industry, A_k, and the corresponding productivity of a commodity, A'_k, we must say, however, that the effect of a change of the second type upon the price of the commodity directly affected by it would be considerably smaller (see p. 63). In 1919 the reaction of agricultural prices $\left(\dfrac{dP_1}{dA'_1} \cdot \dfrac{1}{P_1} \right)$ would in this instance equal -0.031 instead of

—1.031, i.e., point 1 would be at the upper end of the scale between points 2 and 3.

ii. General Price Reactions

The vertical spread of the separate point scatters on Chart 2 varies from one distribution to another. It is very wide for $k = 1$ and $k = 3$; it is quite narrow for $k = 2$. The two first rows of Table 10 contain the magnitudes of the standard deviations of price reactions of the seven significant commodity groups computed separately for each vertical distribution. These figures can well be used as indices of the corresponding

TABLE 10

MAGNITUDE OF GENERAL PRICE AND OUTPUT REACTIONS AS MEASURED BY THEIR STANDARD DEVIATIONS, 1919–1929

Year	Standard deviation of	k 1	2	3	4	5	6	7	10
1919	$\dfrac{dP_{i10}}{dA_k} \cdot \dfrac{1}{P_{i10}}$	0.187	0.027	0.11	0.054	0.042	0.05	0.056	....
1929		0.11	0.033	0.126	0.058	0.02	0.048	0.05	....
1919	$\dfrac{dX_{i10}}{dA_k} \cdot \dfrac{1}{X_{i10}}$	0.106	0.034	0.148	0.070	0.116	0.051	0.047	....
1929		0.101	0.023	0.139	0.082	0.08	0.041	0.032	....
1919	$\dfrac{dX_{i10}}{dB_k} \cdot \dfrac{1}{X_{i10}}$	0.087	0.037	0.122	0.071	0.125	0.042	0.096	0.18
1929		0.065	0.02	0.113	0.071	0.078	0.052	0.031	0.178

spreads. They measure the magnitude of the general effect the different primary changes would have upon the price setup of the whole economic system.

Should the variation in the productivity coefficient of some particular industry k have no indirect influence whatsoever upon the relative prices of any commodity, all points on the corresponding vertical scale would be clustered (on the zero line); that is to say, with the exception of point k which would occupy the position —1.0. (In computing the standard deviations mentioned above, we discounted this direct reaction and added +1.0 to each derivative $\dfrac{dP_{k10}}{dA_k} \cdot \dfrac{1}{P_{k10}}$, which measures the influence of a productivity change within a given industry k upon the price of its own output. What remains can be considered to represent the indirect effect.) Such complete absence of any indirect effect could be expected only from a very small, insignificant industry. The bigger the industry directly affected by the primary change the larger is the resulting scatter of indirect price reactions which may be expected.

In the same way as the standard deviations represent an approximate measure of price scatters, the total net outputs of various industries conventionally indicate their size.

An alternative measure could be found in the corresponding total net outlays. For an industry which neither invests nor saves, the two figures are identical; otherwise they differ by the amount of the net saving or investment. The last pair of vertical distributions in Chart 5 shows the net outlays of the ten industrial groups in 1919 and 1929, each expressed as percentages of the grand total outlays. The two last scales on Chart 6 describe in similar terms the net outputs of the same industries.

Arranged according to the decreasing size of their net outputs in 1919, the eight significant industries follow in this order: 10, 1, 3, 5, 4, 6, 7, 2; revised according to magnitudes of the respective net outlays, the order changes to: 10, 1, 3, 5, 7, 4, 6, 2. The large investment in foreign trade is responsible for the higher place assigned to industry 7 in the second rank list as compared with the first. The corresponding ratings for 1929 are: 10, 1, 3, 4, 5, 6, 7, 2 and 10, 3, 1, 4, 5, 6, 7, 2. Heavy investments in agriculture raised the relative position of industry 1 in the first series.

Judged by the magnitudes of standard deviations presented in Table 10, the computed influence of potential technical changes within the various industries upon the price structure of the American economic system can be described by analogous ranking. For 1919, it is 1, 3, 7, 4, 6, 5, 2; for 1929 3, 1, 4, 7, 6, 2, 5.

A comparison of corresponding series reveals in general a pronounced positive relationship between the size of an industry and the magnitude of its influence upon the price system. Reactions to changes in the productivity, i.e., in the terms of exchange in international trade (7), however, seems to be greater than its size could warrant. On the other hand, the influence of the textile industry (5) is disproportionately weak. Between 1919 and 1929 the fuel and power (4) industry moved up in its potential influence upon the price system, while the textile industry (5) lost some ground. These shifts clearly reflect the change in the relative value of their respective outputs. So far as the difference between the output size and the outlays size of an industry is concerned, the last measure shows apparently a better correlation with the intensity of the corresponding price reactions.

iii. Secondary Price Reactions

The largest secondary price reactions are experienced by the products of industries which spend the largest proportions of their total outlays on the output of the industry directly affected by the given primary change. The price of household services (10) is excluded from this rule for reasons already mentioned.

Chart 5 shows the 1919–29 changes in the output distribution of each industry in terms of corresponding technical coefficients. Exports (7) and textiles (5) are the two largest non-household (10) consumers of agricultural (1) commodities; they display also the strongest (negative) secondary price reactions to changes in the agricultural coefficient of production, A_1. The two largest buyers of metal products (3) — railroads (6) and foreign trade (7) — are also most sensitive in their price reactions to technical changes within this particular industry.

In general, in 11 of the total 14 significant cases (counting 1919 and 1929 separately and excluding, as usual, industries 8 and 9), the industry which spends the largest portion of its outlays on the product directly affected by the primary change shows also the strongest price reaction. If first and second places are counted, the ratio is 25 out of 28.

This simple correspondence between product distribution and the magnitude of price reactions becomes somewhat less pronounced with the third and higher places on the respective scales. The explanation lies obviously in the influence of indirect cost relationships. An industry A might not sell anything to industry C directly, but at the same time it can supply industry B which in its turn sells a substantial part of its output to industry C. This type of roundabout relationship cannot compete in importance with the main channels of direct cost connections, but it can compare with their thinner branches.

Technical changes in railroad transportation (6) affect the price of mining products (2) practically as much as the price of fuel and power (4), although the latter industry spends relatively much more on railroad services than the former. But the minerals (2) industry pays out a very large proportion of its

, total costs to the fuel and power (4). Thus, through the combination of direct and indirect relationships, the mineral industry (2) becomes one of the largest railroad (6) customers; hence, the strong price reaction.

Similarly, in 1929 mining products (2) occupied a less important position in the cost structure of international trade (7) than in that of the metal (3) industry; but the metal industry (3) itself supplied 30 per cent of all American exports (7). The cumulative effect of the two cost connections proved to be strong enough to make international trade (7) most sensitive in its price reaction toward productivity changes in the mining (2) industry.

5. OUTPUT REACTIONS

i. General Output Reactions

Analysis has shown already that according to our theoretical setup output reactions have a much more complex nature than price reactions. This relative complexity is well reflected in the relative lengths of the two kinds of computation formulae. It is enhanced by the fact that not only technical production coefficients, but also investment, or saving, coefficients can influence the quantitative setup of an economic system.

Chart 3 shows how a change in each of the nine independent productivity coefficients would influence the ten outputs. The setup of this graph is the same as that of Chart 2.

Like its price structure, the quantitative setup of an economic system responds to productivity changes within the larger industries with greater intensity than to similar impulses coming from the smaller branches of production.

The standard deviations of all nine groups of output derivatives are listed in rows 3 and 4 of Table 10. Arranged in the order of decreasing magnitude of these indexes, the seven significant industries make the following array for 1919: 3, 5, 1, 4, 6, 7, 2; for 1929: 3, 1, 4, 5, 6, 7, 2. The second series is nearly identical with the ranking list of the corresponding industries arranged according to their *output* size for 1929 (see p. 86). For 1919 an analogous comparison shows that metals (3), and in particular textiles (5), would have a greater and the agricultural (1) products a smaller potential influence on the quantitative setup of the economic system than the relative size of these industries would lead one to expect.

ii. Direct and Indirect Output Reactions

In contrast to its price reaction, the output variation in an industry directly affected by a technical change is not distinctly different in its magnitude from the indirect reactions of the other industries. As Formulae XLIII and XLIV show, this response is much stronger if the primary change affects the productivity coefficient A'_k of the *commodity* k rather than the productivity coefficient A_k of *industry* k.

Formula XXIb indicates that an induced change in the general investment level β accounts for some part of every output reaction. This element is usually so small in comparison with the total effect of a primary productivity change that it hardly affects the general picture as it is presented in Chart 3. Detailed discussion of this secondary component can conveniently be postponed to the next section. Household services also are excluded from present consideration.

In its indirect output effects, a productivity change within any given industry has the greatest influence upon the commodity of whose output it absorbs the largest proportion. Chart 6 describes the cost structures of the ten industrial groups from this point of view. Comparison with Chart 3 indicates that of the fourteen significant figures which occupy the highest positions on as many vertical scales in Chart 6, ten are on the bottom of the corresponding scales in Chart 3. For the first and second and bottom figures respectively, the similar ratio is 24 out of 28. Most of the exceptions are traceable to indirect cost relationships.

Thus, for example, in 1919, a primary technical change in fuel and power (4) production would have affected mineral (2) output more than the output of the metal (3) industry, and this although the fuel and power (4) industry absorbs a considerably larger proportion of metal (3) goods than of mineral (2) products. Metal (3) industry absorbs, however, 40 per cent of total mineral (2) output. Thus the primary impulse originating in the fuel and power (4) industry is being transmitted to the mineral (2) industry indirectly. The same relationship seems to explain the fact that a variation in the terms of international trade (7) would also have influenced mining (2) production more than metal (3) output.

iii. Output Reactions to
Changes in Saving and Investment Coefficients

The influence of a change in a primary investment coefficient B_k is very similar to the direct output reactions which follow a variation in the corresponding productivity coefficient A_k. The relative intensity of output reaction is nearly the same. Whether in some particular industry the inputs have changed per unit of output because the technique of production was modified or because of additional investment or disinvestment, the direct effect on the quantitative setup of the system is likely to be the same. Comparison of Chart 4, which describes the output variation caused by primary changes in investment coefficients, with Chart 3 reveals a great similarity in the relative position of various points along the corresponding vertical scales. This similarity is particularly great in their lower reaches where the direct effect of both kinds of primary changes are predominantly concentrated.

Whatever difference can be observed in these vertical distributions must be attributed to the more indirect type of reaction.

The influence of technical changes upon outputs through variation in the general investment level β is so small that actually it could have been neglected in the empirical analysis of corresponding output reactions. The dependence of the investment level upon the investment coefficients of various industries is, however, large enough to warrant special investigation.

The reaction of industrial outputs, so far as they are affected by *indirect* investment adjustments, is a product of two distinct elements: the reaction of (a) the general investment level to a given primary change $\left(\dfrac{d\beta}{dA_k} \text{ or } \dfrac{d\beta}{dB_k} \right) \cdot$ and (b) of a particular output upon a given variation in the general investment level $\dfrac{\partial X_{in}}{\partial \beta} \cdot \dfrac{1}{X_{in}}$.

In Chart 7, the first two kinds of derivatives are depicted separately. The influence of the increasing investment coefficient (B_k) upon the general investment level is invariably negative. A decrease in willingness to invest or an increase in willingness to save raises the actual investment ratio in all the other industries, provided their own investment coeffi-

CHART 7

THREE COMPLEX REACTIONS, 1919–1929

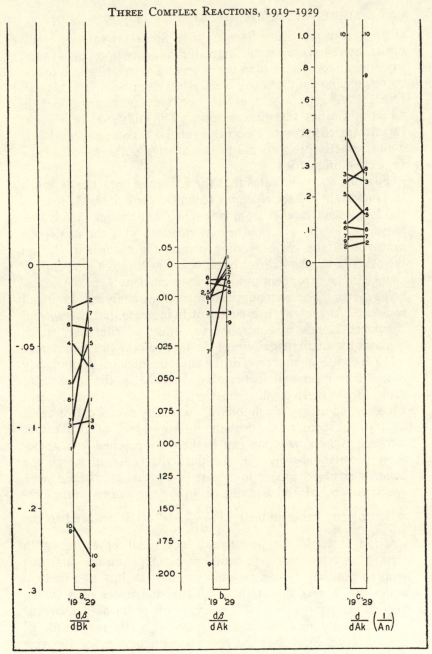

Reaction $\dfrac{d\beta}{dB_k}$ of the general investment (or saving) level, β, to primary changes in investment coefficients B_k; reaction $\dfrac{d\beta}{dA_k}$ of the general investment or saving level, β, to primary changes in technical production coefficient A_k; reaction $\dfrac{d}{dA_k}\left(\dfrac{1}{A_n}\right)$ of the general household consumption level, $\dfrac{1}{A_n}$, to primary changes in technical production coefficient A_k.

cients remain the same (see p. 50). Some investment coefficients, however, exert a much greater influence upon the general investment conditions than the others. The relative size of the corresponding industries is obviously responsible for this difference. A glance at the last two vertical distributions in Chart 5 verifies this presumption. The influence of various investment coefficients B_k on the general investment level β is almost exactly proportional to the relative outlays sizes of the respective industries.

Formula XXIV indicates that the influence (practically much less important) of the changing technical coefficients A_k reaches the investment level β from two sides. On the one hand, it is the direct effect, which is nearly identical with the analogous influence of the corresponding investment coefficient B_k; on the other hand, the indirect effect operates through a secondary change in the dependent productivity coefficient A_n of the households (10). The second phenomenon is analyzed in detail in Sec. 6. At present, it is sufficient to indicate that this second component tends to neutralize the effect of the first, which explains the small magnitude of the total effects (see Chart 7b).

An increase or decrease in the investment level β obviously means a proportional increase or decrease in the investment ratios $\mathcal{B}_k (= B_k \beta)$ of all industries. The effect of this type of variation upon any single output X_i is the sum total of these separate changes. An adequate interpretation of this rather intricate type of reaction can be best approached in a somewhat roundabout way. In the particular case in which the primary change happens to consist in a variation of the saving coefficient B_n of the households (10), the entire output reaction of any other industry $\left(\dfrac{dX_{in}}{dB_n} \cdot \dfrac{1}{X_{in}} \right)$ is reduced to the reaction through the investment level. All other terms in formula XXVIIa vanish when $k = n$. This means that the relative position of various points along the last two vertical scales in Chart 4 depict these isolated influences of a falling general investment level β. The amplitude of the actual spreads will obviously increase and decrease with the magnitude of the variation in β, but the general configuration of the vertical point scatters (except the positions of point 10) does not depend on this magnitude.

The previously mentioned distortion of the direct effects of primary variations of investment coefficients by corresponding indirect reactions can now be visualized as a combination of all the separate vertical scatters of Chart 3 with one of the last two scatters on Chart 4, the latter being weighted by the magnitude of the corresponding reaction of the investment level β (see Chart 7b). The indirect influence tends to increase the relative output of mining products (2) and to diminish the output of agricultural products (1) and textiles (5). This tendency explains why point 2 on most scales of Chart 4 occupies a relatively higher position than in Chart 3 and on the other hand points 1 and 5 in Chart 4 are lower than in Chart 3.

The general amplitude of different point distributions is also considerably modified. Comparison of the relative magnitudes of the standard deviations of these distributions, as given for the eight significant industries in Table 10, leads to the following two rank lists: 10, 5, 3, 7, 1, 4, 6, 2 for 1919, and 10, 3, 5, 4, 1, 6, 7, 2 for 1929. Both show close relationship to the ranking of the relative outlay sizes of the corresponding industries (see p. 86). A variation of the agricultural (1) investment coefficient B_1 seems to cause a smaller general output reaction than the size of this industry would lead us to expect, while the influence of a similar variation in textiles (5) on the contrary is disproportionately strong. In the first case, the indirect reaction through the general investment level reduces the effect of the direct influence, while in the second, it works in the opposite direction. Similar but smaller disparities observed in connection with the analysis of technical productivity changes (see p. 89 above) are obviously of the same origin.

6. BEHAVIOR OF INDIVIDUAL INDUSTRIES

i. Households

a. *Reactions of real remuneration of the household services.* A detailed survey of the price and output behavior of individual industries can well be begun with the analysis of households (10). Households deserve particular attention, first of all because the nature of this particular branch of the economic system is in our theoretical setup fundamentally different from that in any other industry. According to our classification it is also the biggest single industry within the system.

The theoretical peculiarity of households is due to the fact that the productivity coefficient A_n of this industry is not a datum, but rather a dependent variable. Its magnitude is a function of the technical productivity coefficients of all other industries; it changes with the variation of any and every one of these coefficients (see also p. 95 below).

Chart 7c shows how the reciprocal $\dfrac{1}{A_{10}}$ of the productivity coefficient A_{10}, i.e., the real wage rate of household services (see p. 42), would change with every increase in the technical productivity of the various industries. The magnitude of these reactions are computed according to formula xxv. As should be expected, an increase in technical productivity, wherever located, always raises the real wage rate of household services: all points of the distribution in Chart 7c are above the zero line. Their relative position is very similar to the spread of corresponding points along the last two scales in Chart 6. That means that the larger the output size of an industry, the more an advance in its productivity contributes to the increase of the real remuneration rate of household services. Not only the order of magnitudes, but even the relative numerical values seem to correspond rather closely between the two scatters. The net output of the agriculture and foods (1) industry in 1919 was six and one-half, and in 1929 four and one-half times as large in its dollar value as the net output of the mineral (2) industry. The ratio between the magnitudes of corresponding derivatives as plotted on Chart 7c is seven to four and one-half. Similar equality of proportions characterizes the distribution of all other points.

b. Price reactions. In choosing the price of household services, P_{10}, to be used as a *numéraire*, we made their relative price $P_{10 . 10}$ equal 1 and constant by definition. Any actual price variation which, on the basis of a different *numéraire*, would have affected the relative price of household services will, in the present setup, lift or reduce all the other prices relative to this fixed base (see p. 77 above).

What actually matters is the variation of the price of household services in its relation to all the other prices and this relation obviously does not depend upon the arbitrary choice of the *numéraire*. In Chart 2, the magnitude of this variation is revealed in the position of each vertical point distribution in relation to the horizontal zero line to which point 10 is permanently affixed.

The fact that each and every productivity increase reduces

the prices of all other commodities in relation to the price of the household services has been mentioned before; now it can be analyzed in detail. An increase in the productivity of any industry automatically raises the real remuneration rate of household services, i.e., it reduces the productivity coefficient A_{10} of the household industry. But as observed above each reduction (rise) of a technical productivity coefficient invariably leads to a very considerable rise (fall) in the relative price of the commodity directly affected by such change. Hence, the reduction in the productivity coefficient of households must invariably increase the price of household services in relation to all other prices — or, which is the same thing, reduce all the prices in relation to the price of household services.

As observed before, the productivity coefficient A_{10} of households changes in proportion to the size of the industry in which the primary technical variation originated. Thus, the larger the ouput size (see the last two scales in Chart 6) of an industry, the more will point 10 in Chart 2 tend to be elevated over all other points, i.e., the more will the cluster of all these other points be pushed down along the particular vertical scale.

On the other hand, the change in any productivity coefficient must obviously also exercise the usual indirect influence upon the price of household services. On the basis of the preceding analysis, it is known that the magnitude of such effect will in this instance depend upon the proportional amount of the household expenditures which is spent on the product directly affected by the primary change. The larger this proportion (see position of point 10 in various vertical scales of Chart 5), the more will point 10 in Chart 2 be pushed downward in relation to the other points, i.e., the higher will the rest of the points be in relation to the zero line.[1]

An arithmetic average (center of gravity) can be used as a good index of the general position of a whole cluster of points in its relation to the zero line. Special M points placed on all

---

[1] Formula xviia, which describes price reactions, with a commodity other than household services used as a *numéraire*, reveals the nature of the two components of a price reaction of household services explicitly. If $i = n$, the formula is reduced to

$$\frac{dP_{n1}}{dA_k} \cdot \frac{1}{P_{n1}} = \left(-\frac{\Delta_{kk}}{\Delta_{nn}} \cdot \frac{\Delta_{11 \cdot nn}}{\Delta_{11}} \right) + \left(\frac{\Delta_{11 \cdot kk}}{\Delta_{11}} - \frac{\Delta_{1n \cdot kk}}{\Delta_{1n}} \right)$$

The first element on the right side of this equation describes the reaction *via* the coefficient A_{10}, while the rest expresses the secondary response through the household purchases of the commodity directly affected by the primary change.

the vertical scales in Charts 2, 3, and 4 mark the location of these averages.

The two tendencies described above work in some cases in the same direction; in other instances they cancel each other's effects. Agriculture (1) is the largest single industry and metals (3) the second. Thus, via the change in the real remuneration rate $\dfrac{1}{A_{10}}$ of households, a productivity increase in agriculture (1) should have raised the relative price of household services more than a similar productivity change in the metals (3) industry. Actually, the metals industry occupies the first and agriculture the second place, so far as the intensity of such price effects is concerned. The reversed order is due to the secondary effect via household purchases: agricultural (1) products absorb over 20 per cent of total household purchases while only between 5 and 7 per cent are devoted to acquisition of metal (3) products.

In 1919, textiles (5) and minerals (2) seem to influence the relative price of household services by approximately the same amount: the averages of the two point distributions in Chart 2 are on the same level. According to the relative output size of the two industries, the first average should have been much lower than the second. Chart 5 shows, however, that nearly 16 per cent of total household expenditures was absorbed by textiles (5), while only half of one per cent was spent on mineral (2) products. This disparity obviously compensates for the inequality of size. From 1919 to 1929, the latter inequality was considerably reduced and in 1929 an increase in the productivity of the mineral industry (2) would have raised the relative price of household services more than an analogous primary change in textiles (5).

In general, those industries which increased their relative output (see Chart 6) size from 1919 to 1929 also increased their influence upon the relative price of household services; and vice versa, those industries which lost in size sacrificed also some of their influence.

c. Output reactions. The analysis of the output reactions of household services leads to the same two basic considerations which dominated the discussion of the corresponding price variations.

Since this particular output serves as a *numéraire* in the measurement of the relative sizes of all outputs, including its own, point 10 in Chart 3 is invariably fixed on the zero line; the relative output reaction of households is measured by the position of the rest of the points on the same vertical scale in relation to this origin.

Like their price, the output of household services is affected by any outside technical variation through two channels. On the one hand, it is the influence via the changing earning ratio A_{10}; on the other hand, it is the usual output reaction through direct or indirect cost relationships (see p. 89).

In view of such highly intricate interrelationships, it is hardly possible to discern the separate influences of all these various components by simply observing the total effects. The mechanism of these changes can be best understood if it is remembered that the earning ratio A_{10} is made to adjust itself so as to preserve the consistency of the system (see p. 47). It takes up the slacks and relieves the strains caused by primary technical variation and the corresponding reactions in the other parts of the system. In particular, it enables the total output of household services to be adjusted as any other cost factor.

Indeed, a comparative examination of Charts 6 and 3 shows that the position of point 10, in relation to other points distributed along any vertical scale in the latter diagram, corresponds very closely to its relative location on an analogous vertical scale in Chart 6.

In other words, the indirect output reactions of household services are governed by the same type of cost relationships as determine the adjustment of all other outputs.

The location of the M signs, which indicate the averages of the separate point distributions in Chart 3, shows that increase in agricultural (1) productivity tends to reduce the relative output of household services more than any other similar technical change. On the other hand, an improvement in the terms of international trade (7) would have raised the quantity of household services in relation to most other outputs.

The relative position of the averages M obviously depends upon the amplitudes of the various scatters (see Table 10), on the one hand and the relative location of points 10 within these scatters, on the other. In other words, the magnitude of the output reaction of households to various primary technical changes is determined on the one hand by the output size of the industries directly affected, and on the other, by the relative amounts of household services purchased by these industries (see Chart 6). Incidentally, a very pronounced parallelism exists between the two (compare the position of point 10 on various scales of Chart 6 with the relative position of the corresponding points on the last two scales).

The shift in the position in the scatter averages (Chart 3) indicates that, with the single exception of agriculture (1), a productivity increase in any other industry would have reduced the relative output of household services in 1929 more (or increased it less) than ten years before. An examination of Chart 6 shows on the other hand that during the intervening decade household services raised their relative position as an important cost factor in all industries except agriculture (1). Thus it appears that the increased influence through cost connections is responsible for the shift mentioned above. The tendency was fortified by the concomitant variation in the size of agricultural (1), fuel and power (2), and mining (2) output. In metals (3), textiles (5), transportation (6), and international trade (7), the influence via the earning ratio changed in the opposite direction, but this could only mitigate, not reverse, the dominating trend of the cost reactions.

d. Effects of changes in the investment coefficients. In contrast to the changes in the technical productivity coefficient, A_k, variations in the investment coefficient, B_k, do not induce any automatic adjustments in the standard of living, $\dfrac{1}{A_{10}}$; thus the specific effect through the change in A_{10} is absent from output reactions induced by this second type of primary variations. The relative quantity of household services will be influenced mainly through the cost relationships modified by the reaction through the investment level β. Comparing the position of point 10 in Chart 4 with the relative location of point 10 on the corresponding scales of Chart 6, we find a definite positive correlation between the two magnitudes.

Changes in these cost ratios are responsible for the difference in the output reaction of household services as they were in 1919 and 1929. Owing to such identity of causes, the direction of these shifts is the same as in the case of analogous output reactions to technical productivity changes.

e. Effects of a changed willingness to save. As already pointed out, an increase in the investment coefficient B_{10}, i.e., an increased willingness to invest on the part of households — influences the quantitative setup of the whole system through a change in the general investment level alone, and this change is equivalent to a proportional increase in all the separate investment ratios of various industries. As should be expected, a change in the saving coefficient of the households produces a stronger general quantity reaction than any other kind of investment or saving variation.

The order in which the separate points are distributed along the last two vertical scales ($k = 10$) in Chart 4 is almost exactly the opposite of the order in which they are located on the corresponding scales ($k = 10$) in Chart 6. Increased willingness to invest reduces most of all the outputs of agricultural (1) and textile (5) products, i.e., of commodities which deliver the largest part of their total output directly to households. It reduces least the relative quantity of mineral (2) products — typical producers goods which occupy the very last place on the list of household purchases. Between these two extremes the other commodities are distributed approximately in the inverse order of their importance for household consumption.

The distinction between producers and consumers goods industries is not emphasized in this study for the simple reason that introduction of terms of uncertain meaning is likely to obscure rather than clarify the line of an argument. However, such distinction can be made either on the basis of the structure of household expenditures or according to the output distributions of the industries concerned. With the basic industrial classification used in this investigation, both criteria lead to approximately the same results.

Ranked according to the decreasing proportion of total household expenditures devoted to the purchases of their products (i.e., according to the relative position of point 10 on the various vertical scales in Chart 5), the seven significant industries take the following order: 1, 5, 4, 3, 6, 7, 2. This order holds for 1929 as well as 1919. Arranged according to the proportions of their respective total net outputs sold to households (Chart 6, $k = 10$), the same industries appear in the following order: 5, 1, 4, 6, 3, 7, 2 in 1919, and 1, 5, 4, 3, 7, 6, 2 in 1929.

The influence of an increased willingness to invest upon the output of household services puts them definitely in the class of producers goods — this particular output increases in relation to almost all other commodities.

The difference in the location of corresponding points along the last two scales in Chart 4 clearly reflects the structural changes between 1919 and 1929. Textiles (5) became less of a consumers goods industry; metals (3), which at the beginning of the decade occupied exactly the same position as railroad transportation (6), shifted downward, while railroad transportation moved in the opposite direction. The last two changes are obviously connected with the spectacular growth of the automobile industry, which brought the metal (3) industry nearer the households consumption and at the same time, in taking away a large part of their passenger traffic, made the railroads (6) more than ever a producers goods industry. According to the change in the magnitude of its output reaction, international trade (7) shifted away from the consumers goods type of behavior, although in 1929 it absorbed a larger percentage of household expenditures and also delivered a larger proportion of its total output to this purpose. Indirect, roundabout connections exercised in this instance apparently a greater influence than the obvious direct relationships.

The average position M of the whole scatter is, in 1929, much lower than in 1919. This indicates that households themselves displayed at the end of this decade even more than before the typical characteristics of a producers goods industry. In 1929 increased willingness to save would have expanded the output of household services in relation to all the other outputs without exception.

ii. Agriculture and Foods Industries

a. Output reactions. The outstanding characteristic of agricultural (1) output reactions is the tendency to expand above all other industries in response to every technical productivity increase, including its own: point 1 is consistently at or near the top of the various vertical distributions in Chart 3, with only two notable exceptions. In 1919 an increase in the productivity of the textile (5) industry would have considerably reduced the relative output of agricultural (1) products. This is obviously a normal reaction through the cost relationship. Since then the significance of the textile (5) industry as a buyer of agricultural (1) products has been considerably reduced: in ten years the corresponding percentage fell one-third (see Chart 6); as a result, point 1 resumed its usual place near the top of the scatter in Chart 3.

An analogous relationship exists between agriculture (1)

and international trade (7). In 1919 international trade (7) absorbed over one-fifth of American agricultural production. Accordingly, an increase in the productivity coefficient A_7 — an improvement in the terms of international trade — would have considerably reduced the relative output of agricultural (1) commodities. In 1929 only 10 per cent of our farm (1) output went abroad — and the negative output reaction became much smaller.

b. Price reactions. An increase in agricultural (1) productivity naturally leads to the usual violent reduction in the relative prices of agricultural commodities (see Chart 2). In combination with the exceptionally great positive output effect mentioned above, primary changes of this kind (for example, fluctuations in crop yields per acre) might account for the typical picture of a negative correlation between agricultural prices and output variations. However, no analysis conducted in terms of *relative* prices and *relative* quantities can possibly lead to any definite statements concerning the variations in *absolute* prices and quantities. Thus, for example, even if points 1 and 10 are at the opposite ends of the first vertical distribution in Chart 2, an increase in the agricultural (1) productivity coefficient A_1 could be accompanied by a *general* price rise as well as by a *general* price fall. In the first case, however, the *absolute* price of household (10) services would rise more, and the price of agricultural (1) products would go up less, than the price of any other goods under consideration; in the second case, agricultural (1) money prices would fall more and the prices of household (10) services less than any other prices. The same applies to the interrelation between the absolute and relative output changes.

Thus the previously mentioned empirical observation, according to which increased productivity in agriculture tends to be accompanied by a considerable expansion in the absolute quantity and a marked fall in the money price of its output, touches the main line of the present analysis only so far as it indicates a reduction of the *relative* price and an increase in the *relative* output of agricultural commodities. The same conclusion could be drawn if the money price actually went up, but by a smaller amount than the prices of any other commodity, and the absolute output dropped, but in a lesser degree than any other output.

iii. Textiles and Leather

a. Output reactions. Textiles and leather (5) products are in their output reaction (see Chart 3) closely connected with agricultural (1) commodities: the outputs of both industries are largely absorbed by household consumption (see Chart 6, $k = 10$) which puts points 1 and 5 at the bottom of most other distributions in the same chart.

Only two kinds of technical changes seem to have opposite effects on agricultural (1) and textile (5) outputs. An increase in the productivity of the textile (5) industry itself would have raised its own relative output far more than the output of agricultural (1) commodities. The explanation lies obviously in the fact that a large percentage of agricultural (1) output is absorbed in textile (5) manufacture (see Chart 6, $k = 5$). Via this cost relationship an increase in the productivity coefficient of the latter industry is bound to have a negative effect on the former. In 1919 the textile (5) industry absorbed a much larger percentage of the total agricultural (1) output than in 1929. Accordingly, the negative output reaction was much greater at the former date.

An improvement in the terms (A_7) of international trade (7) has a tendency to reduce the agricultural (1) output while it leaves point 5 (textile) well at the top of the scale (see Chart 3, $k = 7$).

b. Price reactions. The typical picture of opposite variations in the price and quantity of its own output will accompany any change (increase) in the productivity of the textile (5) industry. The reason is the same as in the case of agriculture — the unusually strong (positive) output reaction.

iv. Metal Industry

In its output reactions the metal (3) industry tends toward the middle range. In no case does point 3 rise to the top or even to the second highest place in any of the seven significant vertical distributions in Chart 3, and only in one instance is it at the very bottom of a vertical scatter. Increased productivity of railroad transportation (6) is likely to produce this effect (Chart 3, $k = 6$). A glance at Chart 6 shows that railroad transportation (6) is the only industry which absorbs a larger percentage of the total output of metal (3) products than of any other cost factor.

b. Price reactions. In its price reactions also the metal industry (3) keeps the middle ground. As should be expected, however, an increase in mining (2) productivity is followed by a considerable drop in metal (3) prices (Chart 2, $k = 2$).

v. Minerals (Mining) Industry

a. Output reactions. A very strong affinity exists between mining (2) and the metal (3) industry. In all but two distributions in Chart 3, points 2 and 3 are near each other. A change in the productivity of the metal (3) industry cuts in between the two and sends point 2 to the bottom of the scale (Chart 3, $k = 3$). Similarly, a technical variation in railroad transportation (6) affects metal (3) output much more than mining (2) production.

b. Price reactions. Not only does the mineral (2) industry sell most of its output to metals (3), but metals constitute a larger percentage of its total costs than any other industry (see Chart 5, $k = 2$). Thus, in its price reaction the mineral (2) industry follows metals (3) nearly as closely as it does in its output variations.

vi. Fuel and Power

a. Output reactions. In seven out of fourteen significant distributions in Chart 3, point 4 is immediately above points 2 and 3; in four its position is between and just below the higher of the other two. Thus, in general fuel and power (4) tends to respond to various productivity increases by increasing its output in relation to mineral (2) and metal (3) production, or at least to one of them. Only an increased productivity coefficient of the mineral (2) industry would reduce the fuel and power (4) output below metals (3) and minerals (2).

b. Price reactions. In its price reactions the fuel and power (4) output is also very close to metals (3) and minerals (2).

vii. International Trade

Between 1919 and 1929 international trade (7) experienced a greater transformation than any other branch of the American national economy. An analysis of the concomitant shift in its price and quantity reactions is therefore particularly interesting.

The great change which modified so fundamentally the position of international trade within the structural setup of the whole system consisted in an increase of its investment ratio $\mathcal{B}_7$ from 0.53 in 1919 to 0.96 in 1929. At the beginning of this decade, the total outlays (exports) of this industry were nearly twice as large as its output (imports); at the end, the two were approximately equal. The adjustment took place through reduction of exports: the output of international trade in 1929 was approximately the same as in 1919 (see the last two vertical distributions in Chart 6); its outlay fell to approximately one-half of the 1919 value (see the last two vertical distributions in Chart 5). The latter variation affected first of all the magnitude of the general price reaction with which the economic system would have responded to a primary change in the productivity coefficient (the terms of) international trade. In 1919 the standard deviation of the corresponding scatter ($k = 7$) on Chart 2 amounted to 0.056; in 1929 it was only 0.050 (see Table 10).

The increase in the investment ratio (reduction of the willingness to invest) reduced also the influence of changing productivity and investment coefficients of international trade upon the output of other industries via the general investment level β (see Chart 7a and 7b). The amplitudes of the corresponding scatters in Chart 3 and Chart 4 diminished from 0.047 to 0.032 and from 0.096 to 0.031 respectively (Table 10).

a. Output reactions. International trade supplies to agriculture (1) a large proportion of its product (imports) than any other industry. The same is true of the use of imported products (7) by the textile (5) industry (see Chart 6, $k = 1$ and $k = 5$). Thus an increase in agricultural productivity tends to reduce the quantity of imports in relation to all other outputs, and the same is true of the primary technical change in textile (5) production (see Chart 3).

On the other hand, improved terms of trade, i.e., an increase in the productivity of international trade (7) itself, raises imports (output of international trade) in relation to all other outputs. This means that, in analogy to agricultural (1) and textile (5) prices and quantities, the relative import prices and quantities will show in such a case definitely opposite movements.

b. Price reactions. Most of the reduction in exports consisted in diminished foreign sales of agricultural (1) products. Although in 1929 it still absorbs a greater proportion of agricultural output than of any other single industry, the lead is considerably reduced (see Chart 6). As a result, the negative reaction of import prices to technical productivity increases in agriculture (1) is in 1929 much smaller than in 1919. On the other hand, metal (3) goods raised their proportion in American exports from 18 to 30 per cent. Accordingly, in 1929, the sensitivity of import prices to technical changes in the metal (3) industry is considerably greater than in 1919.

In general, import prices remained in 1929 as they were in 1919 the most sensitive element of the American price system. Point 7 occupies a very low position on most of the vertical scales of Chart 2.

viii. Railroad Transportation

a. Output reactions. The largest proportions of transportation services are absorbed by such bulky commodities as agricultural (1) products, fuels (4), metals (3), and mineral (2) products (see Chart 6). Thus point 6 is near the bottom of the corresponding distributions in Chart 3. An increase in any of the three technical efficiency coefficients would tend to reduce the relative output of transportation services.

The previously made distinction between the productivity A_k of the industry k and the productivity A'_k of the commodity k acquires from the viewpoint of the transportation (6) industry particularly great significance. It is rather the latter — an increased efficiency of coal utilization, for example — which would lead to a reduction in transportation services. An improvement in methods of coal production would lead, on the other hand, to an increase in the proportional input of transportation services as compared with the other factors involved.

b. Price reactions. Fuel and power (4) and metal (3) products are the most important cost elements of the railroads (6). Thus an increased productivity in either industry would cause a considerable reduction in the relative price of transportation services. Otherwise, point 6 is usually in the upper ranges of the vertical distributions of Chart 2.

B. Structural Changes and Secondary Variations in the American Economic System, 1919–1929

7. STRUCTURAL CHANGES

i. Equivalent Sets of Technical Changes

The numerical results of the analysis summarized in Charts 2, 3, and 4, and examined above make it possible to determine approximately the price and output reactions of various commodities to any given combination of primary changes.

Looking forward, an attempt could be made to determine on the basis of this analysis the probable repercussions of expected technical developments or prospective changes in saving and investment habits. Looking backward, it should be possible to explain the price and quantity variations of recent years in terms of the underlying structural transformation of the whole economic system.

The first task implies the necessity of evaluating the future trends in the development of the basic data of the American national economy — an attempt which lies outside the scope of our investigation. The second problem can be approached on the basis of empirical information already used in the previous analysis.

The simplest way to discover the basic changes responsible for the variation in the price and output relationships, which took place in the American national economy between 1919 and 1929 would be a direct comparison of the magnitudes of the technical and investment coefficients of each particular industry as they were in 1919 and in 1929. As indicated before, the available statistical information excludes the possibility of a direct comparison of this kind.

Discussion in Part II, Section 11 shows that the absence of separate price and quantity data cannot possibly hamper an attempt to determine and to compare the relative price and quantity reactions of various commodities in two systems. All the many technical setups which could correspond to any one given set of value (price × quantity) relationships would produce identical price and quantity reactions. But precisely for this reason, any given variation in the value setup of the economic system could have been caused by any one of the infinitely many equivalent sets of technical changes. The indeterminateness of the problem, formulated in such general terms, becomes obvious if it is realized that any number of mutually compensating technical variations could have taken place without affecting the value setup of the economic system at all.

To determine one of these possible technical variations, it is sufficient, for example, to postulate entirely arbitrarily some definite change in the price of each separate commodity and then divide the empirically given change in the value figures of every particular output and input by the appropriate arbitrarily selected price variation. Each ratio thus obtained will represent the variation of the corresponding physical quantity.

Any other set of equivalent technical changes, that is, changes which would produce identical variations in all the separate value figures, can be obtained from the first by introducing additional compensated technical variation of dimensional type, i.e., by changing the productivity coefficient A_k of each separate *industry* k and the productivity coefficient A'_k of the corresponding *commodity* k in inverse proportions so that the efficiency coefficient $A_k A'_k$ (see p. 64) would remain the same.

ii. Changes of the General Productivity Coefficients Interpreted as Index Numbers

The whole analysis would be considerably simplified in those special cases in which the actual value changes could be described entirely in terms of the general productivity coefficients A_k and A'_k; in other words, if the actual technical transformation had consisted exclusively of *proportional* changes in the productivities of all the inputs of every separate industry or a *proportional* variation of the productivity of each separate commodity in all its various uses, or in some combination of these two simple types of technical change.

As a matter of fact, the analysis of the *value* figures in this, as in any other, case could determine only the variation of the efficiency coefficients $A_k A'_k$. Whether in any particular instance the change of $A_k A'_k$ was due to a variation in A_k, A'_k, or a combination of the two, could not possibly have been discovered without additional empirical information.

In the absence of such additional information, however, it is admissible to assume freely any particular change in the magnitude of one of the two components, say A_k. The variation of the other, A'_k, must be determined so as to make the change in the total coefficient $A_k A'_k$ equal to its empirically given magnitude.

Even if the given shifts in the setup of the economic system were such that they could not be described quite accurately in terms of the two types of the proportionality coefficients alone, an attempt can be made to *approximate* the actual change as closely as possible without allowing any other technical variations except those which could be expressed in terms of A_k and A'_k. If *value* figures alone were available, this task would imply an approximate description of the actual value variations solely in terms of the $n - 1$ independent efficiency coefficients, $A'_1 A_1, A_2 A'_2, A_3 A'_3, \cdots A'_{n-1} A_{n-1}$ and the n saving coefficient $B_1, B_2, B_3, \cdots B_n$.

The problem thus raised is essentially an *index number* problem. In analogy to a price index, which encompasses in a single figure a great number of more or less heterogeneous price changes or a quantity index, which describes the average movement of many separate quantity series, variations of the few general efficiency coefficients can serve as indices of the actual changes in all the many separate technical output and input relationships.

Used in an empirical investigation or theoretical construction, an index number is a short-cut intended to simplify the analysis and presentation of complex quantitative relationships. A short-cut is the better the more it shortens the way, provided it leads approximately to the goal which otherwise could, at least in principle, be reached by the main road of complete, unabridged analysis. Comparing the results obtained by use of index numbers with those which would be achieved without simplifications of this kind, it should be possible to determine the efficacy of the selected short-cut method.

iii. Computing Technical Changes from Value Variations

In accordance with this conceptual scheme, an attempt can be made to determine what changes in the 9 efficiency and the 10 investment coefficients could have reproduced as closely as possible the variations of the value setup of the American economic system as actually observed between 1919 and 1929.

The description of this value setup as used in the present analysis involves nearly 90 separate input and output figures. The task of explaining this number of separate variations requires a solution of a system of as many simultaneous equations. The number of available variables is, however, limited to 19. An exact solution is thus out of the question; were it possible, the whole task would not involve an index problem.

Approximate solutions can be obtained in many ways. The method of least squares is most common. Applied to our task, it would enable us to determine the unknown increments of the 9 efficiency and the 10 investment coefficients in such a way as to minimize the sum total of the squares of the differences between the theoretically derived and the actual changes in each of the 90 separate input figures. The numerical computations required by this type of solution are so great that for practical reasons another somewhat simpler method of approximation was used.

Instead of trying to satisfy approximately the 90 separate equations with 19 variables, we reduced at the very outset the number of equations to 19 and solved those exactly. These 19 were selected in such a way as to dominate the larger system and thus lead to a solution which can be expected to satisfy also this larger system with a reasonable degree of approximation. Of the 19 equations so chosen, 9 describe the observed variations in the relative values of the net outputs of each of the main industrial divisions, except households: the price and quantity of household services are used as a *numéraire* and cannot change by definition. For reasons of homogeneity the values of our unknowns which will fit the 19 other equations will automatically satisfy this last one, too. The other 10 equations describe the observed variation in the saving ratios $B_1, B_2, B_3 \cdots$ of all 10 industries, including households. None of these 19 equations is linear. But linear approximation can be used. If the unknown increments are relatively small, it can be expected to give reasonably accurate results.

iv. Theoretical Formulae

As shown before, the change in any efficiency coefficient $A_k A'_k$ caused by a variation in A_k alone affects the *value* setup of the system exactly in the same way as an equal change in A'_k alone or as any equivalent combination of the two. To avoid unnecessary complexity in the following formal analysis, the productivity coefficients A'_k of the various commodities will be considered as constant and all the variations in the corresponding efficiency coefficients $A_k A'_k$ will be entirely attributed to the industrial coefficients A_k.

The whole calculation deals with known and unknown changes between two periods — the basic or zero (0) and the final or the first (1) period. Appropriate superscripts "0" and "1" are used to indicate the difference between the two sets of values. For example, $v_{ik}{}^0$ represents the input value of commodity k as used in industry i in the base period, $v_{ik}{}^1$ the corresponding value in the final period.

Increment signs Δ (not to be confused with the Δ, the price determinant) are used to indicate the differences between the basic and the final values of the same variables:

$$\Delta A_i = A_i{}^1 - A_i{}^0$$
$$\Delta B_i = B_i{}^1 - B_i{}^0$$
$$\Delta v_{ik} = v_{ik}{}^1 - v_{ik}{}^0$$
$$\Delta \beta = \beta^1 - \beta^0$$
$$\text{etc.}$$

The basic values of the proportionality coefficients $A_1, A_2, \cdots$ and β are — as in all the preceding computations — taken as being equal to 1.

Thus

$$\Delta A_i = A_i{}^1 - 1$$
$$\mathcal{B}_i{}^0 = B_i{}^0$$
$$\text{etc.}$$

The value $v_i{}^1$ of the output of industry i in the final period is (approximately) equal to its original value, $v_i{}^0$ in the base period plus the sum total of the $2n - 1$ partial derivatives of the dependent variable v_i in respect of the independent variables $A_1, A_2, \cdots A_{n-1}$, and $B_1, B_2, B_3, \cdots B_n$, each of them multiplied by the increment of the corresponding independent variable:

$$(\text{XLVIII}) \quad v_i{}^1 - v_i{}^0 = \left(\frac{\partial v_i}{\partial A_1} \right)^M \Delta A_1 + \left(\frac{\partial v_i}{\partial A_2} \right)^M \Delta A_2 \cdots$$

$$+ \left(\frac{\partial v_i}{\partial A_{n-1}} \right)^M \Delta A_{n-1} + \left(\frac{\partial v_i}{\partial B_1} \right)^M \Delta B_1$$

$$+ \left(\frac{\partial v_i}{\partial B_2} \right)^M \Delta B_2 + \cdots + \left(\frac{\partial v_i}{\partial B_n} \right)^M \Delta B_n$$

An analogous expression for the final value of an investment ratio $\mathcal{B}_i$ is:

$$(\text{XLIX}) \quad \mathcal{B}_i{}^1 - \mathcal{B}_i{}^0 = \left(\frac{\partial \mathcal{B}_i}{\partial A_1} \right)^M \Delta A_1 + \left(\frac{\partial \mathcal{B}_i}{\partial A_2} \right)^M \Delta A_2 + \cdots$$

$$+ \left(\frac{\partial \mathcal{B}_i}{\partial A_{n-1}} \right)^M \Delta A_{n-1} + \left(\frac{\partial \mathcal{B}_i}{\partial B_1} \right)^M \Delta B_1$$

$$+ \left(\frac{\partial \mathcal{B}_i}{\partial B_2} \right)^M \Delta B_2 + \cdots + \left(\frac{\partial \mathcal{B}_i}{\partial B_n} \right)^M \Delta B_n$$

The values of all derivatives as indicated by the superscript M refer to some intermediate points between the base and final position of the system. The magnitudes of all these derivatives in these extreme positions are supposed to be known, and the intermediate values can be defined as some averages of these two.

The averaging formulae adopted for the following computations are given below: [1]

(L)

$$\left(\frac{\partial v_i}{\partial A_k}\right)^M = (v_i{}^0 + v_i{}^1)\left[\left(\frac{\partial v_i}{\partial A_k} \cdot \frac{1}{v_i}\right)^0 + \left(\frac{\partial v_i}{\partial A_k} \cdot \frac{1}{v_i}\right)^1\right] \div 4$$

(LI)

$$\left(\frac{\partial v_i}{\partial B_k}\right)^M = (v_i{}^0 + v_i{}^1)\left[\left(\frac{\partial v_i}{\partial B_k} \cdot \frac{1}{v_i}\right)^0 + \left(\frac{\partial v_i}{\partial B_k} \cdot \frac{1}{v_i}\right)^1\right] \div 4$$

$$\text{where} \quad \frac{\partial v_i}{\partial B_k} \cdot \frac{1}{v_i} = \frac{\partial X_i}{\partial B_k} \cdot \frac{1}{X_i}$$

(LII) $\quad \left(\frac{\partial \mathcal{B}_i}{\partial A_k}\right)^M = (\mathcal{B}_i{}^0 + \mathcal{B}_i{}^1)\left[\left(\frac{\partial \beta}{\partial A_k}\right)^0 + \left(\frac{\partial \beta}{\partial A_k}\right)^1\right] \div 4$

(LIII) $\quad \left(\frac{\partial \mathcal{B}_i}{\partial B_k}\right)^M = \left(\mathcal{B}_i{}^0 + \mathcal{B}_i{}^1\right)\left[\left(\frac{\partial \beta}{\partial B_k}\right)^0 + \left(\frac{\partial \beta}{\partial B_k}\right)^1\right] \div 4$

$$+ \left[\left(\frac{\partial B_i}{\partial B_k}\right) + \left(\frac{\partial B_i}{\partial B_k}\right)^1\right] \div 2$$

$$\text{where} \quad \left[\left(\frac{\partial B_i}{\partial B_k}\right)^0 + \left(\frac{\partial B_i}{\partial B_k}\right)^1\right] \div 2 \begin{cases} = 1 \text{ if } i = k \\ = 0 \text{ if } i \neq k \end{cases}$$

Substitution from L and LI in XLVIII and a division of both sides of the resulting equations by $\dfrac{v_i{}^0 + v_i{}^1}{4}$ gives:

---

[1] Partial derivatives $\dfrac{\partial v_i}{\partial A_k} \cdot \dfrac{1}{v_i}, \dfrac{\partial v_i}{\partial B_k} \cdot \dfrac{1}{v_i}$, etc., are *identical* with the total derivative $\dfrac{dv_i}{dA_k} \cdot \dfrac{1}{v_i}, \dfrac{dv_i}{dB_k} \cdot \dfrac{1}{v_i}$. The symbol ∂ of partial differentiation is introduced in the present formulation in place of the previously used sign d of total differentiation because in the present analysis all the separate derivatives appear simultaneously, while in the previous discussion each was considered without any reference to the others.

(LIV)

$$\left[\left(\frac{\partial v_i}{\partial A_1}\cdot\frac{1}{v_i}\right)^0+\left(\frac{\partial v_i}{\partial A_1}\cdot\frac{1}{v_i}\right)^1\right]\Delta A_1$$

$$+\left[\left(\frac{\partial v_i}{\partial A_2}\cdot\frac{1}{v_i}\right)^0+\left(\frac{\partial v_i}{\partial A_2}\cdot\frac{1}{v_i}\right)^1\right]\Delta A_2+\cdots$$

$$+\left[\left(\frac{\partial v_i}{\partial A_{n-1}}\cdot\frac{1}{v_i}\right)^0+\left(\frac{\partial v_i}{\partial A_{n-1}}\cdot\frac{1}{v_i}\right)^1\right]\Delta A_{n-1}$$

$$+\left[\left(\frac{\partial v_i}{\partial B_1}\cdot\frac{1}{v_i}\right)^0+\left(\frac{\partial v_i}{\partial B_1}\cdot\frac{1}{v_i}\right)^1\right]\Delta B_1$$

$$+\left[\left(\frac{\partial v_i}{\partial B_2}\cdot\frac{1}{v_i}\right)^0+\left(\frac{\partial v_i}{\partial B_2}\cdot\frac{1}{v_i}\right)^1\right]\Delta B_2$$

$$+\cdots+\left[\left(\frac{\partial v_i}{\partial B_n}\cdot\frac{1}{v_i}\right)^0+\left(\frac{\partial v_i}{\partial B_n}\cdot\frac{1}{v_i}\right)^1\right]\Delta B_n$$

$$=-\frac{4\,\Delta\,v_i}{v_i{}^0+v_i{}^1}$$

Similarly, XLIX can be transformed on the basis of LII and LIII into

(LV)

$$\left[\left(\frac{\partial\beta}{\partial A_1}\right)^0+\left(\frac{\partial\beta}{\partial A_1}\right)^1\right]\Delta A_1+\left[\left(\frac{\partial\beta}{\partial A_2}\right)^0+\left(\frac{\partial\beta}{\partial A_2}\right)\right]\Delta A_2$$

$$+\cdots+\left[\left(\frac{\partial\beta}{\partial A_{n-1}}\right)^0+\left(\frac{\partial\beta}{\partial A_{n-1}}\right)^1\right]\Delta A_{n-1}$$

$$+\left[\left(\frac{\partial\beta}{\partial B_1}\right)^0+\left(\frac{\partial\beta}{\partial B_1}\right)^1\right]\Delta B_1$$

$$+\left[\left(\frac{\partial\beta}{\partial B_2}\right)^0+\left(\frac{\partial\beta}{\partial B_2}\right)^1\right]\Delta B_2+\cdots$$

$$+\left[\left(\frac{\partial\beta}{\partial B_i}\right)^0+\left(\frac{\partial\beta}{\partial B_i}\right)^1+\frac{4}{\mathcal{B}_i{}^0+\mathcal{B}_i{}^1}\right]\Delta B_i+\cdots$$

$$+\left[\left(\frac{\partial\beta}{\partial B_n}\right)^0+\left(\frac{\partial\beta}{\partial B_n}\right)^1\right]\Delta B_n=-\frac{4\,\Delta\,\mathcal{B}_i}{\mathcal{B}_i{}^0+\mathcal{B}_i{}^1}$$

There are $(n-1)$ equations of the type LIV and n of the type LV. There are $n-1$ unknown productivity increments ΔA_1, ΔA_2 $\cdots$ and n unknown increments ΔB_1, ΔB_2 $\cdots$ of all the investment coefficients.

The solution of this system of $2\,n-1$ equations with $2\,n-1$ unknowns determines the magnitudes of the efficiency changes and variations of all the investment coefficients.

v. Efficiency Changes in Different Industries, 1919–1929

In our particular empirical setup, there are 9 unknown technical changes and 10 unknown changes in investment coefficients to be determined. The solution of the 19 simultaneous equations gives the results shown in Table 11.

The year 1929 is used as the base and 1919 as the final period. Thus, the first figure in the first row shows that, if the efficiency level of agricultural (1) products in 1929 is taken to be equal to 1, in 1919 it is $1 - 0.516 = 0.484$. On the other hand, if the efficiency of foreign trade (7) equals 1 in 1929, in 1919 it is $1 + 0.318 = 1.318$. The efficiency of agriculture (1) increased more than that of any other significant industry, while the efficiency of international trade (7) showed the greatest shift in the opposite direction. Ranked according to the size of their efficiency changes from 1919 to 1929, the seven significant industries follow one another in this order:

> Agriculture and Foods (1)
> Textiles and Leather (5)
> Metals (3)
> Railroad Transportation (6)
> Mining (2)
> Fuel and Power (4)
> International Trade (7)

The last two suffered an actual decrease in efficiency.

vi. Changes in the Saving and Investment Coefficients, 1919–1929

The second row in Table 11 shows the increments of the 10 various investment or saving coefficients. As pointed out before, these coefficients can be interpreted as expressing the *willingness* to invest or to save and the change in their magnitudes is not identical with the variation in the directly observable saving and investment ratios. The latter depend also upon the shift in the equilibrating proportionality coefficient β.

Had β remained the same, the changes in the investment coefficients $B_1, B_2 \cdots$ would lead to identical changes in the corresponding saving ratios $\mathcal{B}_1, \mathcal{B}_2 \cdots$ $(= B_1 \beta, B_2 \beta \cdots)$. Actually, however, β did not remain the same. Computed as a sum total of the average derivative of the type $\dfrac{\partial \beta}{\partial A_k}$ and $\dfrac{\partial \beta}{\partial B_k}$,

TABLE 11

Technical Changes and Changes in the Investment Coefficients between the Years 1919 and 1929 *

i	1	2	3	4	5	6	7	8	9	10
ΔA_i	−0.516	−0.017	−0.160	+0.196	−0.456	−0.074	+0.318	+0.086	−0.044	..
ΔB_i	−0.004	−0.046	+0.043	−0.008	+0.016	+0.016	−0.381	+0.058	+0.089	+0.175

* Note that the year 1929 is used as a base period. The actual computation was performed in three successive approximations. While the values of ΔB_i did not show any significant variation from one stage of approximation to another, some of the values of ΔA_i change considerably with successive corrections.

	i	1	2	3	4	5	6	7	8	9
	1st approximation	−0.667	−0.032	−0.152	+0.196	−0.447	−0.014	+0.319	+0.094	−0.053
ΔA_i	2nd approximation	−0.445	−0.019	−0.144	+0.204	−0.437	−0.014	+0.309	+0.106	−0.063
	3rd approximation	−0.516	−0.017	−0.160	+0.196	−0.456	−0.074	+0.318	+0.086	−0.044

The computed change in the efficiency coefficient of the railroad transportation seems to contain a particularly large margin of error; it is very likely that the final magnitude −0.074 obtained for ΔA_6 exaggerates considerably the actual magnitude of this negative change.

each multiplied by the corresponding increments $\Delta A_k \cdots$, $\Delta B_k \cdots$, the increment in β equals -0.045. If the value of this proportionality coefficient is taken to be equal to 1 in 1929, in 1919 it was $1 - 0.045 = 0.955$. From 1919 to 1929 β changed in such a way as to encourage saving and to discourage investment in all industries (at any given willingness to save or to invest). Had β not risen, aggregate savings would have been smaller than total investments, which is impossible by definition.

Arranged according to the magnitude of the changes in their investment coefficients (see Table 11), the seven significant non-household industries follow one another in this order:

> Metal Industry (3)
> Railroad Transportation (6)
> Textiles and Leather (5)
> Agriculture and Foods (1)
> Fuel and Power (4)
> Mining (2)
> International Trade (7)

The large increase in the willingness to invest by the railroads (6) probably reflects the fact that in 1919 this willingness was artificially held down by governmental control.

The last four industries were, in 1929, less willing to invest than in 1919. The spectacular drop in American enthusiasm for foreign loans puts international trade (7) at the very bottom of the list. Metals (3) and textiles (5) were willing to invest a larger proportion of their receipts in 1929 than in 1919; the opposite change in the general investment level β shifted the actual investment ratios in the contrary direction.

The saving coefficient B_{10} of households (10) showed a 17 per cent decrease from 1919 to 1929. It was mainly this decrease which caused the rise in the general investment level β: of the total change of -0.045, this decrease contributed -0.042. Because of the compensating rise in β the actual directly observable investment ratio $\mathcal{B}_{10}$ of households fell only 10 per cent.

vii. Structural Changes and Cost Variations

Like any other kind of index numbers, the computed changes in the 9 efficiency and 10 investment coefficients are significant only so far as they lead approximately to the results which could have been obtained through a non-abridged, exhaustive type of analysis.

The test of significance requires, in other words, a comparison of the actual variation in the value of all the separate inputs and outputs with the corresponding changes computed on the basis of our indices.

The first 9 equations of the type XLVIII used to derive these indices guarantee a complete agreement between the two sets of changes so far as the values of the net outputs $v_1, v_2, \cdots v_9$ are concerned.

The variation in all the separate input figures as computed on the basis of the previously determined primary changes could fit the observed variations exactly only if these increments of the 9 efficiency and 10 investment coefficients were 100 per cent representative of the actual primary changes. Thus the magnitude of the discrepancies between the computed and the actual input values reveals the discrepancy between our indices and the actual primary changes.

The formulae used to compute the theoretical value changes on the basis of the previously derived increments of the 19 independent variables are very similar to those which served to derive these increments from the known value changes. Now we deal, however, with the 90 separate inputs, instead of the 9 total output figures.

As in the former computation, all primary technical variations can be conveniently expressed in terms of the productivity coefficients $A_1, A_2, \cdots A_{n-1}$; $A'_1, A'_2, \cdots A'_n$ are assumed to be constant.

If v^0_{ik} is the value of the (relative) input of commodity k into industry i as given for the base period and if v^1_{ik} is the corresponding value in the final period, then

$$(\text{LVI}) \quad v^1_{ik} - v^0_{ik} = \sum_{e=1}^{e=n-1} \left(\frac{\partial v_{ik}}{\partial A_e} \right)^M \Delta A_e + \sum_{e=1}^{e=n} \left(\frac{\partial v_{ik}}{\partial B_e} \right)^M \Delta B_e$$

where the derivatives are, as indicated by superscript "M", taken at some intermediate, average point between the base and the final period.

Remembering that $v_{ik} = x_{ik} P_{kn} = \dfrac{a_{ik} X_{in}}{A_i B_i} P_{kn}$

$$\text{(LVII)} \quad \frac{\partial v_{ik}}{\partial A_e} = a_{ik}\left[\frac{\dfrac{\partial X_{in}}{\partial A_e}A_iB_i - \dfrac{\partial A_i}{\partial A_e}B_iX_{in} - \dfrac{\partial B_i}{\partial A_e}A_iX_{in}}{(A_iB_i)^2}P_{kn}\right.$$

$$\left. + \frac{X_{in}}{A_iB_i}\cdot\frac{\partial D_{kn}}{\partial A_e}\right]$$

Factoring out $\dfrac{X_{in}}{B_i}P_{kn}$

$$\text{(LVIII)} \quad \frac{\partial v_{ik}}{\partial A_e} = v_{ik}\left[\frac{\partial X_{in}}{\partial A_e}\cdot\frac{1}{X_{in}} - \frac{\partial A_i}{\partial A_e}\cdot\frac{1}{A_i} - \frac{\partial B_i}{\partial A_e}\cdot\frac{1}{B_i}\right.$$

$$\left. + \frac{\partial P_{kn}}{\partial A_e}\cdot\frac{1}{P_{kn}}\right]$$

where

$$\frac{\partial A_i}{\partial A_e}\cdot\frac{1}{A_i}\begin{cases} = +\dfrac{\Delta_{ee}}{\Delta_{nn}}\cdot\dfrac{1}{A_i} & \text{if } i = n \\[2ex] = \dfrac{1}{A_i} & \text{if } i = e \\[2ex] = 0 & \text{in all other cases.}\end{cases}$$

Similarly

$$\text{(LIX)} \quad \frac{\partial v_{ik}}{\partial B_e} = v_{ik}\left[\frac{\partial X_{in}}{\partial B_e}\cdot\frac{1}{X_{in}} - \frac{\partial B_i}{\partial B_e}\cdot\frac{1}{B_i}\right]$$

Substituting LVIII and LIX in LVI:

$$\text{(LX)} \quad v^1{}_{ik} = v^0{}_{ik} + v^0{}_{ik}\left[\sum_{e=1}^{e=n-1}\left\{\left(\frac{\partial X_{in}}{\partial A_e}\cdot\frac{1}{X_{in}}\right)^M - \left(\frac{\partial A_i}{\partial A_e}\cdot\frac{1}{A_e}\right)^M\right.\right.$$

$$\left. - \left(\frac{\partial B_i}{\partial A_e}\cdot\frac{1}{B_i}\right)^M + \left(\frac{\partial P_{kn}}{\partial A_e}\cdot\frac{1}{P_{kn}}\right)^M\right\}\Delta A_e$$

$$\left. + \sum_{e=1}^{n=1}\left\{\left(\frac{\partial X_{in}}{\partial B_e}\cdot\frac{1}{X_{in}}\right)^M - \left(\frac{\partial B_i}{\partial B_e}\cdot\frac{1}{B_i}\right)^M\right\}\Delta B_e\right]$$

The derivatives are averaged according to the following formulae:

$$\text{(LXI)} \quad \left(\frac{\partial X_{in}}{\partial A_e}\cdot\frac{1}{X_{in}}\right)^M = \left[\left(\frac{\partial X_{in}}{\partial A_e}\cdot\frac{1}{X_{in}}\right)^0 + \left(\frac{\partial X_{in}}{\partial A_e}\cdot\frac{1}{X_{in}}\right)^1\right]\div 2$$

$$\text{(LXII)} \quad \left(\frac{\partial X_{in}}{\partial B_e}\cdot\frac{1}{X_{in}}\right)^M = \left[\left(\frac{\partial X_{in}}{\partial B_e}\cdot\frac{1}{X_{in}}\right)^0 + \left(\frac{\partial X_{in}}{\partial B_e}\cdot\frac{1}{X_{in}}\right)^1\right]\div 2$$

$$(\text{LXIII}) \quad \left(\frac{\partial A_i}{\partial A_e} \cdot \frac{1}{A_i} \right)^M = \begin{cases} = \left(\frac{\Delta_{ee}}{\Delta_{nn}} \right)^0 + \left(\frac{\Delta_{ee}}{\Delta_{nn}} \right)^1 \right] \div 2 \\ \qquad \text{if } i = n \\ = 1 \quad \text{if } i = k \\ = 0 \quad \text{in all other cases.} \end{cases}$$

$$(\text{LXIV}) \quad \left(\frac{\partial P_{in}}{\partial A_e} \cdot \frac{1}{P_{in}} \right)^M = \left[\left(\frac{\partial P_{in}}{\partial A_e} \cdot \frac{1}{P_{in}} \right)^0 + \left(\frac{\partial P_{in}}{\partial A_e} \cdot \frac{1}{P_{in}} \right)^1 \right] \div 2$$

$\left(\dfrac{\partial B_i}{\partial A_e} \cdot \dfrac{1}{B_i} \right)^M$ and $\left(\dfrac{\partial B_i}{\partial B_e} \cdot \dfrac{1}{B_i} \right)^M$ were previously defined by formulae LII and LIII.

Formulae LX has been used in actual computations with 1929 taken as the base period.

viii. Comparison of Actual and Computed Cost Changes

Chart 8 enables us to compare the value changes of all the separate inputs, as computed on the basis of the previously determined indices of primary technical and investment changes, with the corresponding actual variations.

All figures are relatives with the net dollar value of household services used as *numéraire*. Each pair of vertical point distributions describes the cost structure of one particular industry. Actual value relationships of 1929 are plotted on the right side. Computed values for 1919 are shown on the left scale. Broken lines connect the corresponding actual 1929 and computed 1919 values. Actual 1919 figures are also plotted on the left scales. Solid lines connect them with the analogous base-year figures.

All broken lines would coincide with the solid if the 9 efficiency and 10 investment increments in Table 11 had quite accurately described the actual structural changes in the American economic system between 1919 and 1929. A perfect fit of this kind can hardly be expected. The prevalent similarity, if not in the magnitude at least in the direction of the two types of movement, seems to indicate that the basic indices of primary changes are not devoid of significance.

The deviations of the computed figures from the actual figures deserve special attention. Each individual discrepancy of this kind shows that the actual change of the particular technical coefficient (a_{ik}) differed from the average change of all the other coefficients describing the inputs of the same

CHART 8

Comparison of Computed and Actual Input Values of Separate Cost Elements in All Industries, 1919–1929

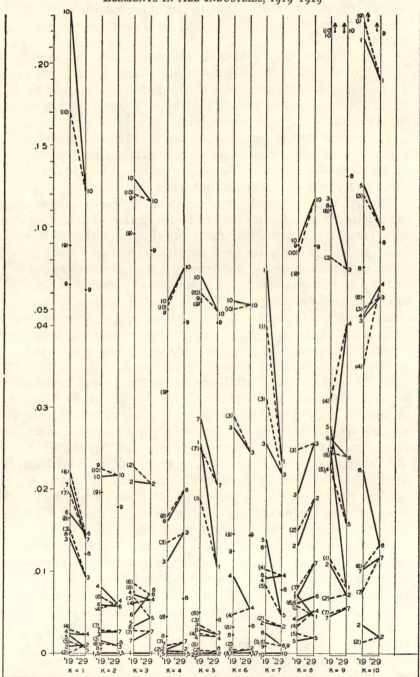

Basic classification of industries.   Data not reproduced here.

commodity (k) in all the other industries $(i = 1, 2, 3 \cdots)$ as well as from the average change in the input coefficients of all the other commodities $(k = 1, 2, 3 \cdots)$ used in the same industry (i).

As the theoretically computed changes in the net values of each of the 10 industrial outputs are exactly equal to their actual variations, the sum total of the positive deviations between the two types of points on every 1919 scale is equal to the sum total of the negative deviations.

The same is true of the discrepancies between the computed and the actual input values of any particular commodity in all the various industries. The aggregate surpluses are necessarily equal to the cumulated deficiencies.

The relative magnitude and direction of each particular deviation indicates the magnitude and direction of the difference between the actual technical variation and the average index of structural change as shown in Table 11.

An examination of the discrepancy between the computed and the actual input values of household (10) services in various industries $(k = 1, 2, 3)$ reveals a rather general underestimate of the increase and overestimate of the decrease in this element in the cost structures of various industries. A very considerable overestimate of the amount of household (10) services assigned to the undistributed (9) industry in 1919 (i.e., the underestimate of the corresponding input increase between 1919 and 1929) explains these other deviations. This underestimate is due to the spectacular growth of the distributive and other types of so-called service industries, all of which are assigned to our undistributed (9) group (see Appendix II). This change was bound to increase the input of household services in this industry far out of proportion to other cost factors, and thus cause an underestimate of the actual increment between 1919 and 1929. The overestimates in other industries appear by way of compensation.

In other instances the discrepancy between the computed and the actual cost allocations to the undistributed (9) industry as well as the corresponding differences between the actual and estimated input figures of undistributed (9) products simply reflects the greater completeness of our statistical distribution for 1919 as compared with 1929. The actual input of metal (3) products into the undistributed (9) industry fell from 1919 to 1929 by a larger amount than theoretically computed. The implied reduction in the corresponding technical coefficient simply indicates improvement in the statistical 1929 distribution of metal (3) products as compared with that of 1919. This discrepancy in its turn pulled down the average input coefficient of metal products and contributed an opposite difference between the theoretical and actual input values of metals (3) in all the other industries.

A closer examination of Chart 8 reveals several discrepancies of material significance. The actual expenditure on railroad transportation (6) by households (10) decreased between 1919 and 1929, while the theoretical estimate shows a marked increase of this figure. Indeed, if all the individual technical consumption coefficients had changed in the same proportion or if the input of railroad (6) services in all the other industries had changed in the same proportion as their input into households (10), this discrepancy would be much smaller. Actually, the increasing use of automobiles reduced the consumption coefficient of railroad transportation (6) in relation to all the other technical coefficients of the household (10) industry. This coefficient was reduced also in comparison with the technical input coefficients of railroad (6) services in all the other industries. Hence the underestimate of the household expenditures on this particular type of commodity in 1919 as compared with 1929.

The disparity between the actual and the computed change in the costs of textiles (5) to the metal (3) industry reflects the disproportionately great increase in the physical input of cloth, leather, and rubber used in automobile manufacture.

A disproportionately great improvement in the fuel economy of the railroads (6) reduced their fuel and power (4) bill far beyond the computations based on proportional technical changes.

8. PRICE CHANGES AND PHYSICAL OUTPUT VARIATIONS, 1919–1929

i. Theoretical Computation of Price and Output Changes

On the basis of the previously computed increments of the 10 investment and 9 efficiency coefficients, it was possible to estimate with a significant degree of approximation the changes in the *values* of separate cost elements used by various industries. These value changes could be expressed in terms of separate price and physical input changes only if it were possible to split the variation of each particular efficiency coefficient $A_k A'_k$ into its two parts — the variation of the productivity coefficient A_k of industry k and the variation of the productivity coefficient A'_k of the commodity k (see p. 64).

On the basis of value figures used in this investigation the distinction of this kind cannot be made. By venturing however beyond the narrow margins of factual analysis into the limitless realm of common-sense speculation, it might be interesting to make some reasonable guesses.

Given a definite increase (decrease) in the combined coefficient $A_k A'_k$ of some industry k, neither of the two components could have increased (decreased) in a larger proportion unless the other had decreased (increased) simultaneously. If it were known that A_k and A'_k do not move in opposite directions, then it would necessarily follow either that (a) one of these two elements shifted in the same direction and in the same proportion as the combined coefficient $A_k A'_k$ while the other remained unchanged, or that (b) both A_k and A'_k shifted in the same direction but each in a smaller proportion than the combined coefficient $A_k A'_k$.

Now there is good reason to believe that the productivity (A_k) of an industry k and the corresponding productivity (A'_k) of the commodity k more often than not will have the tendency to move in the same direction, particularly if this direction is that of technological progress — a progress which hardly ever reverses itself.

In cases of negative variations — such as the observed deterioration in the terms $(A_7 A'_7)$ of international trade or the slightly reduced efficiency $(A_4 A'_4)$ of the fuel and power industry — the situation is much more complex and no attempt should be made in such instances to rationalize any simplified assumptions.

On the basis of such ignorance let it now be assumed that the change in the industrial productivity A_k and the variation in the commodity productivity A'_k have in every single instance contributed equal amounts to the known total increment of the combined efficiency coefficient $A_k A'_k$.[1] Thus, for example, the total change $\Delta(A_3 A'_3)$ in the efficiency coefficient of the

---

[1]
$$\Delta(A_k A'_k) = 1 - (1 + \Delta A_k)(1 + \Delta A'_k)$$

If ΔA_k and $\Delta A'_k$ are so small that the product $\Delta A_k \Delta A'_k$ can be neglected, and if at the same time $\Delta A_k = \Delta A'_k$, it follows that

$$\Delta A_k = \Delta A'_k = \frac{\Delta(A_k A'_k)}{2}$$

metals (3) industry between 1919 and 1929 equals 0.16 (see Table 11). According to our assumption it can be split into an 0.08 increase in the productivity of metal manufacture (ΔA_3) and an equal, 0.08 increase in the productivity of the metal goods as used in other industries ($\Delta A'_3$).

Once the increments of all three types of primary coefficients — A_k, A'_k and B_k — are given, the relative changes in the (relative) prices and the relative magnitude of the (relative) physical outputs of all the commodities can be computed separately.

(LXV)

$$\frac{\Delta X_{in}}{X_{in}} = \sum_{e=1}^{e=n-1} \left(\frac{\partial X_{in}}{\partial A_e} \cdot \frac{1}{X_{in}} \right)^M \Delta A_e + \sum_{e=1}^{e=n-1} \left(\frac{\partial X_{in}}{\partial A'_e} \cdot \frac{1}{X_{in}} \right)^M \Delta A'_e$$

$$+ \sum_{e=1}^{e=n} \left(\frac{\partial X_{in}}{\partial B_e} \cdot \frac{1}{X_{in}} \right)^M \Delta B_e$$

(LXVI)

$$\frac{\Delta P_{in}}{P_{in}} = \sum_{e=1}^{e=n-1} \left(\frac{\partial P_{in}}{\partial A_e} \cdot \frac{1}{P_{in}} \right)^M \Delta A_e + \sum_{e=1}^{e=n-1} \left(\frac{\partial P_{in}}{\partial A'_e} \cdot \frac{1}{P_{in}} \right)^M \Delta A'_e$$

(See also formulae XLII, XLIII, XLIV).

Average values of all price and quantity derivatives are used throughout (see formulae LXI, LXII, LXIII and LXIV).

ii. Comparison of Actual and Computed Price and Output Changes

Table 12 contains in its first row price and in the second row (physical) output indices of the 7 significant commodity groups computed for 1919 with 1929 taken as a base. Household services (10) are used as the *numéraire*.

The figure 129 obtained for the agricultural (1) price level in 1919 indicates that if the ratio of agricultural (1) prices to the prices of household services (10) were taken to equal 1 in 1929, this ratio would have been 1.29 in 1919. In other words, between 1919 and 1929 the prices of agricultural (1) products in relation to the prices of household (10) services fell 29 per cent. The corresponding index of the physical output of agricultural commodities for 1919 is 109. It shows that, according to our computations, the ratio of agricultural and food (1) output to the output of household (10) services fell 9 per cent.

The last two rows of Table 12 contain ordinary indices of prices and physical outputs compiled for the same commodity groups on the basis of separate statistical price and quantity data. These statistical indices are described in detail in the

TABLE 12

COMPARISON OF THE ACTUAL WITH THE INDIRECTLY COMPUTED PRICE
AND QUANTITY CHANGES BETWEEN 1919 AND 1929

Industry	1	2	3	4	5	6	7
Indirectly computed 1919 price index 1929 = 100	129	105	115	99	134	111	116
Indirectly computed 1919 physical output index 1929 = 100	109	95	98	75	99	96	92
Actual price index for 1919 1929 = 100	136	118	132	105	165	91	147
Actual physical output index for 1919 1929 = 100	84	61	64	47	80	91	60

Supplement. Whenever prices and quantities of smaller commodity groups are averaged in computing one of these seven indices, the values of their net sales outside this particular group were used as weights. This type of weighting corresponds to our method of eliminating intra-industrial sales in the process of consolidation of accounts (see p. 15).[1]

These empirical indices describe the change in the *absolute* price and output levels of the seven significant commodity

[1] A complicated index number computation inevitably involves many more or less arbitrary decisions concerning the selection of the primary sources, determination of the averaging formulae, etc. In instances like the present, where the results of such index computation are used in checking some more or less theoretical estimates, the problem always arises of real subjective independence of the two experiments.

Conscious of this difficulty, the author delegated the whole computation of these statistical indices to a person who was ignorant not only of the results of our theoretical estimates but also of the general purpose of this particular task. The instructions given to Mr. F. H. Sanderson, who computed these indices contained only the desired classification of industries and defined the appropriate method of weighting. The averaging formula was chosen by Mr. Sanderson. In the mimeographed Supplement his report is presented without changes.

groups. Thus they cannot be directly compared with the theoretical indices, which show the changes in *relative* prices and relative quantities with households prices and household output used as the point of reference.

The two types of figures are comparable, however, so far as the order of magnitudes is concerned. If the theoretical computations show, for example, that in 1919 the physical output of metal (3) products was in its relation to the output of household services (10) 2 per cent (100 − 98) lower than in 1929, while in 1919 the similar relative figure for fuel and power (4) production was 25 per cent (100 − 75) lower than in 1929, the absolute level of power (4) output in 1919, computed on the 1929 base, must have been lower than the corresponding absolute level of metal (3) output.

Thus, if the theoretically derived price and physical output indices were in complete agreement with the actual directly computed price and quantity changes, the rank list of industries arranged according to the relative magnitudes of one type of figures should be identical with the corresponding rank list based on the other kind of indices.

Arranged according to the decreasing magnitude of the corresponding actual and indirectly computed price and quantity indices, the seven significant industries follow one another in this order.

PRICE CHANGES		PHYSICAL OUTPUT CHANGES	
Actual	*Indirectly computed*	*Actual*	*Indirectly computed*
Textiles (5)	Textiles (5)	Railroads (6)	Agriculture (1)
Imports (7)	Agriculture (1)	Agriculture (1)	Textiles (5)
Agriculture (1)	Imports (7)	Textiles (5)	Metals (3)
Metals (3)	Metals (3)	Metals (3)	Railroads (6)
Mining (2)	Railroads (6)	Mining (2)	Mining (2)
Fuel, Power (4)	Mining (2)	Imports (7)	Imports (7)
Railroads (6)	Fuel, Power (4)	Fuel, Power (4)	Fuel, Power (4)

A comparison of the two right-hand columns shows that, with the exception of railroad transportation (6), the indirectly computed changes of physical outputs correspond exactly as to rank with the actual variations. The index of railroad transportation (6) appears to be underestimated by three places.

The two left-hand columns reveal an analogous similarity

between the actual and the computed price changes. In this instance, however, there are two exceptions. The index of transportation prices (6) was overestimated by two places, while the indirectly derived index of import (7) prices is one place lower than the actual change.

C. Special Problems

9. the problem of industrial classification

i. Theoretical Analysis

For the purpose of detailed numerical analysis, the 44 industries represented in the main statistical tables (5 and 6) were consolidated into 10 large groups. The decision concerning the composition of these groups is for obvious reasons arbitrary. The question naturally arises, to what extent the results obtained would vary if our industrial classification were modified.

The theoretical problem involved can be formulated in the following terms: Given a basic statistical setup describing some particular economic system as composed of n separate industrial accounts; by consolidation of two of these n industries this setup is transformed into another which consists of only $n - 1$ industries. What is the difference between the analogous price and quantity derivatives as computed on the basis of the complete and the consolidated setup?

The general solution of this problem is rather intricate and, what is more important, the practical application of the criteria indicated by such a solution is equivalent to an actual computation and comparison of the two sets of derivatives. For the present purposes, it is sufficient to indicate the general nature of the theoretical considerations involved.

Let, for example, the industries 1 and 2 of our basic theoretical setup be consolidated into a new combined industry $(1 + 2)$. If the accounting rules described on p. 15 ff. are followed, the net output value v_{1+2} of the new consolidated industry will equal $v_1 + v_2 - v_{12} - v_{21}$; the input value $v_{(1+2)i}$ of any outside cost factor i used in $(1 + 2)$ can be defined as $v_{1i} + v_{2i}$ and the input value $v_{i(1+2)}$ of its product used in some outside industry i — as $v_{i1} + v_{i2}$. The total outlays of the consolidated industry will be $\dfrac{v_1}{B_1} + \dfrac{v_2}{B_2} - v_{12} - v_{21}$; its investment ratio

$\mathcal{B}_{1+2}$ defined in terms of the original setup is

$$\dfrac{v_1 + v_2 - v_{12} - v_{21}}{\dfrac{v_1}{\mathcal{B}_1} + \dfrac{v_2}{\mathcal{B}_2} - v_{12} - v_{21}}$$

From the known input and output figures, all the technical coefficients of the consolidated industry and commodity $(1 + 2)$ can be computed, and on the basis of these coefficients it is possible to determine the general formulae for the price and output derivatives.

A comparison of these formulae with those previously obtained for the basic non-consolidated setup shows that — in the simplified case of no saving and no investment $(\mathcal{B}^0_1 = \mathcal{B}^0_2 = \cdots \mathcal{B}^0_n = 1)$ — the price and the output derivatives of all commodities *not directly involved* in the process of consolidation, will remain the same if, for example, (a) neither of the two consolidated industries uses the product of the other and at the same time their output distributions and their cost structures are proportionally equal:

$$v_{21} = v_{12} = 0 \text{ and}$$
$$\dfrac{v_{i1}}{v_{i2}} = \dfrac{v_{1i}}{v_{2i}} = \dfrac{v_1}{v_2} \quad \text{for } i = 3, 4, \cdots, n$$

or if (b) the outlays of one of the two industries are devoted exclusively to the purchase of the products of the other, while at the same time the other industry does not buy any of its products:

$$v_{12} = v_1 \text{ and } v_{1i} = 0, \text{ for } i = 3, 4, \cdots, n, \text{ and } v_{21} = 0$$

The two cases mentioned above do not exhaust the list of all the particular setups in which the price and the output derivatives of industries not directly affected by consolidation are entirely invariant toward it. They indicate, however, the type of interrelationships which could account for invariance of this kind.

No actual statistical classification ever contains two industries which would strictly satisfy any such conditions. In many instances, however, they might be closely approximated. In those cases, the magnitudes of various prices and the output reactions computed on the basis of one consolidated setup can be expected to be rather similar to those obtained from a more detailed classification or from a somewhat differently consolidated setup.

ii. Comparison of Empirical Results Obtained on the Basis of Various Industrial Classifications

In order to determine the stability of the price and output relationships in respect to changes in industrial classification, the main grouping described on p. 69–72 was alternatively modified in three ways. A complete set of price and output derivatives was computed on the basis of each classification. Table 13 describes the three auxiliary classifications in terms of the first (basic) setup.

TABLE 13

COMPARISON OF THE FOUR CLASSIFICATIONS OF INDUSTRIES, 1929

1ST (BASIC) CLASSIFICATION GROUP NUMBER	2ND CLASSIFICATION		3RD CLASSIFICATION		4TH CLASSIFICATION	
	Group number	Content in terms of the 1st classification	Group number	Content in terms of the 1st classification	Group number	Content in terms of the 1st classification
1	1	1	1	1	1	1
2			2 + 3a	2 + 3 excl. Automobile industry	2	2
3	(2 + 3)	2 and 3	3b	Automobile industry		
4	4	4	4	4	3 + 4	3 + 4
5	5	5	5	5	5	5
6	6	6	6	6	6	6
7	7	7	7	7	7	7
8	8	8	8	8	8	8
9	9	9	9	9	9	9
10	10	10	10	10	10	10

Two of the three auxiliary classifications are obtained through simple consolidation; the second group combines the minerals (2) and metals (3) industries, while the fourth lumps metals (3) with the fuel and power (4) industry. The third setup involves an actual rearrangement. The automobile industry is treated as a separated class, while the rest of the metals (3) industry is combined with the minerals (2).

The magnitudes of the various price and output reactions as computed on the basis of these four classifications are presented in Charts 9 and 10. The figures for the third classification — with automobile manufacture treated as a separate industrial group — are listed in Appendix III.

Agriculture (1), textiles (5), railroad transportation (6), and international trade (7) are the four significant industries which, besides households (10), retained their identity through all the changes in classification; fuel and power (4) is the same in the first, second, and third setup, while minerals (2) as a separate commodity group can be found in only the first and the fourth. No two classifications contain the metals (3) industry in an identical form.

Accordingly, the influence of primary changes in agriculture $(k = 1)$, textiles $(k = 5)$, railroad transportation $(k = 6)$, and international trade $(k = 7)$ are traced in Charts 9 and 10 through all the four types of classifications, while for fuel and power $(k = 4)$ and minerals (2) only three and respectively two strictly comparable scatters could be constructed. The same applies to comparability of separate points on any two neighboring vertical scales; only those which retain their identity through all the four, three, or two distributions grouped together are interconnected with solid lines.

The charts show that most reaction patterns are only slightly affected by these particular changes in industrial classification. They indicate also that the price and output behavior of a consolidated industry tends to represent an average of the reaction patterns of its component parts. This phenomenon is revealed very clearly in the behavior of the combined minerals and metals (2 + 3) industry of the second classification as compared with the automobile (3b) and the mineral and metals excluding automobiles (2 + 3a) groups of the third setup.

In its output reaction, the automobile (3b) industry stays at the top of most scatters (see Chart 10) close to agriculture (1) and textiles (5), while the rest of the metals and minerals (2 + 3a) industry pulls down toward the lower end of the corresponding point distributions. Combined in 2 + 3 they keep to the middle ground with the greater weight of the latter group obviously prevailing. The fact that most of the household sales of the metals (3) industry are made on account of its automobile (3b) branch explains the marked difference in

CHART 9

PRICE REACTIONS TO PRIMARY PRODUCTIVITY CHANGES $\frac{dP_{in}}{dA_k} \cdot \frac{1}{P_{in}}$. COMPUTED

ON THE BASIS OF FOUR DIFFERENT CLASSIFICATIONS OF INDUSTRIES, 1929

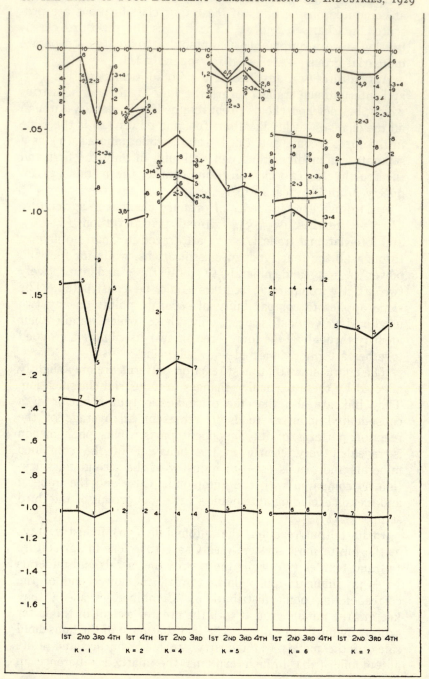

For detailed description of each classification see Table 13. The data for the first and third classifications of industries are in Appendix III, Tables 6 and 13. The data for the second and fourth classifications are not reproduced here.

CHART 10

Output Reactions to Primary Productivity Changes $\dfrac{dX_{in}}{dA_k} \cdot \dfrac{1}{X_{in}}$. Computed on the Basis of Four Different Classifications of Industries, 1929

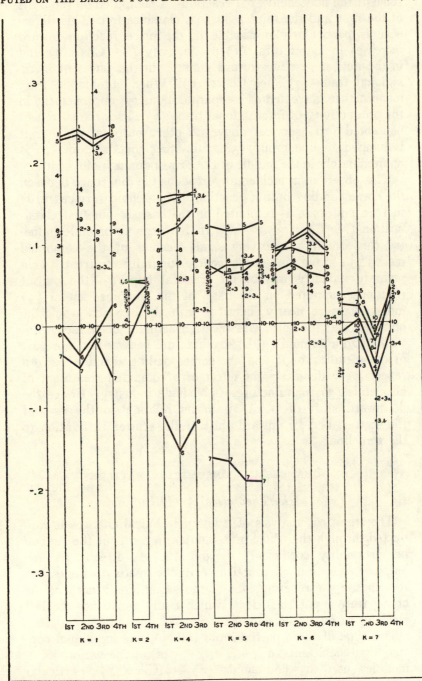

For detailed description of each classification see Table 13. The data for the first and third classifications are in Appendix III, Tables 8 and 12. The data for the second and fourth classifications are not reproduced here.

some of the household (10) reactions as computed on the basis of the first and the third industrial classification. This difference is particularly noticeable in the price reaction toward increases in agricultural (1) productivity (see Chart 9) and in the output reaction toward changes in the terms of international trade (7) (see Chart 10). When automobile (3b) manufacture is treated as a separate industry, improvement in the productivity of international trade (7) raises the output of household (10) services above all other outputs, while if it is lumped in one group (3) with other metals, point 10 is approximately in the middle of the corresponding point scatters.

This observation incidentally explains the difference between the corresponding output reaction of household services (10) in 1919 and 1929 as computed on the basis of our first classification (see Chart 3, $k = 7$). In 1919 the automobile industry constituted a relatively small element of the combined metals (3) group, and consequently our failure to treat it as a separate industry was of no practical import — the output reactions computed on the basis of the combined metal (3) industries were nearly identical with those which would be obtained had the third classification actually been used. Toward 1929 automobile (3b) manufacture became a major part of the metals group; and the corresponding reaction pattern reflects very definitely the effect of a combined treatment of all metals (3) manufactures as a single industry. Hence the downward shift of point 10 in its relation to the rest of the scatter, i.e., an upward shift of the scatter in relation to the zero line.

10. CHANGES IN CONSUMPTION PATTERNS

i. Theoretical Analysis

The empirical analysis of primary technical changes is conducted through the whole investigation in terms of the *general* proportionality coefficients A_k and A'_k. As already pointed out, consideration of practical exigency made it impossible to compute the repercussions of the variations in each of the 90 separate input coefficients which really constitute the last elements of our basic setup (see Part II, section 7).

One type of these partial input ratios — the individual consumption coefficients, a_{n1}, a_{n2}, a_{n3}, $\cdots$, of all the various commodities used by households (n) — attracts the particular attention of many investigators. Changes in consumers' tastes have often been considered one of the most important features in the recent development of the American economy. Thus an empirical analysis of this type of partial technological variations might be of particular interest.

The general formulae of the price and output reaction to partial technical changes are very similar to those derived for proportional variations (see p. 59). Remembering that a coefficient a_{nk} — which describes the input of commodity k per unit of output of the household services (n) — is in the nth row and the kth column of the price determinant Δ and in the kth row and the nth column of the quantities determinant D, we have

$$(\text{LXVII}) \qquad \frac{dP_{in}}{da_{nk}} \cdot \frac{a_{nk}}{P_{in}} = a_{nk} \left[\frac{\Delta_{ni \cdot nk}}{\Delta_{ni}} \right] = 0$$

The price reactions are identically equal to zero.

$$(\text{LXVIII}) \qquad \frac{dX_{in}}{da_{nk}} \cdot \frac{a_{nk}}{X_{in}} = a_{nk} \left\{ \left[\sum_{e=1}^{e=n} \left(\frac{D_{nn \cdot ee}}{D_{nn}} - \frac{D_{ni \cdot ee}}{D_{ni}} \right) B_e \right] \frac{d\beta}{da_{nk}} \right.$$
$$\left. + \frac{D_{ni \cdot kn}}{D_{ni}} + \frac{A_n}{A_i} \cdot \frac{d}{da_{nk}} \left(\frac{A_i}{A_n} \right) \right\}$$

where

$$(\text{LXIX}) \qquad \frac{dA_n}{da_{nk}} = \frac{\Delta_{nk}}{\Delta_{nn}}$$

and

$$(\text{LXX}) \qquad \frac{d\beta}{da_{nk}} = - \frac{\dfrac{D_{kn}}{D_{nn}} - B_n \dfrac{\Delta_{nk}}{\Delta_{nn}}}{\displaystyle\sum_{e=1}^{e=n} \frac{D_{ee}}{D_{nn}} B_e}$$

All the output derivatives are expressed in relative, i.e., elasticity, terms. In the previous formulae of this type, the basic value of the proportionality coefficient A_k was assumed to equal 1; thus the numerical multiplication of the straight derivatives $\dfrac{dX_{in}}{dA_k}$ and $\dfrac{dX_{in}}{dA_k}$ by A_k could have been omitted. In the present case, however, the independent variable (a_{nk}) is in general smaller than 1. Thus it must be explicitly introduced in the final elasticity expression $\dfrac{dX_{in}}{da_{nk}} \cdot \dfrac{a_{nk}}{X_{in}}$.

Only the output derivatives for 1929 are actually computed. Chart 11 presents the results in graphic form; the underlying figures are tabulated in Appendix III.

ii. Influence of Changes in the Consumption Pattern upon the General Level of Consumption Computed for 1929

An increase in the technical coefficient a_{nk} would indicate an increase in the physical input of commodity k per unit of household (10) services produced — provided the general productivity coefficient A_n (i.e., all the other separate input ratios a_{n1}, a_{n2}, $\cdots$) had remained the same. Actually, it cannot

TABLE 14

EFFECTS OF CHANGING TASTES UPON THE GENERAL LEVEL OF HOUSEHOLD
PRODUCTIVITY AND CONSUMPTION, 1929

k	1	2	3	4	5	6	7	8	9
$\dfrac{dA_{10}}{da_{10k}} a_{10k}$	0.220	0.002	0.068	0.076	0.115	0.015	0.014	0.105	0.379

possibly remain the same; depending upon value of all really independent coefficients of the system (including a_{nk}), A_n is bound to change with every variation of a_{nk}. The derivatives $\dfrac{dA_n}{da_{nk}}$, computed according to formula LXIX with $n = 10$, and put in the form of a corresponding elasticity expression $\dfrac{dA_{10}}{da_{10k}} a_{10k}$ are listed in Table 14.

The figures are positive throughout. That means that if the householders attempt to increase the amount of some commodity k consumed per unit of services supplied, the actual consumption level $\left(\dfrac{1}{A_{10}} \right)$ of all other commodities will necessarily decrease (see p. 42). This adjustment is very similar in its nature to the adjustment of the actual saving ratios $\mathcal{B}_1$, $\mathcal{B}_2$, $\cdots$ to any change in the willingness to save (or to invest), B_k, in any single industry k (see p. 90).

Householders, in other words, are not free to decide that

CHART 11

OUTPUT REACTIONS $-\dfrac{dX_{in}}{dA_{nk}} \cdot \dfrac{A_{nk}}{X_{in}}$ TO VARIATIONS IN THE HOUSEHOLD CONSUMPTION COEFFICIENTS, A_{nk}, 1929

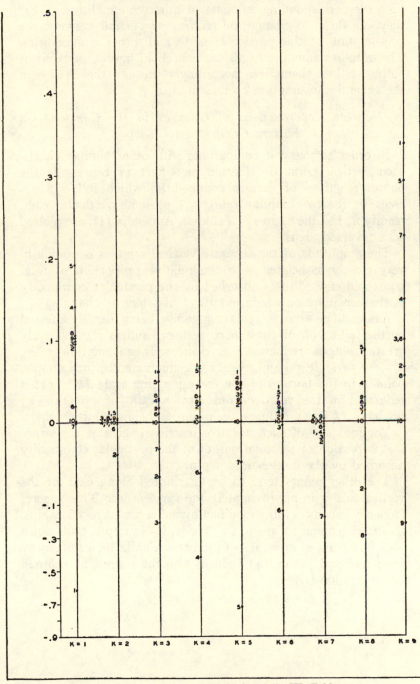

Basic classification of industries.   Data in Appendix III, Table 14.

they are going to increase the consumption of one commodity, per unit of services supplied, without changing at the same time the corresponding amounts of other commodities. What they can do is to change the *relative proportion* between the consumption of this particular and of all other commodities. The *absolute* amounts of all the household inputs, per unit of output, adjust themselves accordingly through the change in the general consumption coefficient A_n.

iii. Indirect Repercussions of Changes in the Consumption Pattern Computed for 1929

In order to make it comparable with other similar charts, each vertical point distribution on Chart 11 represents the output reactions of various commodities which follow a *decrease* in the consumption ratio, a_{10k}, of some particular commodity k; i.e., the figures of Table 14, Appendix III, are plotted with reversed signs.

The amplitude of the separate vertical scatters is obviously very closely associated with the relative proportion of total household expenditures absorbed by the particular commodity k, the consumption coefficient (a_{nk}) of which is changing.

As should be expected, this commodity, being directly affected by the falling off of consumers' demand, suffers the relatively greater output reduction. A decreased consumption ratio, $a_{10\ 1}$, of agricultural and food (1) products, sends, for example, point 1 to the bottom of the corresponding scale ($k = 1$); a reduction in the relative consumption ratio of mineral (2) products ($k = 2$) reduces their output below all the others.

The intensity of such negative reaction is greater the larger the proportion of the total output of the particular commodity absorbed by the households (see p. 89).

The other points tend to be distributed along each of the vertical scales in approximately the same order. This general tendency is considerably modified by indirect cost relationships. Reduced demand for metal (3) goods, for example, pulls down also the output of mineral (2) products. Similarly, a shift away from fuel and power (4) reduces also the output of railroad transportation (6).

PART IV

PART IV

APPLICATION OF INPUT-OUTPUT TECHNIQUE
TO THE AMERICAN ECONOMIC SYSTEM IN 1939

A. OUTPUT, EMPLOYMENT, CONSUMPTION, AND INVESTMENT

1. QUANTITATIVE RELATIONSHIP BETWEEN THE PRIMARY DEMAND FOR PARTICULAR PRODUCTS AND TOTAL OUTPUT AND EMPLOYMENT

How will the cessation of war purchases of planes, guns, tanks, and ships — if not compensated by increased demand for other types of commodities — affect the national level of employment? How many new jobs will be created by the consumers' demand for an additional one million of passenger cars, how many of these jobs can be expected to be located is the automobile industry itself, and how many in other industries such as Steel and the Chemicals, the Coal and the Petroleum industries? How much additional freight traffic and revenue can the American railroads expect to derive from every billion dollars worth spent on post-war housing construction?

These are the kind of questions which arise with any practical discussion of the immediate as well as of the long run prospects of our post-war economy. In an attempt to indicate a possible approach to a factual statistical answer to these questions this article describes a method of estimating the quantitative relationship which exists between the primary demand for the products of all the various branches of the national economy, on the one hand, and the total output and employment in each of them, on the other.

Given the annual bill of goods which is to be made available for consumption (and for new investment), the total outputs of various industries requisite for its actual production depends primarily upon the technical structure of all the many branches of agriculture, mining, manufacture, transportation, and service which directly or indirectly contribute to the output of the various commodities included in this final bill of goods.

Table 15 below depicts the input-output relationships of the

TABLE 15.—INPUT AND OUTPUT RELATIONS IN THE ECONOMIC SYSTEM OF THE UNITED STATES, 1939[1]

(Consolidated Industrial Classification)

DISTRIBUTION OF OUTLAYS (INPUT) OF CLASSES LISTED AT LEFT OF TABLE	DISTRIBUTION OF OUTPUT OF CLASSES LISTED AT LEFT OF TABLE											
	1 Agriculture and foods	2 Minerals	3 Metal fabricating	4 Fuel and power	5 Textiles, leather and rubber	6 Railroad transportation	7 Foreign trade (exports)	8 Industries, n.e.c.	9 Government	10 All other industries	11 Household consumption	12 Total net output
1. Agriculture and foods	112	...	...	...	555	...	643	585	9	650	14,522	16,964
2. Minerals	718	...	1,190	12	4	...	190	1,250	...	856	149	3,763
3. Metal fabricating	417	69	...	342	118	302	1,070	2,142	337	4,186	3,020	12,304
4. Fuel and power	82	282	355	...	138	265	700	402	195	2,581	3,541	8,876
5. Textiles, leather, and rubber	1,294	...	315	5	17	6	197	95	27	824	5,442	6,993
6. Railroad transportation	967	346	368	971	238	...	...	514	100	4	689	4,303
7. Foreign trade (imports)	853	366	46	81	459	...	...	488	...	647	...	2,833
8. Industries, n.e.c.	1,073	77	352	1,033	8	630	376	...	...	5,198	5,625	19,226
9. Government (taxes)	...	...	185	191	...	32	...	53	4,623	9,659	2,594	13,795
10. All other industries	8,155	1,490	3,366	3,099	3,149	723	88	9,078	2,812	...	28,937	60,896
11. Household services:												
A. Persons employed	(11,893)	(576)	(2,825)	(1,493)	(2,447)	(1,019)	...	(3,510)	(924)	(20,306)	...	(44,993)
B. Wages and salaries	3,466	792	5,461	2,311	2,543	1,863	...	4,210	6,197	21,269	...	48,112
C. Profits and interest	701	314	1,192	1,252	347	685	...	1,322	1,700	13,223	...	20,736
Total net outlays (input)	17,838	3,736	12,830	9,297	7,576	4,506	3,264	20,139	16,000	58,745	64,519	

[1] All figures are in millions of dollars and, in addition to manufacturers' value, include transportation costs, but exclude trade margins. A description of the consolidated industrial group in terms of their components is given in the appendix.

Source: United States Department of Labor, Bureau of Labor Statistics, Employment and Occupational Outlook Branch, Postwar Division. All figures are preliminary and subject to change.

different industries as they existed in the American national economy of 1939. Each row of figures shows the distribution of the total output of one particular industry among the different users of its products, these consisting of other industries, foreign countries (exports), households, etc. The total net output of Agriculture and Foods, for example, amounted to 16,964 million dollars. Of this, 555 million dollars worth went to the Textile, Leather and Rubber industries, 585 million to Industries, n.e.c., 643 million dollars worth were exported, and so on, while 14,522 million dollars worth were destined for direct household consumption. Commodities and services absorbed in the industry which produced them are not included in the net total output figure.

Column 11 of the table contains what might be called the 1939 consumption bill of goods, i.e. it shows the amounts which all the different industries contributed *directly* to the satisfaction of the final household demand. The *indirect* contribution of each industry to the household and new investment demand is indicated by that portion of its output which is absorbed by all the non-household users.

With the thorough-going division of labor characteristic of the modern industrial economy, the secondary effect of any change in the demand for consumers' and investment goods upon industries contributing to their production mainly in an indirect way is no less significant than the direct effect upon those branches of the national economy which are principally engaged in the production of commodities and services which directly enter the final bill of goods. The tracing of these indirect repercussions can be achieved through examination of the statistical data presented above in Table 15; an evaluation of their numerical magnitude requires, however, application of a rather elaborate analytical technique.

Actual computations of prospective demand [1] and employment are frequently based on certain assumptions concerning the magnitude of the net national product and its distribution by separate family income levels. Combined with households expenditure studies showing the composition of consumers' budgets, these basic assumptions can be translated into a definite bill of goods similar to that listed in column 11 of Table 15.

Instead of attempting to compute employment figures from

[1] See, for example, The Structure of American Economy, Part I. Basic Characteristics (National Resources Committee, 1939), pp. 14–16.

a given list of consumers' purchases (and net investments), it is possible, of course, to reverse the analytical procedure and, having assumed a given level of total employment, compute the bill of goods which would have been produced if available labor forces were apportioned among the various branches of production with a view to supplying the households with finished consumers' goods in certain anticipated proportions, while providing at the same time for net investment of a certain fraction of the resulting net national income. Both of the above-mentioned alternative approaches are partial. They both take explicitly into account the existence of one definite relationship between the outputs and employment figure of various industries and the magnitude of the net national income — the relationship which is determined by the *technical structure* of all the industries — but both neglect the other relationship between the same two aggregates — the relationship which is established via the *income flow* from the productive sectors of the national economy to the ultimate household consumers and investors.

This second relationship combined with the first one determines uniquely what might be called the equilibrium situation characterized by one particular equilibrium amount of total employment distributed in one particular way among all the various industries and associated with one particular bill of goods. Economic policies aimed at establishment and maintenance of a high level of employment can influence the position of all these equilibrium values only by affecting one or both of the underlying relationships.

The relationship between employment and consumption (and net investment) via income payments can be influenced by means of economic intervention more readily than that which links the same two variables via the technological structure of the national economy. Most instrumentalities of modern economic policies aimed at full employment are thus designed to modify the volume and direction of flow of various income (and investment) streams. The nature and magnitude of the final effects of such measures upon output and employment depend, however, on the character of the above-mentioned structural relationships, which, in themselves, cannot be easily affected by deliberate central action. For that reason an accurate knowledge of these relationships appears to be indispensable for an accurate appraisal of the probable results of any particular type of policy.

2. DERIVATION OF BASIC EQUATIONS AND ASSUMPTIONS INVOLVED

The proposed method of statistical computation of the total outputs and corresponding employment figures of all the various industries from a given bill of goods is based on the assumption that the production of a given quantity of any particular type of goods requires a definite technically determined amount of direct labor combined with certain also technically determined amounts of products of other industries. Thus, there must exist one, and only one, combination of outputs of various industries which makes the total output of each industry just large enough to make its direct contribution to the final bill of goods and satisfy at the same time the requirements of all the other industries. Once the output of each separate industry is thus computed, the magnitude of the appropriate labor force can be easily determined. The summation of the separate employment figures of all the various industries gives the employment figure for the national economy as a whole.

Let X_1 represent the total physical output of industry 1, X_2 the total output of industry 2, and so on; each of these magnitudes being expressed in terms of appropriate physical units, such as tons, yards, barrels, or "quantity purchasable for $1,000,000 at given prices."

The amount of the product of industry 2 absorbed by industry 1 can be designated as x_{12}, the number of units of the product of industry 3 used by industry 2 as x_{23}. In general x_{ik} will indicate the amount of product k used in industry i.

If x_{n1} stands for the amount of output of industry 1 which is used for direct household consumption and thus is entered into the final bill of goods, x_{n2} indicates the corresponding amount of product 2, and so on, the necessary balance between the total output and total input (absorption) of the products of each of the m different industries can be described through the following self-explanatory system of equations:

$$
\begin{aligned}
+X_1 - x_{21} - x_{31} - \cdots - x_{m1} &= x_{n1} \\
-x_{12} + X_2 - x_{32} - \cdots - x_{m2} &= x_{n2} \\
-x_{13} - x_{23} + X_3 - \cdots - x_{m3} &= x_{n3} \\
&\ \,\cdots\cdots\cdots\cdots\cdots\cdots\cdots \\
&\ \,\cdots\cdots\cdots\cdots\cdots\cdots\cdots \\
&\ \,\cdots\cdots\cdots\cdots\cdots\cdots\cdots \\
-x_{1m} - x_{2m} - x_{3m} - \cdots + X_m &= x_{nm}
\end{aligned}
$$

(1)

The relation between the total output of any particular industry, say X_1, and the amounts x_{12}, x_{13}, $\cdots$ of the products of other industries absorbed in the process of its production depends primarily upon the technical structure of this industry 1. Accordingly, let a_{12} represent the technical input coefficient determining the amount of the product of industry 2 absorbed by industry 1 per unit of its output, i.e. $a_{12} = \dfrac{x_{12}}{X_1}$, and in general, $a_{ik} = \dfrac{x_{ik}}{X_i}$.

The amount of labor services absorbed by an industry can also be related to its total output and thus expressed in terms of a corresponding labor input coefficient. If x_{in} stands for the amount of labor absorbed by industry i, $a_{in} = \dfrac{x_{in}}{X_i}$ is the labor input coefficient showing the labor requirements of the particular industry per unit of its output.[2] Thus, the technical structure of each industry can be described by a series of technical input coefficients — one for each separate cost element.

The technical relationships describing the inputs absorbed by all the m different industries as determined by the magnitude of their respective total outputs constitute our second system of equations:

$$x_{12} = a_{12}X_1; \; x_{13} = a_{13}X_1; \; \cdots; \; x_{1m} = a_{1m}X_1; \; x_{1n} = a_{1n}X_1$$
$$x_{21} = a_{21}X_2; \quad \cdots \quad ; \; x_{23} = a_{23}X_2; \; \cdots; \; x_{2m} = a_{2m}X_2; \; x_{2n} = a_{2n}X_2$$
$$x_{31} = a_{31}X_3; \; x_{32} = a_{32}X_3; \qquad \cdots \qquad \cdots; \; x_{3m} = a_{3m}X_3; \; x_{3n} = a_{3n}X_3$$

$$(\text{II}) \quad \cdots\cdots\cdots\cdots\cdots\cdots\cdots\cdots\cdots\cdots\cdots\cdots$$

$$x_{m1} = a_{m1}X_m; \; x_{m2} = a_{m2}X_m; \; x_{m3} = a_{m3}X_m; \; \cdots; \; \cdots x_{mn} = a_{mn}X_m.$$

Thus, on the basis of information contained in system II system I can be rewritten in the following form:

$$X_1 - a_{21}X_2 - a_{31}X_3 - \cdots - a_{m1}X_m = x_{n1}$$
$$-a_{12}X_1 + X_2 - a_{32}X_3 - \cdots - a_{m2}X_m = x_{n2}$$
$$-a_{13}X_1 - a_{23}X_2 + X_3 - \cdots - a_{m3}X_m = x_{n3}$$

$$(\text{III}) \cdots \cdots\cdots\cdots\cdots\cdots\cdots\cdots\cdots\cdots\cdots\cdots$$

$$-a_{1m}X_1 - a_{2m}X_2 - a_{3m}X_3 - \cdots + X_m = x_{nm}$$

[2] The use of the same subscript "n" in designating the amounts of commodities absorbed by Households (x_{n1}, x_{n2}, $\cdots$) and the input of labor services

The column on the right-hand side of the m equations represents the given bill of goods, and its elements are, for the purposes of our particular computation, given constants; so are also all the technical coefficients on the left-hand side. By solving this system of m simultaneous equations, it is possible to compute the unknown outputs, $X_1, X_2, X_3, \cdots X_m$ of all the separate industries.

The solution of the basic system of equation III can be written in the following form:

$$X_1 = A_{11}x_{n1} + A_{12}x_{n2} + \cdots + A_{1m}x_{nm}$$
$$X_2 = A_{21}x_{n1} + A_{22}x_{n2} + \cdots + A_{2m}x_{nm}$$
$$X_3 = A_{31}x_{n1} + A_{32}x_{n2} + \cdots + A_{3m}x_{nm}$$

(IV)

$$X_m = A_{m1}x_{n1} + A_{m2}x_{n2} + \cdots + A_{mm}x_{nm}$$

Inserting in the right-hand side of the first of these equations the values of x_{n1}, x_{n2}, etc., as given in the assumed bill of goods, we can compute X_1, i.e. the total output of industry 1. The same values, $x_{n1}, x_{n2}, \cdots, x_{nm}$, inserted in the subsequent equations determine the total outputs, $X_2, X_3, \cdots, X_m$, of all the other industries.

The term $A_{11}x_{n1}$ represents that part of the total output of industry 1 which is due to the x_{n1} units of commodity 1 entered in the final bill of goods; $A_{12}x_{n2}$ represents that part of this output which derives from the ultimate demand for x_{n2} units of commodity 2 and so on. In other words the coefficient A_{12} shows by how much the output of industry 1 would increase (or decrease) if the amount x_{n2} of commodity 2 which is entered into the bill of goods is raised (or reduced) by one unit (while the remaining parts of the bill of goods remain unchanged).

The magnitude of each of these coefficients A as computed from system III depends upon the technical characteristics of

---

in various industries (x_{1n}, x_{2n}, $\cdots$) is not accidental. From the point of view of general equilibrium analysis, Households can be treated as an "industry" engaged in production of services (among them labor services) and purchase of consumer goods. Thus, the former represent its output, while the latter constitute the corresponding inputs.

all the industries,[3] i.e. upon all the technical input coefficients — a's — of the basic system of equations III. The effect of additional consumers' demand for metal products upon total output of fuels depends, for example, among other factors upon the technical coefficient describing the use of agricultural products as cost element of the textile industry.

To compute the *employment* in the separate industries it is only necessary to insert the total output figures in the last column of technical equations in system II. The employment in industry 1 (x_{1n}) is obtained, for example, by inserting the previously determined magnitude of X_1 in equation $x_{1n} = a_{1n}X_1$. Substituting for X_1 in this latter equation its equivalent as given in system IV, it is possible to show explicitly the dependence of the number of workers employed in industry 1 (x_{1n}) upon the given bill of goods.

(v) $\qquad x_{1n} = a_{1n}A_{11}x_{n1} + a_{1n}A_{12}x_{n2} + \cdots + a_{1n}A_{1m}x_{nm}$

A similar relationship can be derived for every other industry. The magnitude of total national employment is obtained by summation of the labor requirements of all the separate industries:

$$
\begin{aligned}
x_{1n} + x_{2n} + \cdots + x_{mn} &= (a_{1n}A_{11} + a_{2n}A_{21} \\
&+ \cdots + a_{mn}A_{m1})x_{n1} + (a_{1n}A_{12} + a_{2n}A_{22} + \cdots + a_{mn}A_{m2})x_{n2} \\
&+ \cdots + (a_{1n}A_{1m} + a_{2n}A_{2m} + \cdots + a_{mn}A_{mm})x_{nm}
\end{aligned}
$$

(VI)

The coefficient $(a_{1n}A_{11} + a_{2n}A_{21} + \cdots + a_{mn}A_{m1})$ of x_{n1} measures the contribution to the total national employment of any additional unit of commodity 1 entered into the final bill of goods, coefficient $(a_{1n}A_{12} + a_{2n}A_{22} + \cdots + a_{mn}A_{m2})$ shows the corresponding contribution per unit of final demand for commodity 2, and so on. The significance of these employment coefficients from the point of view of employment policies hardly needs to be dwelt upon; it is obvious.

[3] If D represents the determinant

$$
\begin{vmatrix}
1 & -a_{21} & -a_{31} & \cdots & -a_{m1} \\
-a_{12} & 1 & -a_{32} & \cdots & -a_{m2} \\
-a_{13} & -a_{23} & 1 & \cdots & -a_{m3} \\
\cdots & \cdots & \cdots & \cdots & \cdots \\
-a_{1m} & -a_{2m} & -a_{3m} & \cdots & 1
\end{vmatrix}
$$

of the linear system III and D_{ik} — the algebraic complement (minor) of the element $-a_{ik}$ in this determinant, then

$$A_{ik} = \frac{D_{ik}}{D}$$

The concept of final demand (output) which is used here synonymously with that of the bill of goods needs some further clarification. Its counterpart is the concept of intermediate demand (output), while total demand (output) embraces both. The final demand for a commodity represents that part of its total output which is treated — within the framework of a given analytical scheme — as an independent variable, while the derived or intermediate demand comprises the other part, which is considered to be a dependent variable.[4] Fuel oil used in private homes, for example, is treated as final demand and entered into the bill of goods, while fuel oil burned in industrial furnaces is not. It is usually considered to be a cost element of the various industries — the dependence of each particular oil input upon the output of the corresponding industry being characterized by the magnitude of the appropriate technical input coefficient.

Household consumption is not the only kind of demand which can be considered as final. Commodities used for expansion of plant or building up of inventories, i.e. for net investment, for example, might also be conveniently included in the bill of goods. An alternative approach would require knowledge of some direct or indirect relationships between the final demand for various commodities (exclusive of those used for net investment) and the demand for investment goods. On the basis of such relationships, the amount of various commodities used for new investment could be computed indirectly from the given bill of goods. In mathematical language this means that introduction of additional equations in our system would make it possible to consider as dependent some of the variables which previously had to be treated as independent.

As already pointed out, the "independence" of the bill of goods could be entirely eliminated if additional relationships were introduced in the analysis connecting consumers' spending and net investment with outputs and employment in all the various industries *via the income flow*. In such a setting, the distinction between a "given" bill of goods and "derived" output and employment figures becomes non-existent; both appear to be uniquely determined by the system of given struc-

---

[4] A distinction which, incidentally, should not be confused with that of cause and effect.

tural relationships.[5] As indicated before, this type of approach is not suited to the analysis of problems of economic policy. Only a system containing one or more free, independent variables opens opportunities for comparative appraisal of alternative courses of purposeful action.

Ignorance as well as design might make it necessary to transfer — for purposes of empirical investigation — into the given bill of goods, items which otherwise would better be counted among the derived variables. For example, if the value of some particular input coefficient, say a_{12}, were unknown, the input of commodity 2 into industry 1 could obviously not be evaluated analytically on the basis of the previously derived technical relationships. It might still be possible, however, to ascertain the magnitude of this input directly or to estimate it on the basis of some other, outside information. In this case the unknown production coefficient can be simply omitted (i.e. assumed to be zero) in all the equations, and, at the same time, the directly estimated input added to the bill of goods. Thus, although the magnitude of this particular item is now being placed among the *given* data, its influence upon the outputs of all the other industries — via the corresponding input requirements — will still be taken account of in the rest of the computation.

3. COMPUTATION FROM 1939 DATA

Input-output data of the kind assembled in Table 15 supply the primary information required for the actual performance of computations outlined in the previous section. Although presented in terms of millions of dollars, these figures can also be interpreted as representing physical quantities measured in terms of units defined as the "amount (of particular commodities or services) purchasable for one million dollars at 1939 prices." In the subsequent computation of the labor input coefficient, actual figures of number of persons employed rather than value, i.e. wage figures, are used.

Dividing each cost figure in column 1 by the last — net total output — figure in row 1, we obtain a series of technical coefficients describing the input of all the various cost factors used by the Agriculture and Food industries per unit of output.

[5] An attempt to approach the empirical analysis of the American national economy from the point of view of general equilibrium, i.e. treating it as a completely determined system, is presented in Parts I-III of this volume.

TABLE 16.—TECHNICAL COEFFICIENTS FOR THE YEAR 1939

Input of Items at the Left of Each Row Per Unit of Product Listed at the Top of Each Column

	Agriculture and foods	Minerals	Metal fabricating	Fuel and power	Textiles and leather	Transportation (railroad)	Foreign trade	Industries n.e.c.	Government	All other industries
Agriculture and foods	...	...	...	...	0.0794	...	0.2270	0.0304	0.0007	0.0064
Minerals	0.0066	...	0.0967	0.0014	0.0006	...	0.0671	0.0650	...	0.0092
Metal fabricating	0.0423	0.0183	...	0.0385	0.0169	0.0702	0.3777	0.1114	0.0244	0.0717
Fuel and power	0.0246	0.0749	0.0289	...	0.0197	0.0616	0.2471	0.0209	0.0141	0.0430
Textiles, leather, and rubber	0.0048	...	0.0256	0.0060	0.0024	0.0014	0.0695	0.0049	0.0020	0.0129
Transportation (railroad)	0.0763	0.0919	0.0299	0.1094	0.0340	...	...	0.0267	0.0072	0.0001
Foreign trade	0.0570	0.0973	0.0037	0.0091	0.0656	...	0.1327	0.0254	...	0.0106
Industries, n.e.c.	0.0503	0.0205	0.0286	0.1164	0.0011	0.1464	...	...	0.3351	0.0858
Government	0.0633	...	0.0150	0.0215	...	0.0074	0.0028	0.0028	...	0.1586
All other industries	0.4807	0.3960	0.2736	0.3490	0.4504	0.1680	0.0311	0.4722	0.2038	...
Household services: employment	0.7011	0.1531	0.2296	0.1682	0.3499	0.2368	...	0.1826	0.0670	0.3334

Thus, for example, $a_{12} = \dfrac{112}{16,964} = 0.0066$. A division of the figures in all the other columns by the last entries of the corresponding rows gives the basic set of numerical technical coefficients as reproduced in Table 16. These can be inserted in the basic system of equations III in place of the algebraic coefficients a_{12}, a_{32}, etc.

The first equation will read now as follows:

(VII)

$$X_1 - 0.0794X_5 - 0.2270X_7 - 0.0304X_8 - 0.0007X_8 - 0.0064X_{10} = x_{n1}$$

The other nine appear also in a similar numerical form.

The solution [6] of the system of these ten equations leads us finally to the following relationships showing the dependence of the output of each of the ten separate industries upon any given bill of goods. (See page 151.)

These correspond to the final general solution IV of our problem with actual coefficients computed on the basis of the 1939 data inserted in place of their algebraic counterparts, A_{11}, A_{12}, etc.

The significance of these numerical values has already been elucidated in general terms (see p. 145). Coefficient 0.1266 in the third equation shows, for example, that an increase of the final bill for Textile and leather products (x_{n5}) by "one dollar's worth" would lead to an increase in the total net output of Metals (X_3) by 0.1266 "dollars' worth."

Given a definite bill of goods, i.e. a set of definite numerical values to be inserted in VIII in place of x_{n1}, x_{n2}, x_{n3}, etc., the corresponding total net outputs of all the ten separate industrial divisions can be readily computed. Insertion of the actual 1939 consumption figures as shown in column 11 of Table 15 (14,522 for x_{n1}, 149 for x_{n2}, $\cdots$) obviously would result in total output figures listed in the last column of the same table. A different bill of goods, on the other hand, will require a different combination of industrial outputs and result in different employment figures for various industries.

How stable are the technical relationships which constitute the framework of the whole proposed system of analysis? With

---

[6] Using a modified Doolittle method adjusted to operation with a modern computing machine of the usual type (Marchand), an experienced computer obtained this numerical solution of the ten simultaneous equations in five hours. Solution of much larger systems involving for example forty equations can be considered to be entirely practicable.

TABLE 17

(VIII)

Output		Agriculture	Minerals	Metals	Fuel	Textiles	Railroad transportation	Foreign trade	Industries, n.e.c.	Government	Other industries
1. Agriculture	$x_1 =$	$1.0325x_{n1}+$	$.0409x_{n2}+$	$.0161x_{n3}+$	$.0190x_{n4}+$	$.1049x_{n5}+$	$.0141x_{n6}+$	$.2628x_{n7}+$	$.0539x_{n8}+$	$.0241x_{n9}+$	$.0215x_{n10}$
2. Minerals	$x_2 =$	$.0513x_{n1}+$	$1.0415x_{n2}+$	$.1186x_{n3}+$	$.0380x_{n4}+$	$.0372x_{n5}+$	$.0332x_{n6}+$	$.1536x_{n7}+$	$.1060x_{n8}+$	$.0474x_{n9}+$	$.0388x_{n10}$
3. Metals	$x_3 =$	$.1735x_{n1}+$	$.1538x_{n2}+$	$1.0720x_{n3}+$	$.1356x_{n4}+$	$.1266x_{n5}+$	$.1387x_{n6}+$	$.5297x_{n7}+$	$.2177x_{n8}+$	$.1292x_{n9}+$	$.1316x_{n10}$
4. Fuel	$x_4 =$	$.1025x_{n1}+$	$.1566x_{n2}+$	$.0759x_{n3}+$	$1.0552x_{n4}+$	$.0822x_{n5}+$	$.0969x_{n6}+$	$.3432x_{n7}+$	$.0912x_{n8}+$	$.0636x_{n9}+$	$.0755x_{n10}$
5. Textiles	$x_5 =$	$.0268x_{n1}+$	$.0478x_{n2}+$	$.0366x_{n3}+$	$.0155x_{n4}+$	$1.0183x_{n5}+$	$.0126x_{n6}+$	$.1001x_{n7}+$	$.0253x_{n8}+$	$.0164x_{n9}+$	$.0227x_{n10}$
6. Railroad transp.	$x_6 =$	$.1076x_{n1}+$	$.1264x_{n2}+$	$.0568x_{n3}+$	$.1320x_{n4}+$	$.0330x_{n5}+$	$1.0256x_{n6}+$	$.0982x_{n7}+$	$.0622x_{n8}+$	$.0366x_{n9}+$	$.0243x_{n10}$
7. Foreign trade	$x_7 =$	$.0805x_{n1}+$	$.1192x_{n2}+$	$.0268x_{n3}+$	$.0280x_{n4}+$	$.0581x_{n5}+$	$.0159x_{n6}+$	$1.0550x_{n7}+$	$.0531x_{n8}+$	$.0242x_{n9}+$	$.0250x_{n10}$
8. Industries, n.e.c.	$x_8 =$	$.2306x_{n1}+$	$.1820x_{n2}+$	$.1306x_{n3}+$	$.2452x_{n4}+$	$.2021x_{n5}+$	$.2289x_{n6}+$	$.3467x_{n7}+$	$1.1481x_{n8}+$	$.4337x_{n9}+$	$.1966x_{n10}$
9. Government	$x_9 =$	$.1955x_{n1}+$	$.1185x_{n2}+$	$.0961x_{n3}+$	$.1228x_{n4}+$	$.1257x_{n5}+$	$.0758x_{n6}+$	$.1513x_{n7}+$	$.1316x_{n8}+$	$1.0903x_{n9}+$	$.2019x_{n10}$
10. Other industries	$x_{10} =$	$.7813x_{n1}+$	$.6854x_{n2}+$	$.4826x_{n3}+$	$.6004x_{n4}+$	$.7156x_{n5}+$	$.3937x_{n6}+$	$.7409x_{n7}+$	$.7520x_{n8}+$	$.5292x_{n9}+$	$1.2372x_{n10}$

what coefficients, for example, can a set of equations computed on the basis of the 1939 input-output relationships be used for evaluation of production and employment figures based on a hypothetical 1945 bill of goods? Two conceptually distinct types of change in technical coefficients have to be distinguished — those which occur in response to output or price variations and those which originate spontaneously, i.e. independently of such variations.

The first — manifestation of the well-known substitution phenomenon — could be easily taken care of if, in describing the basic technical characteristics of the various branches of production, we could use non-linear, multivariate production functions, rather than the simplified linear equations of set II. Lack of sufficient factual information, however, makes an introduction of such refinements hardly practicable. It is also quite possible that in general discussion the importance of this kind of variation has been exaggerated beyond the limits of its practical significance.

The second type of variation, representing genuine technological change and innovation, cannot possibly be accounted for, even with the help of most refined analytical devices. This does not mean, however, that this kind of change cannot be anticipated with a fair degree of accuracy. On the contrary, anybody familiar with the economies of industry and agriculture knows that most of the major technological developments are well discernible far in advance of their actual culmination, while minor innovations are frequently planned by leading enterprises well ahead of their general adoption.

Leaving a detailed analysis of changing input-output relationships for a separate empirical investigation, we can still inquire into the effects which such changes — whatever their nature and their causes — might have upon the applicability of the proposed method of estimating employment from a given national bill of goods. A test designed to supply an at least preliminary answer to this question is described below.

4. "PREDICTION" OF 1929 OUTPUTS BY USE OF 1939 TECHNICAL RELATIONSHIPS

A quantitative statistical description of the American economy comparable with that given in Table 15 for the year 1939 is available also for the year 1929.[7] This table contains, in

[7] See p. 71.

particular, consumption and total output figures comparable (with one exception to be mentioned later) with those placed in the last two columns of the 1939 input-output chart, i.e. the 1929 bill of goods as well as the corresponding net total output are known.

How closely is it possible to estimate the total net output of various industries in the year 1929 from the known 1929 bill of goods by using the 1939 technical relationships as a basis of this estimate?

The fact that what is being tested is not a forward, but rather a backward, "prediction" is of secondary importance. Had a bill of goods for some future year, say 1949, been given, and the corresponding total net outputs estimated on the basis of 1939 input-output relationships, the final comparison of "fact" with prediction could not have taken place before the year 1949, and by that time the whole period of time covered by such computations would have become a matter of past experience.

The following analysis consists of four separate operations: (a) description of the 1929 bill of goods in terms of the 1929 value figures, (b) translation of these figures into the 1939 units in which all our computation formulae are expressed, (c) indirect computation of the 1929 net total outputs on the basis of the above-mentioned formulae, (d) comparison of the computed 1929 net total outputs with the actual, the latter also translated into 1939 units.

In the 1929 industrial classification, Government is not represented as a separate "industry," as is done in 1939; it is included among the Other industries. This discrepancy in classification necessitates introduction of a special adjustment which will be commented upon in due course.

The selection of the items to be included in the 1929 bill of goods is predetermined by the previously derived numerical computation formulae VII. These are based on the 1939 technical coefficients, which in their turn have been derived from the 1939 input-output table. In this table the input (costs) incurred on current account are combined with those made on capital account, i.e. with new investments. The technical coefficients, and consequently also the final computation formulae based on these figures, automatically provide for a certain amount of net investment — the amount defined by the investment relationships which prevailed in the year 1939. That means that if we had included in the 1929 bill of goods only household consumption and no net investment, the corresponding total net outputs of the different industries computed on the basis of formulae VIII would have provided for as much net investment per unit of output of each investing industry as was invested in 1939. Actually, the 1929 investments were very different from those of 1939, and there is no reason to believe that the above-mentioned ratios remained unchanged. A larger proportion of the national product was invested in 1929 than in 1939.

The most clear-cut method of dealing with investment would be that of treating all net investment as an independent variable, i.e. freeing the 1939 input figures and technical coefficients of all the investment items and including the actual 1929 net investment in the final bill of goods on a par with household consumption. Unfortunately the 1939 input figures available at the present time do not lend themselves readily to the introduction of the rather refined distinction between current production inputs and new investment. The following compromise procedure has therefore been adopted. The 1929 bill of goods used in the present computation consists of (a) the 1929 household consumption and (b) the excess of the (larger) 1929 over the (smaller) 1939 net investment. This is done on the assumption that the magnitude of the numerical constants in the computation formulae VIII takes care of new investments up to the 1939 level.

Column 1 and column 2 in Table 18 show the actual household consumption and the total net output for the year 1929 in 1929 prices. For purposes of subsequent computations, however, this 1929 bill of goods must be described in terms of the same physical units which are used to describe the 1939 technical coefficients, i.e. in terms of the "amounts purchasable for one million dollars at 1939 prices" (see p. 148 above). In other words, these 1929 figures must be corrected for the 1929–1939 price changes. Column 3 of the same table contains the necessary price indices — one for each of the ten groups of industries. Multiplying each entry of Column 1 with the appropriate index, we translate the 1929 household consumption figures in 1939 prices. The resulting data are entered in column 4.

To obtain the 1929 final bill of goods these consumption figures must be augmented by the excess of 1929 over the 1939

TABLE 18*

	1	2	3	4	5	6	7	8
	1929 Household consumption in 1929 prices	1929 Total net outputs in 1929 prices	1939 Price indices 1929 = 100	1929 Household consumption in 1939 prices	Excess of the 1929 over the 1939 new investment in 1939 prices	1929 Bill of goods in 1939 prices	1929 Computed total net outputs in 1939 prices	1929 Actual total net outputs in 1939 prices
1. Agriculture	13,669	17,031	67.5	9,227	...	9,227	11,512	11,496
2. Mineral industries	149	3,866	96.0	143	...	143	3,647	3,711
3. Metal fabricating	4,196	16,729	95.1	3,990	1,039	5,029	13,964	15,909
4. Fuel and power	4,643	10,246	86.1	3,998	...	3,998	8,992	8,822
5. Textiles, leather, and rubber	7,150	9,139	84.0	6,009	...	6,009	7,465	7,677
6. Railroad transportation	950	6,666	85.5	812	...	812	4,081	5,699
7. Foreign trade (imports)	842	4,997	73.5	619	...	619	3,115	3,673
8. Industries, n.e.c.	6,548	19,003	100.0	6,548	3,007	9,555	20,972	19,003
9. Government ⎫ 10. Other industries ⎭	23,346	48,836	100.0	23,346	...	23,346	52,563	48,836
Total	61,493	136,623	...	54,692	4,046	58,738	126,311	124,826

* All value figures are in millions of dollars.

investments. Of the three major net investment items — plant and equipment, business inventories, and the export surplus on merchandise and services account — the former is by far the most important. The difference between the 1939 and the 1929 export surplus is quite small. Net addition to business inventories in 1929 amounts to 1,600 million dollars as against 800 million dollars in 1939. The difference would appear to be substantially smaller if expressed in fixed prices. Lack of sufficient detailed information makes it impossible to use the figure in the present computation.

Annual figures for total investment in new equipment, plant, and other non-residential construction (residential construction constitutes part of the consumers' purchases) are available both for 1929 and 1939.[8] To put these on a net basis it would be necessary to know the expenditures on replacement of worn-out plant and equipment. No reliable figures of this kind are available. Estimates of depletion and depreciation charges in the two years indicate, however, that the total real replacement expenditures of 1929 did not differ much from those of 1939. Thus, the difference between the gross investments of the two years can be assumed to be approximately equal to the corresponding difference in net investment. Accordingly, the gross 1929 totals are translated into 1939 prices and subtracted from the corresponding 1939 amounts. Thus, two separate excess investment figures are obtained, one for industrial equipment, the other for plant and construction. The first constitutes predominantly a product of Metal Fabrication industries, the second of the Industries, n.e.c. They are entered in the appropriate rows of column 5. Column 6 contains the final 1929 bill of goods — household consumption plus excess investment — expressed in 1939 prices. These are the figures which have to be inserted in place of $x_{n1}, x_{n2}, \cdots$ etc. in the computation formulae VIII.

As indicated before, the 1929 bill of goods includes Government among Other industries, while formulae VIII provide for treatment of Government as a separate industry. Thus, in the present computation x_{n9} is taken to be equal zero, while the figure substituted for x_{n10} includes government as a part of Other industries. This procedure would be quite accurate only if the coefficients of x_{n9} and x_{n10} in equations VIII were identical, which is not the case. An examination of the formulae

[8] Federal Reserve Bulletin, February, 1941.

shows, however, that the difference between the two sets of constants is not very great.

Column 7 in Table 18 shows the indirectly computed total net outputs of various industrial groups for the year 1929 in terms of the 1939 prices. In the actual computation separate figures are obtained for Government and the Other industries — 9,683 million dollars and 53,307 million dollars, respectively. The sum total of these two amounts would include some governmental services absorbed by the Industries, n.e.c. and the part of the product of the latter industries absorbed by the Government. Both of these items must be eliminated if the combined total output is to represent a net and not a gross figure. According to the basic 1939 relationships (Table 16), the input coefficient of governmental services into Industries, n.e.c. is 0.1586, and the corresponding coefficient describing the use of the products of these latter industries by the Government is 0.2038. Thus, the net combined total output of the two is

$$53,307 \ (1 - 0.1586) + 9,683 \ (1 - 0.2038) = 52,563.$$

The actual total net outputs for the year 1929 expressed in 1939 prices are shown in the last column of the same table. In six out of the nine instances the indirectly computed figure shows a very close agreement with the actual one.

The marked disparity between the estimated and the observed output of Metals is to a large extent due to inadequacy of the industrial classification used in this analysis. A considerable proportion of the Metals output is absorbed by Industries, n.e.c. and Other industries — the two largest and least homogeneous of our industrial classes. Any outside influence acting upon the Metal output via industries included in either one of these groups is bound to be damped and "averaged out" because of artificial linking with many other unrelated industries. This might partly explain why the underestimate of Metal production coincides with a marked over-estimate in the two latter groups.

The discrepancy between the actual and the computed output of Railroad services is obviously due to technical change. Introduction of long distance trucking after 1929 makes the demand for railroad transportation computed for that year on the basis of the 1939 technical standards far short of the actual requirements.

The discrepancy between the computed and actual amount of the 1929 imports is explainable by a "technical change" of a different kind. The result of the indirect computation would be much more accurate if the use of imported commodities per unit of-output in each industry in 1929 had been the same as is 1939.[9] Actually, the introduction of the Smoot-Hawley tariff (1930) and subsequent protective measures caused an all-round shift from imported to domestic commodities, i.e. to a general reduction of the technical input coefficients of imports. The difference between the actual 1929 imports and imports computed on the basis of the 1939 relationships represents a fair measure of our changed "propensity to import."

The foregoing observations show two principal reasons for the discrepancy between the actual and the indirectly estimated output figures: (a) the insufficiently refined classification of industries, and (b) the disregard of some rather obvious technical changes. As a third reason we have to add (c) the inaccuracy of our basic statistical data on the input-output relationships of various industries.

The use of the 1939 input-output relationships for the computation of the 1929 outputs has been made with the avowed purpose of revealing the effects of the changes in the basic structure of the American industries which have actually taken place during the intervening decade of vigorous technological development. Whenever the methods developed above are actually utilized for prognostication of future output and employment figures, the technical coefficient used in such computations must be adjusted for anticipated changes. Analysis of previous technological trends, combined with direct information on pending innovations in various branches of industry, can supply a solid factual basis for such adjustments. The structure of our analytical formula makes it possible to utilize such information in a rather simple and straightforward way. It obviates, in particular, the necessity of trying to anticipate, more or less intuitively, the effect of such technological changes upon future output and employment — these repercussions are worked out quasi-automatically on the basis of the internal logic of the analytical apparatus used in these computations.

---

[9] Imports competing with the output of a domestic industry are treated in the Input-Output table as if they were imported by this industry and distributed by it, i.e. they are charged from foreign countries to the industry as a cost element and also added to its net total output as a part of its product.

The industrial classification underlying the present example [10] had to be adopted for reasons of practical expediency. A summary inclusion of industries of vastly different technological structure in such amorphous groupings as "Industries, n.e.c." or "Other industries" is bound to cause abnormal strains and stresses in the structure of the empirical computation formulae, and thus naturally lead to greatly distorted results.[11] For purposes of practical application a much more detailed subdivision of industries is definitely preferable.[12]

The combination of many small industries in one single group adds certain elements of stability to the technical input coefficients, since it averages out the variations of its separate components. This observation, however, cannot be used as an argument against refinement of industrial classification. Even if the actual computations were performed on the basis of a very detailed industrial breakdown, all the statistical stability of a less refined subdivision could be recaptured by subsequent combination of the computed output figures into larger groupings. The combination of the output of Government with that of the Other Industries, as described above, illustrates the method to be followed in such cases. This procedure makes it possible to combine the analytical advantages of a refined industrial classification with desired stability of larger statistical aggregates.

5. TOTAL AND DIRECT EMPLOYMENT COEFFICIENTS

The influence of the magnitude and composition of the final bill of goods upon total employment can be determined on the basis of formula VI. The numerical values of the small a's (labor input coefficients) can be found in the last row of Table 16, while the capital A's are represented by the previously computed numerical coefficients of the system VIII. Thus, on the basis of the structural characteristics of the American economy of the year 1939, we obtain the relationships connecting the final purchases of various types of commodities and serv-

[10] See Appendix.
[11] A detailed discussion of the problems of industrial classifications from the point of view of analysis of inter-industrial relationships can be found in Part III, section 9.
[12] A detailed input-output table describing the structure of the American economy in terms of ninety-five separate industries is being presently completed by the Post-War Division of the Bureau of Labor Statistics, United States Department of Labor.

ices with the magnitude of total employment (Table 19). An additional million dollars worth of final purchases of Agricultural and food products would increase total national employment by 1.1395 thousand men; an equal additional expenditure on transportation services, however, would increase the national employment figure by only 0.4886 thousand men.

Employment figures are expressed in terms of man-years, i.e. they are not adjusted for differences in the length of the work days, and work week in various industries. When a worker shifts from one industry to another, he, as a rule, automatically changes his annual number of labor hours. Thus the Agricultural employment figure and the corresponding employment coefficients might contain a considerable amount of "hidden unemployment."

It is interesting to compare these total employment coefficients with the direct employment coefficients of the corresponding industries. (Table 19, second row.) The latter cover only labor employed by the industry immediately affected by the given demand variation,[13] while the former show the reaction of total national employment, including the increased (or reduced) employment in industries indirectly affected by the primary change in demand.

In interpreting these two rows of figures it is important to keep in mind that both of them relate employment, not to the magnitude of the total net output of the corresponding industries (as do the labor input coefficients listed in the last row of Table 16), but to that part of output which enters the final bill of goods. As has been shown before, the change in the total net output of an industry as a rule exceeds the corresponding variation in final demand for its products.

It is worth noticing that the indirect employment — as measured by the difference between the two figures — is in most instances (with the notable exception of Agriculture) much larger than the direct one. The relationship between the two varies, however, from industry to industry.

The labor requirements of an industry do not change, of course, in direct proportion to the increase or decrease in its output, although, if corrected for variations in the length of the working day and week, the relationship is, in many instances, more constant than it appears to be at first sight. For purposes

---

[13] Expressed as a_{1n}, A_{nn} for industry 1 (see formula v above), a_{n2}, A_{22} for industry 2, and so on.

TABLE 19.—Total and Direct Employment Coefficients of the Various Branches of Production Per Unit of the Final Demand for Their Respective Outputs

Units: Thousands of Persons per One Million Dollars Worth of Final Demand

FINAL DEMAND FOR ONE MILLION DOLLARS WORTH OF	Agriculture and foods	Minerals	Metal fabricating	Fuel and power	Textiles and leather	Railroad transportation	Foreign trade (imports)	Industries n.e.c.	Government services	Other industries
Total employment coefficient	1.1393	0.5659	0.5057	0.5176	0.7701	0.4886	0.7657	0.6120	0.4076	0.5394
Direct employment coefficient	0.7239	0.1595	0.2461	0.1775	0.3563	0.2429	...	0.2029	0.0739	0.4125

of further, more detailed analysis average labor input figures should be replaced by full-length schedules based on a detailed study of labor requirements of separate industries at different levels of output.

APPENDIX

The following table describes the ten large industrial groups used in this study in terms of their components. Numbers attached to the separate industries are those used in the statistical study referred to in footnote 12 (page 159) above.

1. AGRICULTURE AND
    FOODS
    1. Field Crops
    2. Vegetables
    3. Fruits and Nuts
    4. Horticultural Specialties
    5. Forest Products
    6. Dairy Products
    7. Poultry and Poultry
        Products
    8. Livestock and Livestock
        Products
    9. Fishing
    10. Flour and Grist Mill
        Products
    11. Canning and Preserving
    12. Bread and Bakery Products
    13. Sugar Refining
    14. Starch and Glucose
        Products
    15. Alcoholic Beverages
    16. Nonalcoholic Beverages
    17. Tobacco Manufactures
    18. Slaughtering and Meat
        Packing
    19. Milk and Manufactured
        Dairy Products
    20. Edible Fats and Oils, N.E.C.
    21. Other Food Products

2. MINERALS
    22. Iron Mining
    23. Blast Furnaces
    39. Nonferrous Metal Mining
    40. Smelting and Refining of
        Nonferrous Metals
    43. Nonmetallic Mining
    44. Nonmetallic Mineral
        Manufactures

3. METAL FABRICATING
    24. Steel Works and Rolling
        Mills
    25. Iron and Steel Foundry
        Products
    26. Shipbuilding
    27. Firearms
    28. Munitions
    29. Agricultural Machinery
    30. Engines and Turbines
    31. Automobiles
    32. Aircraft
    33. Transportation
        Equipment, N.E.C.
    34. Industrial and Household
        Equipment, N.E.C.
    35. Machine Tools
    36. Merchandising and Service
        Machines
    37. Electrical
        Equipment, N.E.C.
    38. Iron and Steel, N.E.C.
    41. Aluminum Products
    42. Nonferrous Metal Manu-
        factures and Alloys

4. FUEL AND POWER
    45. Petroleum and Natural Gas
    46. Petroleum Refining
    47. Anthracite Coal
    48. Bituminous Coal
    49. Coke and Manufactured
        Solid Fuel
    50. Manufactured Gas
    51. Communications
    52. Electric Public Utilities

5. TEXTILES, LEATHER,
    AND RUBBER

58. Cotton Yarn and Cloth
59. Silk and Rayon Products
60. Woolen and Worsted
    Manufactures
61. Clothing
62. Other Textile Products
63. Leather
64. Leather Shoes
65. Leather Products, N.E.C.
66. Rubber Products

6. RAILROAD TRANS-
   PORTATION
   73. Steam Railroad Transpor-
       tation

7. FOREIGN TRADE
   75. Foreign Trade

8. INDUSTRIES, N.E.C.
   53. Chemicals
   54. Lumber and Timber
       Products
   55. Furniture and Other
       Manufactures of Wood
   56. Wood Pulp, Paper and
       Paper Products
   57. Printing and Publishing

67. Industries, N.E.C.
68. Residential Construction
69. Commercial and Industrial
    Construction

9. GOVERNMENT
   92. Government

10. ALL OTHER INDUSTRIES
    76. Banking
    77. Insurance
    78. Business Services Other
        Than Advertising
    79. Advertising
    80. Services Allied to
        Transportation
    81. Automotive Repair and
        Services
    82. Other Repair Services
    83. Rental Agencies
    84. Commercial Renting
    85. Home Renting
    86. Hotels, etc.
    87. Laundry, etc.
    88. Personal Services
    89. Professional Entertainment
    90. Motion Picture Theatres
    91. Amusement Places
    95. Undistributed

B. EXPORTS, IMPORTS, DOMESTIC OUTPUT, AND EMPLOYMENT [1]

I. STRUCTURAL CHARACTERISTICS OF THE NATIONAL ECONOMY AND THE EFFECTS OF FOREIGN TRADE

The effects of foreign trade upon output and employment are based on the same structural characteristics of the national economy as those which determine the parallel effects of domestic demand. A previous article devoted to the study of this latter type of relationship contained a detailed exposition of the general theoretical scheme of what might be called the input-output approach to the empirical analysis of a national economy.[2] There it was shown that the relevant structural elements of a national economy can be quantitatively described in terms of "technical input coefficients." Each co-

[1] The reader interested in general economic and quantitative analysis of the problem, but not in details of technical procedure, is advised to read part 1 and part 3 of this article, omitting part 2, which contains a mathematical formulation of the general theory presented in part 1.

[2] See Part IV, A.

efficient represents the amount of one particular kind of commodity or service — product of one particular "industry" — used by another industry per unit of its output. The statistical data required for computation of a complete set of technical input coefficients for all branches of the national economy can be presented in the form of an input-output table (see Table 20, below). This table shows the distribution of the output of each separate segment of the national economy among all its different users, i.e. all the other segments of the economy, including not only extractive and manufacturing industries and transportation, but also households and foreign countries. Foreign trade is considered in this connection to be a separate industry, with imports representing its output and exports its input. All the investment purchases of durable goods are segregated in a separate column at the end of the table. Only current inputs are listed in the other columns. All construction is assigned to investment.

i. Allocation of Imports

The allocation of imports among the various branches of the national economy is complicated by the fact that many commodities coming in from abroad are nearly identical with similar goods of domestic origin. The technical structure of separate industries determines only the input ratios of the various types of goods and services, irrespective of their individual origin. It is only the allocation of the combined foreign and domestic supply which really matters from the point of view of each consuming industry taken separately. The obvious way to take account of the internal logic of these relationships is that of distributing competitive imports, not directly to their respective uses, but rather indirectly *through* the domestic industries producing similar types of goods. Thus all competitive agricultural imports can, for example, be charged first to domestic agriculture. The same amount has in this case to be added to the domestic net output of agriculture. The total supply thus obtained is then distributed between the consuming industries. This method of presentation has been used in the 1939 input-output table reproduced in the previously cited article.

Operationally, this approach can be shown to be equivalent to another based on the explicit assumption that all the consuming industries absorb the domestic output of any given type of commodity combined in a fixed proportion with a certain amount of its competitive imports, the proportion itself being determined by the ratio of the total import of the particular type of goods to their total supply (i.e. total imports plus the domestic output).

This observation suggests an alternative method of entering competitive imports in the input-output table. It consists of direct allocation of competitive imports to consuming industries, and is based on the fictitious assumption that each one of these industries absorbs the same relative combination of imports of any particular kind and of corresponding competitive domestic output. This method of allocation has the advantage of greater flexibility, since it allows deviation from proportional distribution of imports in all those instances in which specific, nonproportional allocation is actually possible and thus is obviously preferable. Since the reëxport of foreign goods, for example, is excluded from our basic statistics beforehand, a proportional allocation of imported commodities to exports has little sense, even in those instances in which they are being spread among all other — i.e. domestic — users in direct proportion with the similar products of domestic origin.

Considerations developed above in relation to imports apply also to the allocation of domestic trade services, i.e. the distribution of trade margins. These can be charged to the industry, the product of which is being handled by trade, or they can be allocated directly to the industry purchasing these products. In the first instance, for example, the charge from Trade to the Ferrous Metals industry would comprise the total trade margins realized on all the Ferrous Metals sales; in the second, it would show the aggregate margins paid by the Ferrous Metals industry on all its purchases.

Table 20 shows the input-output relationships of the American economy of 1939 with all imports charged directly to the consuming and all Trade margins directly to the purchasing industries. Each one of the separate entries in the foreign trade — i.e. the imports — row represents a combination of all types of imports absorbed by the particular consuming industry. The heterogeneous nature of these import figures has no damaging influence on the results of our computations, so long as the technical input coefficients of all the various industries, as well as the import ratios of all the various types of commodities are known, i.e. are considered as given.

TABLE 20.—ALLOCATION OF GOODS AND SERVICES BY INDUSTRY OF ORIGIN AND DESTINATION, 1939[1]

(Employment figures, thousands of persons; all other figures in millions of dollars)

INDUSTRY PURCHASING

INDUSTRY PRODUCING	(1) Agriculture and fishing	(2) Food, tobacco, etc.	(3) Ferrous metals	(4) Motor vehicles	(5) Metal fabrics	(6) Nonferrous metals	(7) Nonmetallic minerals	(8) Fuel and power	(9) Chemicals	(10) Lumber, paper	(11) Textiles and leather	(12) Rubber
1. Agriculture and fishing	…	4,656	…	…	…	…	…	…	154	179	522	…
2. Food, tobacco and kindred products	499	…	…	…	…	…	…	…	45	6	143	…
3. Ferrous metals	19	…	…	465	839	42	…	…	…	61	3	1
4. Motor vehicles, industrial and heating equipment	6	5	1	…	…	…	…	21	2	4	4	…
5. Metal fabricating	5	299	…	497	…	…	2	36	29	49	1	…
6. Nonferrous metals and products	4	18	84	89	170	…	…	38	69	4	1	…
7. Nonmetallic minerals and products	13	117	27	33	43	6	3	…	117	44	2	5
8. Fuel and power	373	160	295	…	141	6	…	6	177	163	117	26
9. Chemicals	276	118	34	…	102	60	172	12	…	104	307	30
10. Lumber, paper products, printing and publishing	83	214	1	102	57	3	16	4	59	…	49	4
11. Textiles and leather	53	42	…	…	8	6	38	…	13	75	…	56
12. Rubber	33	3	…	192	15	…	2	…	4	1	27	…
13. All other manufacturing	1	…	…	11	20	1	…	1	1	8	96	…
14. Construction	342	70	41	24	42	8	18	821	18	42	22	4
15. Transportation	762	377	256	104	130	72	284	2,115	213	372	50	30
16. Trade	378	313	24	63	78	8	38	35	113	168	190	8
17. Foreign countries imports	116	423	52	48	78	304	25	122	81	124	280	199
18. Business and consumer services	550	376	13	85	77	4	12	39	183	63	83	41
19. Government	200	1,481	157	314	335	96	70	1,973	115	269	195	59
20. Unallocated and stock	1,342	1,945	534	721	2,240	597	620	1,378	816	1,771	1,628	163
21. Households—(a) Incomes	5,424	2,103	886	2,048	2,743	625	709	2,710	1,011	2,097	2,626	280
(b) Employment[2]	(62)	(1,260)	(480)	(960)	(1,570)	(270)	(440)	(1,220)	(430)	(1,740)	(2,510)	(150)
Net total	10,479	12,720	2,404	4,973	7,118	1,832	2,009	9,311	3,220	5,604	6,345	906

[1] Prepared in the U. S. Department of Labor by the Bureau of Labor Statistics; a detailed description of all the industrial groups is given in the Appendix.

[2] This is a gross figure, since it includes the 1,440,000 of domestic workers.

TABLE 20.—ALLOCATION OF GOODS AND SERVICES BY INDUSTRY OF ORIGIN AND DESTINATION, 1939[1] (Continued)

(Employment figures, thousands of persons; all other figures in millions of dollars)

INDUSTRY PURCHASING

INDUSTRY PRODUCING	(13) All other manufacturing	(14) Construction	(15) Transportation	(16) Trade	(17) Foreign countries	(18) Business and consumer service	(19) Government	(20) Unallocated	(21) Households	Used in investment	Net total
1. Agriculture and fishing	7	159	...	...	415	...	10	439	3,249	...	9,790
2. Food, tobacco and kindred products	2	...	...	...	248	1	1	370	11,309	...	12,624
3. Ferrous metals	...	564	67	...	159	1	11	372	1	1	2,602
4. Motor vehicles, industrial and heating equipment	...	230	...	1	379	...	1	1,238	1,907	1,130	4,930
5. Metal fabricating	9	1,010	181	3	510	22	112	1,391	826	1,824	6,807
6. Nonferrous metals and products	39	108	...	...	158	5	10	455	20	2	1,277
7. Nonmetallic minerals and products	7	1,167	13	2	60	2	3	147	160	40	2,037
8. Fuel and power	40	108	730	501	488	88	243	1,638	3,546	...	9,154
9. Chemicals	38	347	15	...	191	33	17	588	919	9	3,192
10. Lumber, paper products, printing and publishing	25	765	8	225	123	1,305	64	1,006	1,262	263	5,595
11. Textiles and leather	15	2	...	8	149	22	28	386	4,857	54	5,873
12. Rubber	1	3	26	13	34	28	13	229	222	45	890
13. All other manufacturing	...	11	23	39	56	254	3	243	696	111	1,573
14. Construction	11	...	828	189	...	251	4,207	...	3,151	(10,089)	10,089
15. Transportation	8	...	...	4	103	...	96	474	1,964	...	7,414
16. Trade	46	635	47	...	244	103	43	948	11,651	...	15,134
17. Foreign countries imports	21	140	15	37	...	80	32	311	1,262	...	3,750
18. Business and consumer services	16	4	73	686	2	2,389	25	2,151	15,684	...	20,167
19. Government	62	71	800	1,755	...	3,430	...	1,259	3,700	...	15,300
20. Unallocated and stock	562	630	4,667	5,390	...	12,121	8,343	6,148	5,242	...	23,767
21. Households—(a) Incomes	750	3,869	...	9,268	...	...	...	...	...	...	73,676
(b) Employment	(430)	(1,750)	(1,980)	(5,680)	...	(4,130)	(3,880)	...	(1,410)	...	(30,352)[2]
Net total	1,659	9,825	7,493	18,121	3,319	20,141	13,262	19,793	71,628	3,479	235,641

[1] Prepared in the U. S. Department of Labor by the Bureau of Labor Statistics; a detailed description of all the industrial groups is given in the Appendix.

[2] This is a gross figure, since it includes the 1,440,000 of domestic workers.

Every variation in world market conditions, every change in the import duties or quotas can have some effect on the share of competitive imports of any particular kind of commodity in its total domestic supply. The highly complex nature of the causal relationships involved makes impractical any attempt to introduce them explicitly in our theoretical set-up, i.e. to treat the import coefficients as dependent variables. While considering them as given, one still can investigate the effects of the possible changes of such coefficients. It is in this sense that the question could be asked: "How will the output and employment in all the different branches of the national economy be affected by a shift from imported commodities to corresponding domestic products?"

Given a complete set of input coefficients describing the technical structure of all the branches of the national economy, it is possible to compute how much additional output and employment would result in all the different industries from increased ultimate demand for the product of any one of them.

ii. Four Definitions of "Ultimate Demand"

The definition of "ultimate" demand, as well as the corresponding definition of "derived" output and employment, is obviously relative. From the point of view of entirely comprehensive general equilibrium approach, all demand is derived and none is ultimate, i.e. independent: the size of consumers' purchases is determined through their double connection with the rest of the economic system via

(a) the direct and indirect demand for labor services, generated by a given consumers' and net investment bill of goods, conditioned by the technical structure of the system, and described by the given technical set of input coefficients.

(b) the relationship, established via the income flow, between the level of employment and the demand for all the various types of consumers' and investment goods.

It is the conscious omission of the second set of relationships which enables us to ask: "How much employment will correspond to any *given* level of domestic consumers' and investment demand?" The answer to this question represents nothing but a quantitative description of the first (a) type of relationships. In every particular instance it can be computed from a known set of technical input coefficients of all the different branches of the national economy. Exports enter these calculations as inputs of the "Foreign Trade" industry; the structure of this industry is described by a series of technical coefficients, each of which shows the amount of exports of one particular type of commodity or service required — according to the prevailing conditions on the world markets — to "produce," i.e. to obtain one unit of imports.[3] In the older — now unfashionable — terminology, the amounts of commodities and services which a country has to export in order to secure a unit of imports were referred to as its "terms of foreign trade."

Viewed as an intermediate link in the chain of industrial interrelationships, exports cannot be treated as an element of final demand. The question "How much output and employment is created by a given amount of exports?" is inadmissible in this context, since the exports themselves are not "given" but rather derived from a given bill of domestic demand.

In contemporary economic discussion, exports are frequently treated as an independent variable, that is, they are considered to be a part of the final bill of goods. A combination of institutional changes, most of which took place since the First World War, has indeed brought about what might be called an autonomy of exports. Governmental loans to foreign countries, gold imports of unprecedented volume supplemented by various exchange stabilization devices, and lately the lend-lease arrangements have weakened the close quid pro quo relationship which hitherto has been supposed to exist between the size of the imports of a country and the level of its exports, to such an extent that in many instances it became practically non-existent.

The problems involved in the treatment of exports as an independent variable are analogous to those discussed above (p. 168) in connection with the treatment of domestic household and investment purchases as final demand. In both instances, a relationship which otherwise uniquely determines the magnitude of the variable in question is deliberately omitted from consideration, and thus this particular variable becomes free and independent. In the case of domestic demand, the

---

[3] The amounts referred to are physical amounts, or indexes of physical amounts. For reasons of operational convenience, the physical unit of any given commodity, or any given combination of commodities, can be defined as "the amount purchasable for one million dollars at the prices of some given year, say 1939."

omitted relationship is that between the level of employment
and income, on the one hand, and the corresponding level of
consumers' demand and of net investment, on the other; in the
case of foreign trade, it is the direct input-output relationship,
the terms of trade, between imports and exports.

If both the domestic consumers' and investment demand, as
well as the exports, are viewed as the independent variables
of our system, the two can be merged in a single magnitude of
final demand. An increase of this combined bill of goods, say
by one thousand tons of coal — be it caused by increased
domestic household purchases, by additional exports, or by any
combination of the two — will affect output and employment
in all the different branches of the domestic economy in one
definite way. So long as both are treated as independent variables, the employment coefficients of exports (i.e. additional
employment required per unit of specific exports) are identical
with the corresponding employment coefficients of the domestic
households and investment demand.

Two distinct approaches to the analysis of exports in their
relation to the domestic economy in general and to domestic
households and investment demand in particular have been discussed above. In the first,[4] only the domestic household purchases and all the investment demand are entered into the final
bill of goods. Exports, "hitched on" to the import requirements through a set of given input-output coefficients (the
"terms of trade"), are — along with the output and employment figures of all domestic industries — accounted for among
the other dependent variables of the system. According to the
second approach, terms of trade relationships are omitted from
consideration, and the export demand is included in the final,
independent bill of goods alongside the "free" domestic consumers' and investment demand.

To these can be added a third case. Here only the exports
are treated as an independent variable, the domestic demand
being relegated to the status of dependence. This is achieved
through reintroduction of the previously omitted domestic employment-income-consumption relationship (see p. 168, above).
The employment figures computed from this point of view
show more than the *primary* demand for labor *directly* and
indirectly derived from the given export bill of goods on the

---

[4] Discussed in detail in the previously cited article.

basis of existing interindustrial relationships. They also include the *secondary* employment *directly* and *indirectly* dependent upon the additional household demand resulting — via the income flow — from the higher level of primary employment.

Instead of being included in toto in the final bill of goods, exports, for purposes of a certain type of analysis, can be conveniently split into two parts — independent exports and the dependent exports. The latter are taken to be subject to the quid pro quo relationship of the international net terms of trade, while the former are free and thus independently given. In contemplating the possible consequences of various foreign lending and lend-lease policies, it might be well to consider the exports "given away" on credit as an independent variable, but at the same time take into account the fact that additional, dependent exports must pay for imports required — in accordance with the existing import ratios of foreign goods — for maintenance of expanded domestic production and consumption.

The distinction between independent-primary and dependent secondary exports has its counterpart in the separation of domestic investment from household consumption. From the point of view of a certain type of analysis (and policy), the latter constitutes a dependent set of variables linked up to the rest of the system through given employment-income-consumption relationships, while the former — through omission of "investment determining" relationships — is entered into a given final bill of goods.

Thus in this fourth and last type of approach to be considered in this paper, neither the domestic household consumption nor that part of exports which is used to pay for the imports are entered into the final bill of goods. This means that both the domestic-employment-income-consumption relationships as well as the terms of foreign trade relationships are included among the given structural data of the problem and only the export surplus is treated as the independent demand factor.

The basic operational distinction between the different possible approaches to the analysis of exports in their relation to the other elements of the economic system has been elucidated above in terms of inclusion of household consumption, invest-

ment, exports and export surpluses, etc., in the set of dependent or, alternatively, in the group of independent variables of
our theoretical system. A closer examination of the foregoing
analysis shows, however, that it is really the description of the
quantitative interrelationships connecting the dependent variables of the system with each other and with the given bill of
goods — not the exact enumeration of all the various kinds of
economic variables of which any given bill of goods is actually
composed — which makes it possible to distinguish one type
of theroetical approach from another. Each dependent variable is identified through the peculiar relationships which connect it with the rest of the system, a combination of relationships which distinguishes it from any other dependent variable
as well as from the set of all the *in*dependent variables (i.e.
from the bill of goods). A change in the theoretical approach
which removes a variable from the former and transfers it to
the latter set causes it to lose most of its individual characteristics. When counted among the dependent variables, for example, exports or domestic consumption are clearly distinguishable from each other, and have to be treated as separate
entities; once included in the given independent bill of goods,
they become indistinguishable. Exports of an additional million dollars' worth of textiles will — from the point of view of
an approach which treats both as final demand — affect the
rest of the system exactly in the same way as an equivalent
amount of textiles absorbed in domestic household consumption. As a matter of fact, any million dollars' worth of textiles
absorbed within the economic system, but not explicitly identified with any one of the variables treated as dependent will —
be it invested at home, purchased by the Government or simply
dumped into the sea — have the same effect on outputs and
employment. In short, any independent demand otherwise
unspecified would affect the dependent variables of the economic system in the same way as any other physically similar
elements explicitly included in the independent, final demand.
This explains why an empirical study aimed at establishment
of quantitative relationships between the final demand and the
outputs and employment dependent upon it could, strictly
speaking, content itself with a purely negative definition of
final demand as including all demand not explicitly listed as
dependent.

2. MATHEMATICAL FORMULATION OF THE ANALYSIS

Before they can be applied to the analysis of actual statistical data, the results of the foregoing theoretical discussion must be formulated in precise quantitative terms. To avoid unnecessary repetition, the general theoretical formulae fully developed in the previous article will be referred to below without detailed interpretation. As before $X_1, X_2, \cdots, X_f, \cdots X_m, X_n$ represent the total net outputs of all the various branches of the national economy; X_n is the figure of total employment (the "labor" output of households); X_f stands for aggregate imports; x_{ik} indicates the amount of the product of industry k used in industry i: $x_{1f}, x_{2f} \cdots$, for example, are the amounts of imports absorbed by industry 1, industry 2, etc.; a_{ik} is the coefficient describing the use of commodity k by industry i, per unit of its total output: $a_{ik} \equiv \dfrac{x_{ik}}{X_i}$. Thus, $a_{1f}, a_{2f} \cdots$ are the import coefficients of industry 1, industry 2, etc.; $a_{1n}, a_{2n} \cdots$ are the employment (labor input) coefficients of industry 1, industry 2, etc. The labor input coefficient of foreign trade, a_{fn}, for obvious reasons equals zero.

The structurally determined system of interindustrial relationships can be described by m equations of the following type:

$$(\text{III}) \quad -a_{1k}X_1 - a_{2k}X_2 - \cdots - a_{fk}X_f - \cdots + X_k - \cdots - a_{mk}X_m \equiv D_k$$
$$(k = 1, 2, \cdots, f, \cdots, m)$$

$D_1, D_2, \cdots, D_k, \cdots, D_m$ are the separate components of the final bill of goods, here defined as comprising domestic household consumption as well as domestic and foreign investment.

If solved for the dependent variables $X_1, X_2, \cdots, X_m$ in terms of a given bill of goods, the system leads to the following expression:

$$(\text{IV}) \quad X_k = {}_{nn}A_{k1}D_1 + {}_{nn}A_{k2}D_2 + \cdots + {}_{nn}A_{kf}D_f + \cdots + {}_{nn}A_{kk}D_k + \cdots$$
$$+ {}_{nn}A_{km}D_m$$
$$(k = 1, 2, \cdots, f, \cdots, m)$$

Inserting on the right-hand side the given bill of goods, i.e. the given numerical magnitudes of $D_1, D_2 \cdots$, it is now possible to compute the total output $X_1, X_2 \cdots$ of all the various industries.

Each of the capital A's appearing in IV obviously depends in its magnitude upon the technical input coefficients — the small a's — entered on the left-hand side of equations III.[5]   The subscripts nn on the left of all the A's indicate that no technical coefficients describing the output or the input of the industry n (households) enter in the computation of these constants.

Exports are treated here as dependent variables.   This is indicated by the fact that the terms $a_{f1} X_f, a_{f2} X_f, \cdots$ describing the dependence of exports upon the imports X_f appear on the left-hand side of structural equation III.

Employment figures for all the separate industries can be computed by multiplying the previously obtained output figures by the corresponding labor input coefficients:

$$(\text{v}) \quad x_{kn} = a_{kn}X_k = a_{kn\ nn}A_{k1}D_1 + a_{kn\ nn}A_{k2}D_2 + \cdots + a_{kn\ nn}A_{km}D_m$$
$$(k = 1, 2, \cdots, f, \cdots, m$$

Every widening of the bill-of-goods concept finds its mathematical expression in the transfer of the corresponding variables from the left to the right side of equations in System III. The accompanying omission of certain relationships — an omission which has been shown to be the logical prerequisite of every transfer of a variable from the category of dependent into that of independent, i.e. given magnitudes — finds its expression in the elimination of the corresponding equations from System III.   On the other hand, every narrowing of the bill-of-goods concept means the introduction of new dependent variables on the left-hand side and addition of new equations.

The discussion of particular cases might begin with case 2, in which not only domestic household consumption and investment but also all the exports are included in the final bill of goods.   The addition of exports to the list of independent variables means that the expressions $a_{fk}X_f$ describing the dependence of exports of all the different kinds of products ($k = 1, 2,$

---

[5] If D represents the determinant

$$
\begin{vmatrix}
1 & -a_{21} & -a_{31} & \cdots & -a_{m1} & -a_{n1} \\
-a_{12} & 1 & -a_{32} & \cdots & -a_{m2} & -a_{n2} \\
-a_{13} & -a_{23} & 1 & \cdots & -a & -a_{n3} \\
\cdots & \cdots & \cdots & \cdots & \cdots & \cdots \\
\cdots & \cdots & \cdots & \cdots & \cdots & \cdots \\
-a_{1m} & -a_{2m} & -a_{3m} & \cdots & 1 & -a_{nm} \\
-a_{1n} & -a_{2n} & -a_{3n} & \cdots & -a_{mn} & 1
\end{vmatrix}
$$

while D_{nn} stands for the algebraic complement (minor) of element $-a_{nn}$, and $D_{nn \cdot ik}$ for the algebraic complement of the two elements $-a_{nn}$ and $-a_{ik}$ then
$$_{nn}A_{ik} \equiv \frac{D_{nn \cdot ik}}{D_{nn}}.$$

$\cdots, m$) upon the magnitude of total imports X_f must be transferred from the left to the right side of System III. As elements of a given bill of goods, these exports become, as has been explained above, indistinguishable from the similar commodities (used in domestic household consumption and investment) already included in it: they must be considered now as being included in $D_1, D_2, \cdots$.

The fth equation ($k = f$) in System III has to be eliminated, since the "terms of trade" relationships, to which it gives — in combination with the suppressed terms in other equations — a quantitative expression, are now dropped from consideration. Thus a new, reduced system of $m - 1$ basic structural equations is obtained:

$$(\text{VI}) \quad -a_{1k}X_1 - a_{2k}X_2 - \cdots - a_{f-1\,k}X_{f-1} - a_{f+1\,k}X_{f+1} - \cdots$$
$$+X_k - \cdots - a_{mk}X_m = D_k$$
$$(k = 1, 2, \cdots, f - 1, f + 1, \cdots, m)$$

The simultaneous solution of these equations leads to $m - 1$ expressions analogous to IV:

$$(\text{VII}) \quad X_k = {}_{nn\cdot ff}A_{k1}D_1 + {}_{nn\cdot ff}A_{k2}D_2 + \cdots + {}_{nn\cdot ff}A_{k\,f-1}D_{f-1}$$
$$+ {}_{nn\cdot ff}A_{k\,f+1}D_{f+1} + \cdots + {}_{nn\cdot ff}A_{km}D_m$$
$$(k = 1, 2, \cdots, f - 1, f + 1, \cdots, m)$$

The subscript $nn \cdot ff$ attached to each A indicates that both the technical coefficients describing the inputs and outputs of industry n (households), as well as those related to industry f (foreign trade), do not enter into the computation of these constants.[6]

Employment figures for all the separate industries can be derived from the following expressions analogous to v above:

$$(\text{VIII}) \quad x_{kn} = a_{kn}X_k = a_{kn}\,{}_{nn\cdot ff}A_{k1}D_1 + a_{kn}\,{}_{nn\cdot ff}A_{k2}D_2 + \cdots$$
$$+ a_{kn}\,{}_{nn\cdot ff}A_{k\,f-1}D_{f-1} + a_{kn}\,{}_{nn\cdot ff}A_{k\,f+1}D_{f+1} + \cdots$$
$$+ a_{kn}\,{}_{nn\cdot ff}A_{km}D_m$$
$$(k = 1, 2, \cdots, f - 1, f + 2, \cdots, m)$$

To determine by how much the total employment will increase from the addition to the given bill of goods of one unit of commodity k, it is necessary to sum up the coefficients of D_k in all the $m - 1$ equations in VIII:

$$(\text{IX}) \quad a_{1n}\,{}_{nn\cdot ff}A_{1k} + a_{2n}\,{}_{nn\cdot ff}A_{2k} + \cdots + a_{f-1\,n}\,{}_{nn\cdot ff}A_{f-1\,k}$$
$$+ a_{f+1n}\,{}_{nn\cdot ff}A_{f+1\,k} + \cdots + a_{mn}\,{}_{nn\cdot ff}A_{mk}$$

[6] In terms of determinantal notation (see footnote 5 above):

$$_{nn\cdot ff}A_{ik} \equiv \frac{D_{nn\cdot ff\cdot ik}}{D_{nn\cdot ff}}$$

Imports, X_f, have to be computed from the output figures in a separate operation:

(x) $x_{kf} = a_{kf}X_k$

$$(k = 1, 2, \cdots, f - 1, f + 1, \cdots, m)$$

These equations, analogous to VIII above, determine the amount of foreign commodities absorbed by each separate industry. Summation of all these imports, supplemented by the amount D_f — if any — directly entered in the final bill of goods, gives the aggregate figure for the national economy as a whole.

If exports and domestic investment alone are entered in the final bill of goods, $D_1, D_2, \cdots$, while domestic consumption is considered to be dependent upon domestic employment via income (case 3), the corresponding amounts of all the separate commodities $x_{n1}, x_{n2}, \cdots, x_{nm}$ can be moved on the left-hand side of the basic system of structural equations. They appear there as functions of the total employment, X_n, i.e., as $a_{n1}X_n$, $a_{n2}X_2, \cdots, a_{nm}X_m$. At the same time a new equation is added to the system:

(XI) $-a_{n1}X_1 - a_{n2}X_2 - \cdots - a_{n\ f-1}X_{f-1} - a_{n\ f+1}X_{f+1} - \cdots$
$- X_{nm}X_m + X_n = D_n.$

It shows the relationships between the outputs of all the separate industries (exclusive of foreign trade), $X_1, X_2, \cdots$, total employment, X_n, and the amount of labor, if any, entered in the final bill of goods, D_n. The complete structural system thus consists of m equations of the following form:

(XII) $-a_{1k}X_1 - a_{2k}X_2 - \cdots - a_{f-1\ k}X_{f-1} - a_{f+1\ k}X_{f+1} - \cdots$
$+ X_k - \cdots - a_{mk}X_m - a_{nk}X_n = D_k$
$$(k = 1, 2, \cdots, f - 1, f + 1, \cdots, m, n)$$

and its solution similar to IV and VII is:

(XIII) $X_k = {}_{ff}A_{k1}D_1 + {}_{ff}A_{k2}D_2 + \cdots + {}_{ff}A_{k\ f-1}D_{f-1} + {}_{ff}A_{k\ f+1}D_{f+1}$
$+ \cdots + {}_{ff}A_{km}D_m + {}_{ff}A_{kn}D_n$
$$(k = 1, 2, \cdots, f - 1, f + 1, \cdots, m, n)$$

The subscript ff under the A's indicates that no input coefficients related to foreign trade affect the magnitude of these constants. The absence of the subscript nn, on the other hand, signifies that the labor input and the household consumption coefficients do enter into their computation.[7]

---

[7] In terms of determinantal notation (see footnotes 5 and 6, above)

$$_{ff}A_{ik} \equiv \frac{D_{ff \cdot ik}}{D_{ff}}$$

The last of the expressions in set XIII determines directly the magnitude of total employment X_n. The imports figure might be obtained separately on the basis of import relationships similar to x, above.

If both the domestic employment-consumption relationships and the international terms of trade relationships are taken into consideration, only investment — domestic and foreign — can be entered in the final bill of goods. In this case both employment, X_n, and imports, X_f, must be included as dependent variables on the left-hand side of the basic structural equations, and the number of these equations is increased to n. The computational formula is similar to those developed above; it is even simpler, since the enlarged set of the n equations includes all the variables, which obviates the necessity of computing either employment X_n or imports X_f in separate operations:

$$(\text{XIV}) \quad X_k = A_{k1}D_1 + A_{k2}D_2 + \cdots + A_{kn}D_n$$
$$(k = 1, 2, \cdots, m, n)$$

The assumption of strict, direct proportionality between all the inputs and outputs implied by the use of constant production coefficients lends to our theoretical models a high degree of artificial rigidity. Some significant implications of this rigidity become apparent if one considers the extreme case in which the values of all the independent variables D_1, D_2, $\cdots$ representing the given bill of goods are assumed to be equal to zero. All the outputs determined by either one of the three sets of linear equations VII, XIII or XIV must then necessarily vanish.[8]

In the case represented by equation VII, such a result appears to be quite reasonable — the given bill of goods includes in this instance the entire domestic consumption and investment, as well as all exports. If each of these items is reduced to zero, i.e. is entirely eliminated, all production and employment would naturally cease. In the other two cases, however, the given bill of goods does not include domestic household consumption — the latter being treated as a set of variables dependent on the level of employment. The conclusion that all employment and all production would vanish with cessation of exports and discontinuation of all domestic investment, in the one case, and with the disappearance of export surpluses

---

[8] The determinants $D_{nn \cdot ff}$, D_{ff} and D respectively are *not* equal to zero, since otherwise neither of the three systems could have a consistent solution with any of the D's being non-zero.

and of domestic investment, in the other, is obviously contrary to all reasonable expectations.

Actually the employment-consumption relationship is not linear. If the consumption coefficients a_{n1}, a_{n2}, $\cdots$ do not remain constant, but rather increase with a fall in employment, a parallel reduction in the given bill of goods D_1, D_2, $\cdots$ will lead to a less than proportional fall in domestic consumption and employment, and even a complete elimination of the export and investment demand will result in a new equilibrium with positive production, employment and domestic household consumption.

The preceding considerations thus lead to the conclusion that in empirical application the computation formulae XII and XIV will most probably result in an overstatement of the employment and output dependent upon any given final demand, D_1, D_2, $\cdots$

3. STATISTICAL RELATIONSHIP BETWEEN EXPORTS AND EMPLOYMENT IN THE UNITED STATES IN 1939

Table 21 shows the relationship between exports and employment in the United States in the last normal prewar year, 1939. The statistical data reproduced in Table 20 furnished the empirical base, while the general analysis developed in the first part of this article and summarized in the second supplied the theoretical foundation for the numerical computations, the results of which are shown in Table 21. A separate computation and a different numerical answer correspond to each one of the three sets of theoretical assumptions (with some independent exports) presented above.

i. Variation of Results Computed on Basis of Three Different Definitions of Final Demand

First, the entire exports are treated as a part of the final independently given demand, which includes also all household consumption and domestic investment. Imports are allowed to adjust themselves to the import requirements of all domestic industries, without any regard for the necessity of balancing them — in accordance with the existing international terms of trade — against the volume of exports. Computed on the basis of formulae VII and VIII, the figures entered in column 6 of Table 21 show the *primary employment* dependent on the 1939 exports treated as a set of independent variables; i.e. they

TABLE 21—EXPORT-DEPENDENT EMPLOYMENT IN THE AMERICAN ECONOMY, 1939

INDUSTRY	(1) Total employment — Unit: 1,000 persons	(2) Employment per 1 million dollars of output — Unit: 1,090 persons	(3) Total exports — Unit: $1,000-000	(4) Primary employment directly dependent on exports — Unit: 2 × 3 — 1,000 persons	(5) As per cent of total employment in that industry — 4:1	(6) Primary employment directly and indirectly dependent on exports — Unit: 1,000 persons	(7) As per cent of total employment in that industry — 6:1	(8) Primary and secondary employment dependent on exports — Unit: 1,000 persons	(9) As per cent of total employment in that industry — 8:1	(10) Export surplus[5] — Unit: one million dollars	(11) Primary employment directly dependent on surplus exports — Unit: 2 × 10 — 1,000 persons	(12) As per cent of total employment in that industry — 11:1	(13) Primary and secondary employment dependent on surplus exports — Unit: 1,000 persons	(14) As per cent of total employment in that industry — 13:1
1. Agriculture and fishing[1]	62[1]	.006[1]	415	3	4.24	4	5.98	9	15.12	23	.15	.24	0.6	.99
2. Food, tobacco and kindred products	1,260	.100	248	25	1.95	30	2.41	156	12.40	14	1.40	.11	10.3	.82
3. Ferrous metals	480	.184	159	29	6.11	58	12.03	77	16.06	9	1.66	.35	5.1	1.06
4. Motor vehicles, industrial and heating equipment	960	.195	379	74	7.69	86	8.95	144	15.03	21	4.19	.44	9.5	.99
5. Metal fabricating	1,570	.231	510	118	7.49	149	9.52	214	13.52	29	6.66	.43	14.1	.92
6. Nonferrous metals and products	270	.211	158	33	12.37	48	17.70	62	23.02	9	1.90	.70	4.1	1.52
7. Nonmetallic minerals and products	440	.216	60	13	2.95	21	4.81	35	7.86	3	.73	.17	2.3	.52
8. Fuel and power	1,220	.133	488	65	5.33	101	8.38	198	16.35	28	3.68	.30	13.0	1.08
9. Chemicals	430	.135	191	26	5.98	37	8.68	69	15.95	11	1.46	.34	4.5	1.05
10. Lumber and paper products, printing, publishing	1,740	.311	123	38	2.20	68	3.93	193	11.12	7	2.18	.13	12.7	.73
11. Textiles and leather	2,510	.427	149	64	2.54	82	3.25	322	12.82	8	3.59	.14	21.2	.84
12. Rubber	150	.169	34	6	3.82	12	7.75	23	15.06	2	.32	.21	1.5	.99
13. All other manufacturing	430	.273	56	15	3.56	22	5.02	57	13.35	3	.87	.20	3.8	.88
15. Transportation	1,980	.276	103	28	1.44	130	6.57	294	14.86	6	1.60	.08	18.5	.93
16. Trade	5,600	.375	244	91	1.61	139	2.45	668	11.77	14	5.18	.09	44.0	.77
18. Business and consumer services	4,131	.205	2	0	.01	44	1.06	450	10.90	0	.02	0	29.6	.72
21. Households	1,400	.048[4]	...	0	...	...	...	143	...	...	...	...	9.3	...
Total[2]	30,352[3]	...	3,310	656	2.16	1,114	3.64	3,114	10.10	188	35.60	.117	204.1	.67

[1] Employment figures for Agriculture include only hired help.
[2] Because of rounding-up of decimals, the totals differ from the column sums.
[3] This figure includes 3,870 thousands of governmental employees not listed above.
[4] Domestic household employment per unit of total nondomestic employment.
[5] The export surplus of each industry is obtained by multiplying its total exports by 0.056, which is the ratio of the aggregate export surplus to total exports.

show — industry by industry — the reduction in employment which would result from discontinuance of all exports, on the assumption that domestic household consumption and investment remains unchanged. The same figures expressed as percentages of total 1939 employment in the corresponding industries are shown in column 7. Primary employment includes both persons engaged *directly* in production of the exported commodities and those whose jobs depend on the same exports *indirectly*, through production of materials and other inputs used, with or without intermediate steps, by the final export industries.

This distinction between direct and indirect primary employment is admittedly an arbitrary one. It must necessarily vary with every change in the industrial classification: the more detailed this classification becomes, i.e. the greater the breakdown of larger industries into separate sub-groups, the smaller will be the number of industries working directly for export and the larger the number of those depending on exports only in an indirect way.

It is mainly because of the ease with which the export ratios (i.e. the proportion of total output sold in foreign markets) can be statistically determined that this concept plays such a great rôle in discussion of the actual export dependence of various industries. In order to indicate the quantitative difference between the total *primary* employment and that part of it which, on the basis of the conventional approach, would be defined as *direct* export-dependent employment, the latter has been computed and is shown in column 4 and — in percentage terms — in column 5 of our table. The corresponding measure of indirect primary employment would be given by the difference between the entries of column 6 and column 4, or column 7 and column 5, respectively.

In the next computation, the assumption of independent, i.e. fixed, household consumption is dropped. The domestic demand for consumers' goods is made to vary in direct proportion to the level of total employment. Thus the figures entered in column 8 show all the employment which would be lost with the elimination of all the exports, if the domestic household demand for consumption goods were to fall off in proportion to the aggregate reduction in employment. The difference between these figures (computed on the basis of formula XII) and the (direct and indirect) primary employment figures en-

CHART 12

Amount of Employment in Various Industries Depending on Exports in 1939

unit: one thousand workers

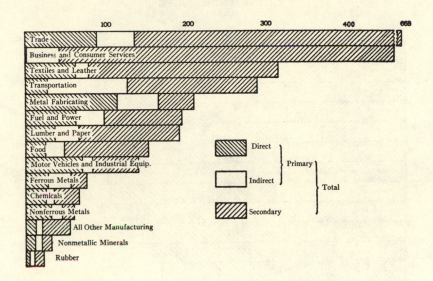

CHART 13

EMPLOYMENT IN VARIOUS UNITED STATES INDUSTRIES DEPENDING ON 1939 EXPORTS EXPRESSED AS A PERCENTAGE OF THE TOTAL 1939 EMPLOYMENT IN THESE INDUSTRIES

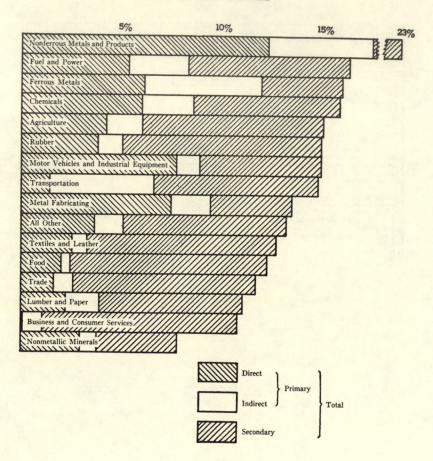

tered in column 6 constitutes what might be called *secondary* employment.

A reduction of exports would naturally affect, not only domestic output, but also the imports. The *primary* effect of a hypothetical elimination of all the 1939 exports (as computed from formulae XII and x) includes a loss of 122 million dollars' worth of imports; the corresponding *total effect,* encompassing also the secondary reduction in the domestic household demand, would be considerably larger. It implies an import reduction of 465 million dollars.

Since the actual 1939 imports amounted to 3700 million dollars, a very substantial import surplus would result in either case. Such a conclusion is not at all surprising, since both import effects are computed on the assumption that all exports are autonomous, an assumption implying the nonexistence of any definite international terms of trade relationship.

These observations lead to the third and last set of computations. Here the net terms of trade, i.e. the relationship between any given volume of imports and the corresponding amounts of goods and services which, according to the 1939 international price ratios, would have to be exported in order to pay for these imports, are introduced in our computational scheme (formula XIV), in addition to all other input-output relationships. Accordingly, instead of the total exports, only the export surplus — which in 1939 amounted to 188 million dollars — is treated as the really autonomous part of American exports. The independent bill of goods used in this computation is reproduced in column 10. The 188 million dollars are arbitrarily distributed between the different kinds of commodities in the same proportion in which these commodities participate in the total 1939 exports listed in column 3.

For reasons mentioned before (p. 177) the secondary employment included in the total export-dependent employment figures entered in columns 8 and 13 is somewhat overestimated. These figures must therefore be considered to represent the upper limits of the actual number of jobs dependent in the year 1939 on the American exports or export surpluses, respectively.

The four graphs drawn on the basis of Table 21 facilitate the examination of the quantitative results obtained. Agriculture is omitted from the two charts showing the absolute employment figures, since the noninclusion of self-employed farmers makes this particular figure unrepresentative; it is entered,

CHART 14

AMOUNT OF EMPLOYMENT IN VARIOUS INDUSTRIES
DEPENDING ON THE 1939 EXPORT SURPLUS
(POSITIVE BALANCE OF TRADE)
The shaded parts represent Primary (Direct and Indirect) Employment

unit: one thousand workers

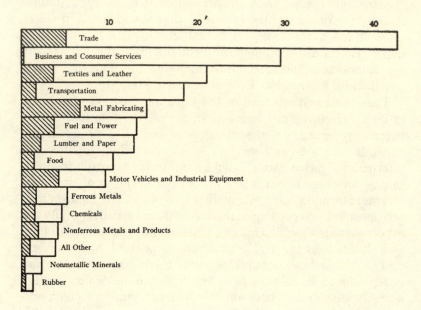

CHART 15

EMPLOYMENT IN VARIOUS UNITED STATES INDUSTRIES DEPENDING ON 1939 EXPORT SURPLUS (POSITIVE BALANCE OF TRADE) EXPRESSED AS A PERCENTAGE OF THE TOTAL 1939 EMPLOYMENT IN THESE INDUSTRIES

The shaded parts represent Primary (Direct and Indirect) employment.

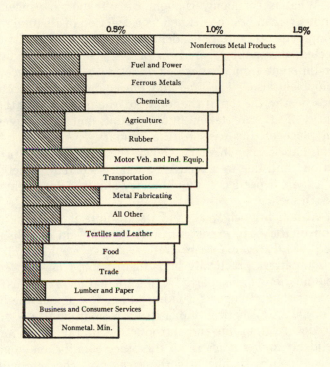

however, in the other two charts, because the disparity disappears when the same effects are described in percentages of the 1939 employment in the respective industries.

ii. General Observations

The following general observations suggest themselves from the examination of these charts:

1. In terms of the absolute number of persons affected, the large industries — that is, the industries with greater total number of employees — show a greater dependence upon exports than the smaller ones.

2. What is commonly thought of as export-dependence of an industry can best be defined as a fraction of its total output or employment figure dependent upon exports. As should be expected, the ranking based on primary employment alone is very different from that which takes into account secondary employment also. The Fuel and Power industry, for example, stands next to the top, if the total, i.e. the primary and the secondary effects, are taken into account, but it occupies the sixth place on the basis of the primary effects alone. The Metal Fabricating industry shows the third largest primary reaction; but, due to a relatively weak secondary effect in its total export dependence, this industry stands below eight other industries.

3. Although much weaker in its absolute impact, the elimination of the 1939 export surplus, resulting in establishment of a perfectly even foreign trade balance, would result in a reaction pattern practically indistinguishable from that caused by elimination of all exports. The explanation is obvious: with both exports and imports ranking rather low among the inputs and outputs of American industries, the addition of the "terms of trade" relationship and introduction of the corresponding dependent exports items in all the other equilibrium equations can not modify significantly the structural characteristics of this economic system.

APPENDIX

Classification of Industries for the Study of Inter-Industry Relations, 1939

1. Agriculture and Fishing
    1. Field crops
    2. Vegetables
    3. Fruits and nuts
    4. Horticultural specialties
    5. Forest products
    6. Dairy products
    7. Poultry and poultry products
    8. Livestock and livestock products
    9. Fishing
2. Food, Tobacco, and Kindred Products
    10. Flour and gristmill products
    11. Canning and preserving
    12. Bread and bakery products
    13. Sugar refining
    14. Starch and glucose products
    15. Alcoholic beverages
    16. Nonalcoholic beverages
    17. Tobacco manufacture
    18. Slaughtering and meat packing
    19. Manufactured dairy products
    20. Edible fats and oils, n.e.c.
    21. Other food products
3. Ferrous Metals
    22. Iron mining
    23. Blast furnaces
    24. Steel works and rolling mills
4. Motor Vehicles, Industrial and Heating Equipment
    31. Motor vehicles
    34. Industrial and heating equipment
5. Metal Fabricating
    25. Iron and steel foundry products
    26. Shipbuilding
    27. Firearms
    28. Munitions
    29. Agricultural machinery
    30. Engines and turbines
    32. Aircraft
    33. Transportation equipment, n.e.c.
    35. Machine tools
    36. Merchandising and service machines
    37. Electrical equipment, n.e.c.
    38. Iron and steel, n.e.c.
6. Nonferrous Metals and Their Products
    39. Nonferrous metal mining
    40. Smelting and refining of nonferrous metals
    41. Aluminum products
    42. Nonferrous metal manufactures
7. Nonmetallic Minerals and Their Products
    43. Nonmetallic mineral mining
    44. Nonmetallic mineral manufactures
8. Fuel and Power
    45. Petroleum and natural gas
    46. Petroleum refining
    47. Anthracite coal
    48. Bituminous coal
    49. Coke and manufactured solid fuel
    50. Manufactured gas
    52. Electric public utilities
9. Chemicals
    53. Chemicals
10. Lumber, Paper and Their Products, Printing and Publishing
    54. Lumber and timber products
    55. Furniture and other manufactures of wood
    56. Wood pulp, paper and paper products
    57. Printing and publishing
11. Textiles and Leather
    58. Cotton yarn and cloth
    59. Silk and rayon products
    60. Woolen and worsted manufactures
    61. Clothing
    62. Other textile products
    63. Leather
    64. Leather shoes
    65. Leather products, n.e.c.
12. Rubber
    66. Rubber products
13. All Other Manufacturing
    67. All other manufacturing
14. Construction
    68. Building construction
    69. Construction other than building

15. Transportation
   71. Coastwise and inland water transportation
   72. Transoceanic transportation
   73. Steam railroad transportation
   70. Transportation, n.e.c.
16. Trade
   74. Trade
17. Foreign Countries
   75. Foreign countries
18. Business and Consumer Services
   51. Communications
   76. Banking
   77. Insurance
   78. Business services other than advertising
   79. Advertising
   80. Services allied to transportation
   81. Automotive repair and services

82. Repair services other than automotive
83. Rental agencies, other than building
84. Commercial building renting
85. Home renting
86. Hotels, tourist courts and camps
87. Laundries, etc.
88. Consumer services
90. Motion picture theatres
89. Other theatres, spectator sports
91. Amusement places
19. Households and Government
   92. Government
   94. Households
20. Unallocated and Stocks
   93. Stocks
   95. Unallocated

C. Wages, Profits and Prices

1. Quantitative Interrelationships Between Wage Rates, Profits, and Prices in the American Economy, 1939

The purpose of this article is to present the measures of certain fundamental interrelationships between the wage rates paid, profits derived, and the prices received by all the various branches of the American economy during the last normal pre-war year, 1939.

The exposition of the actual numerical result of the study is preceded by a short presentation of the simple — some readers may find it all too simple — theoretical background of the analysis. General comments indicating the principal limitations of the theoretical scheme selected and pointing out the probable nature of bias thus introduced in the numerical findings follow at the end.

The cost-price relationship within a separate industry as conditioned by its technical structure constitutes the factual basis of the whole analysis. Let $P_1, P_2, P_3, \cdots, P_i, \cdots, P_m$ be the prices of the products of the m separate industries, and $a_{i1}, a_{i2}, a_{i3} \cdots, a_{im}$, the technical input coefficients showing the amounts of product of industry 1, industry 2, and so on used in production of commodity i, i.e. the physical amounts of these different kinds of goods absorbed by industry i per unit of its own output. The output of an industry, as referred to in all the following discussion, is defined with exclusion of the products consumed by the same industry in which they have been produced. Thus

$$a_{11} = a_{22} = \cdots = a_{ii} = \cdots = a_{mm} = 0 \text{ by definition.}$$

The quantitative relationship between the price P_i of the product of any industry i and the prices of the products of all the other $m - 1$ industries used by it can be described as follows:

(1a) $a_{i1}P_1 + a_{i2}P_2 + a_{i3}P_3 + \cdots + a_{im}P_m + R_i = P_i$
$$(i = 1, 2, 3, \cdots, m)$$

This equation also represents a definition of R_i, which is the difference between the price of the commodity produced by the particular industry and that part of its unit costs which consist of payments for materials and services, in short, for all kinds of products purchased from the other industries. In other words, R_i can be thought of as the "value added" originated in industry i per unit of its product. An accountant would recognize in the above equations the familiar unit cost and profit computations used to determine the appropriate price for, say, a next year's model of a Plymouth four-door sedan. One equation of this type can be set up for each of the m industries comprised in our economic system. Considering, now, the technical coefficients — all the small a's — as known, we arrive at a system of m linear equations with $2m$ yet unknown variables: the m prices, $P_1, P_2, \cdots, P_m$ and the m values added, $R_1, R_2, R_3, \cdots, R_m$.

After having assigned some definite numerical magnitudes to any m of these $2m$ variables, we can solve the system 1a for the remaining m variables. A price-fixing authority, for example, could calculate the combined amount of wages and profits which each of the m separate industries would derive per unit of its output on the basis of any particular set of prescribed m prices. On the other hand, having first decided on the amounts of combined wage and profit income which each of the m industries should be able to earn per unit of its output, the same authority could, on the basis of given technical relationships, determine the one and only system of prices which would have to be established in order to make the attainment of this particular income allocation possible. As a matter of fact, having arbitrarily fixed any k prices and m-k values added, it is possible to solve our m equations for the remaining m-x prices and k values added.

The actual solution of system 1a for all the m prices in terms of the similar number of all the values added can be written down in the form of m equations — one for each of the unknown prices:

$$(2a) \qquad P_i = A_{1i}R_1 + A_{2i}R_2 + \cdots + A_{ii}R_i + \cdots + A_{mi}R_m$$
$$(i = 1, 2, 3, \cdots, m)$$

Each one of the capital A's depends in its magnitude on all the small a's, i.e. it is a function of the technical structure of all the m industries.[1]

A_{ki} shows the relationship between the price P_i and the value added, R_k, derived by industry k per unit of its output. Should R_k, for example, be increased by one dollar, that is, should the combined wages and profits earned in industry k per unit of its product be increased by one dollar (while the R's, that is, wages and profits, in all other industries remain the same as before) the price P_i of the product of industry i will go up by A_{ki} dollars.[2]

To introduce into our system the wage rate, i.e. the price of labor P_n explicitly, it is only necessary to split the value added R_i of each industry into its two component parts, which in this instance are the wages W_i and the non-wage income or, for short, profits π_i. The wage costs per unit of output can,

---

[1] If D represents the determinant

$$
\begin{vmatrix}
1 & -a_{21} & -a_{31} & \cdots & -a_{m1} & -a_{n1} \\
-a_{12} & 1 & -a_{32} & \cdots & -a_{m2} & -a_{n2} \\
-a_{13} & -a_{23} & 1 & \cdots & -a_{m3} & -a_{n3} \\
\cdots & \cdots & \cdots & \cdots & \cdots & \cdots \\
\cdots & \cdots & \cdots & \cdots & \cdots & \cdots \\
-a_{1m} & -a_{2m} & -a_{3m} & \cdots & 1 & -a_{nm} \\
-a_{1n} & -a_{2n} & -a_{3n} & \cdots & -a_{mn} & 1
\end{vmatrix}
$$

while D_{nn} stands for the algebraic complement (minor) of the element $-a_{nn}$ and $D_{nn \cdot ki}$ for the complement of the two elements $-a_{nn}$ and $-a_{ki}$, then

$$A_{ki} = \frac{D_{nn \cdot ki}}{D_{nn}}$$

[2] Comparing the meaning of A_{ki} as a measure of dependence between the price of commodity i and the income derived by industry k with its significance as a coefficient showing the effect of a change in the "final demand" for commodity k upon the physical output of industry i, we observe the notable parallelism existing between the price variation and physical changes as seen from the point of view of the economic system as a whole. The latter aspect of the problem has been discussed in Part IV, A and B.

furthermore, be represented as the wage rate P_n multiplied by the labor input coefficients a_{in}; this coefficient, in analogy with the other technical coefficients, represents the amount of direct labor hired and used by industry i per unit of its output. Thus

$$(3a) \quad R_i = W_i + \pi_i = a_{in}P_n + \pi_i \qquad (i = 1, 2, 3, \cdots, m)$$

Substituting each of these m relationships in the corresponding equations of system 2a we arrive at a new set of equations:

$$(4a) \quad P_i = (A_{1i}a_{1n} + A_{2i}a_{2n} + \cdots + A_{mi}a_{mn})P_n + $$
$$A_{1i}\pi_1 + A_{2i}\pi_2 + \cdots + A_{mi}\pi_m \qquad (i = 1, 2, 3, \cdots, m)$$

Each of these equations describes the price of one commodity as depending upon the wage rate P_n paid in all industries and the profit rates $\pi_1, \pi_2, \cdots, \pi_m$ earned by each one of them. The expression in parentheses shows by how much the particular price P_i would go up (or down) for every dollar added to (or subtracted from) the wage rate P_n, this on the assumption that the profits earned per unit of output in all the industries remain the same as before.

These and other similar formulae enable us to determine the total price effect of all possible combinations of separate and simultaneous changes in wage and profit rates of various industries.

If for some reason it were desirable to disregard in our analysis one particular link in the chain of cost-price relationships, this can be done by solving system 1a for a different set of independent variables and omitting one of the equations. For example, if it is assumed — as it might very well be, from a short-run point of view — that a change in the replacement costs of industrial machinery would be "absorbed" by the machinery-using industries, rather than "passed forward" by means of corresponding adjustment in the prices of finished products, this assumption can be taken care of by shifting the price of machinery, let it be P_2, from the set of dependent into that of the independent variables. The group of m independent variables will consist now of the m-1 other prices and one of the values added, say the value added in the machinery industry, R_2. The price of machinery occupies now, in the solutions of our equations, a position similar to that of the wage rate, P_n, in 4a. If by any chance — and this is frequently the real reason for wanting to disregard these particular elements of the system — the input coefficients describing the amounts of equipment required by various industries for purposes of replacement are unknown, a relationship of the type described by system 2a can still be established:

$$(2b) \quad P_i = \overline{A}_{1i}\overline{R}_1 + \overline{A}_{3i}\overline{R}_3 + \cdots + \overline{A}_{ii}\overline{R}_i + \cdots + \overline{A}_{mi}\overline{R}_m$$
$$(i = 1, 3, 4, \cdots, m)$$

Here the replacement expenditures on machinery $a_{12}P_1$, $a_{32}P_3$, $\cdots$, $a_{m2}P_m$ are considered to be a part of the redefined values added $\overline{R}_1$, $\overline{R}_3$, $\cdots$, $\overline{R}_m$ of the respective industries:

$$(3b) \quad \overline{R}_i = a_{i2}P_2 + a_{in}P_n + \pi_i \qquad\qquad (i = 1, 3, 4, \cdots, m)$$

The price of machinery, as such, P_2 is eliminated from the set of variables; so is R_2, the value added in the machinery industry. At the same time, the equation describing the cost-price relationship within the machinery industry — the equation which would have contained R_2 — is left out of consideration. Thus system 3b includes m-1 equations and $2m$-2 variables, of which m-1 are prices and m-1 the redefined values added.

The new short-circuited theoretical description of our economic system takes, as compared with the complete description 2a, a greater number of elements for granted. Thus it is able to explain a smaller number of dependent variables. At the same time, it offers the practical advantage of requiring for purposes of actual computations a smaller amount of empirical information than the more comprehensive system 2a.

Once a set of price changes has been computed, it can also be expressed in terms of an index number. Let, for example, ΔP_1, ΔP_2, $\cdots$, ΔP_m be a particular set of price changes computed on the assumption of a general 10 per cent wage rise. If P_1^0, P_2^0, $\cdots$, P_m^0 represent the prices of the base period and a_{n1}, a_{n2}, $\cdots$, a_{nm} the fractions of the average consumer's dollar spent during this base period on commodity 1, commodity 2, and so on — then the weighted average

$$(5) \qquad \frac{\Delta P_1}{P_1^0}\, a_{n1} + \frac{\Delta P_2}{P_2^0}\, a_{n2} + \cdots + \frac{\Delta P_m}{P_m^0}\, a_{nm}$$

will give the price index describing the corresponding change in the average cost of living.

2. NUMERICAL MEASURES OF THESE RELATIONSHIPS

The numerical measures of quantitative interdependence between prices, wages and profits shown in the tables and

TABLE 22.—OUTPUT PRODUCED, INCOME DERIVED AND SELECTED EXPENDITURE ITEMS OF AMERICAN INDUSTRIES FOR THE YEAR 1939

Unit: One Million Dollars

INDUSTRY	Total value of product 1	Wages and salaries 2	Non-wage incomes 3	Total income = cols.2+3 4	Expenditures on capital goods 5	Addition to stocks and inventories 6	Taxes 7	Imports 8	Total "value added" = cols. 4+5+6+7+8 9
1. Agriculture and fishing	10,121	1,102	3,927	5,029	954	0	512	337	6,832
2. Food processing	13,282	1,526	653	2,179	154	24	1,583	824	4,764
3. Ferrous metals	2,622	756	127	883	71	29	108	22	1,113
4. Motor vehicles, industrial and heating equipment	4,975	1,575	553	2,128	126	7	302	10	2,573
5. Metal fabricating	6,970	2,395	439	2,834	139	36	350	18	3,377
6. Nonferrous metals and products	1,616	418	198	616	19	48	95	331	1,109
7. Stone, clay and glass products	2,083	563	167	730	34	17	74	63	918
8. Fuel and power	10,988	2,596	1,175	3,771	1,058	26	1,766	72	6,693
9. Chemicals (and munitions)	3,434	647	401	1,048	44	33	185	161	1,471
10. Lumber, paper, printing, publishing	6,411	2,218	396	2,614	140	13	233	259	3,259
11. Textiles and leather	7,631	2,329	318	2,647	134	33	177	381	3,372
12. Rubber	892	,229	53	282	18	0	59	196	555
13. All other manufacturing	1,671	633	153	786	14	2	65	61	928
14. Construction	10,089	3,783	353	4,136	268	0	90	0	4,494
15. Transportation	7,477	3,398	1,219	4,617	1,102	0	854	284	6,857
16. Trade and restaurants	20,723	7,239	3,153	10,392	372	0	1,014	0	11,778
18. Business and consumer services	18,525	3,948	6,668	10,616	1,148	0	2,122	0	13,886
21. All other goods and services	22,192	1,579	871	2,450	2,026	0	1,166	92	5,734

TABLE 23.—PRICE CHANGES RESULTING FROM ASSUMED 10 PER CENT INCREASES IN WAGE RATES AND NON-WAGE INCOMES, COMPUTED ON THE BASIS OF STRUCTURAL RELATIONSHIPS PREVAILING IN THE AMERICAN ECONOMY OF THE YEAR 1939

Unit: One Per Cent

COMMODITIES AND SERVICES PRODUCED BY:	Price change resulting from a 10% wage rise in all industries 1	Price change resulting from a 10% wage rise in the industry producing the commodity 2	Price change resulting from a 10% rise non-wage income in all industries 3	Price change resulting from a 10% rise in the non-wage income in the industry producing the commodity 4	Price change resulting from a 10% rise in agricultural wage and non-wage income 5
1. Agriculture and fishing	2.55	1.12	4.74	3.98	5.10
2. Food processing	3.23	1.18	2.80	0.51	1.88
3. Ferrous metals	4.98	2.92	1.45	0.49	.04
4. Motor vehicles, industrial and heating equipment	5.56	3.21	2.06	1.13	.05
5. Metal fabricating	5.54	3.53	1.56	0.65	.05
6. Nonferrous metals and products	3.87	2.60	1.81	1.23	.03
7. Stone, clay, glass products	4.98	2.72	1.84	0.81	.05
8. Fuel and power	4.28	2.47	1.88	1.12	.03
9. Chemicals (and munitions)	4.14	1.92	2.50	1.19	.31
10. Lumber, paper, printing, publishing	5.20	3.53	1.56	0.63	.22
11. Textiles and leather	4.91	3.08	1.72	0.42	.56
12. Rubber	4.21	2.58	1.45	0.60	.08
13. All other manufacturing	5.41	3.81	1.75	0.92	.09
14. Construction	6.44	3.75	1.41	0.35	.15
15. Transportation	5.21	4.67	1.92	1.68	.01
16. Trade and restaurants	4.95	3.61	2.50	1.57	.24
18. Business and consumer services	3.23	2.19	4.08	3.70	.04
21. All other goods and services	3.19	0.82	1.66	0.45	.13

graphs below are computed on the bases of technical relationships characteristic of the American economic system of the last normal prewar year, 1939. The technical input coefficients used in these calculations are derived from a large input-output chart showing the flow of commodities and services between all branches of production, transportation, distribution and consumption. The chart itself has been reproduced in a previous article.[3]

In setting up the basic equations all the expenditures on durable equipment, all purchases for purposes of inventory accumulation, as well as tax payments, were treated as part of the values added of the respective industries, that is the *indirect* price effects operating through induced changes in these particular cost items have been neglected. For more or less accidental reasons of computational convenience, payments for imported commodities and services have been treated in a similar way. The loose connection which exists between the import and export prices could be used to rationalize this procedure; furthermore, foreign trade plays a relatively minor part in the American economy, so that a different theoretical treatment of export and import prices would introduce a hardly noticeable change in the numerical results of the following computation.

Table 22 shows in column 1 the value of output of the separate goods and services. As stated above, the products sold and consumed within the same industry are excluded from these totals. The other columns show the composition of values added in various industries, as used in our computations.

i. Effect of Changes in Wage Rates

The final results of the quantitative analysis are presented in Table 23. Column 1 shows by how many per cent the price of each kind of goods and services would have increased (or fallen) if the wage rates *in all industries* were raised (or reduced) by 10 per cent — while non-wage incomes as well as

---

[3] "Exports, Imports, Domestic Output and Employment," Part IV, B. A detailed explanation of the individual classifications used in the construction of all our tables is contained in the appendix to that article. The following minor changes in this classification have been made, however, for the purposes of the present computation: Munitions are included in Chemicals and not in Metal Fabricating; Restaurants are taken from Unallocated, and classed with Trade.

all the other components of the values added in all the industries had remained the same as before. Each figure entered in the next column shows the (smaller) price changes which would result, were the wage rates increased by 10 per cent *only in the industry immediately engaged in producing* the particular commodity; the wage in all other industries remaining the same as before. These figures show, in other words, what might be called the *direct* effects of the wage rise in one particular industry on the price of its own output. The differences between these figures and the corresponding entries in column 1 measure the *indirect* effects, on the price of the products of the industry concerned, of a 10 per cent wage rise in all the other industries. The indirect effects are those transmitted through increased costs of materials and supplies purchased from other industries.

ii. Effect of Changes in Profits

Columns 3 and 4 in Table 23 show the total and the direct effects of a hypothetical 10 per cent increase in profits, interest and other types of non-wage income, computed on the assumption that wages as well as the other four components of the values added in all the industries remain constant. The differences between these two parallel sets of figures obviously measure the indirect dependence of the unit cost of production of each industry upon profits and other non-wage incomes included in the prices of output of all the other industries. Figures 1 and 2 facilitate comparison of the different kinds of price effects presented in Table 23.

Lack of space makes it impracticable to tabulate the magnitudes of all the partial relationships between the price of every commodity, on the one hand, and the wage and non-wage incomes earned in each one of many industries, on the other. As a practically important example of this type of dependence, the computed price effects of a 10 per cent increase in total (wage and non-wage) income derived by Agriculture per unit of its output are listed in column 5 of Table 23, and also represented graphically in Figure 3. In this connection it should be observed that the distinction between the wage and the non-wage income in Agriculture does not coincide with the division between labor and non-labor income as it does in most other industries.

iii. Price Changes

The last right-hand bar in each of the three graphs represents the average of the separate price changes shown in the same diagram. With all separate price changes weighted in proportion to the fractions of the consumer's dollar spent in the year 1939 on each kind of commodity, one of these averages shows that a 10 per cent increase in the wages paid by all industries per unit of their respective products would raise the cost of living by 3.7 per cent, the other indicates that a proportionally similar increase in non-wage earnings would reduce the purchasing power of the consumer's dollar by 2.6 per cent, and the last one means that a 10 per cent increase in all agricultural incomes derived per unit of farm products would have added to the cost of living 0.7 per cent.

Since, as has been pointed out above, the distinction between wage and non-wage income in Agriculture has a very special meaning, the first two averages have also been computed with exclusion of products of Agriculture and of the Food Processing industries. The non-agricultural component of the cost-of-living index (taken separately) indicates a 3.8 per cent rise in consequence of a 10 per cent wage increase, and 2.4 per cent are added to it as a result of a general 10 per cent increase in all non-wage incomes. As should be expected, the exclusion of agricultural prices makes the cost-of-living index more sensitive to wage changes and less dependent upon variations in non-wage incomes.[4]

If wage and non-wage incomes constituted the only components of all the values added, as used in these price computations, a simultaneous and proportionally equal increase in both types of earnings would naturally raise, under our assumption,

[4] In computation of the changes in the costs of living, all consumers' expenses, including those which like the tax burden are assumed to be constant per unit of output, are included in the respective averages. If only those consumers' expenses were taken into consideration which are allowed according to our assumptions to change, the computed increases in the cost of living would obviously be larger: 4.1 per cent for the result of a 10 per cent increase in wages and 2.9 per cent for the corresponding increase in the non-wage income. A 10 per cent rise in agricultural income would increase the variable part of the cost of living by 0.72 per cent, which can be compared with the 0.65 per cent increase in the total index (in the text the latter figure has been rounded out to 0.7 per cent). Applying the same argument to the non-agricultural component of the cost-of-living index, i.e. excluding from it the tax payments and other such items, we raise the 3.8 per cent to 4.4 per cent and the 2.4 per cent to 2.8 per cent.

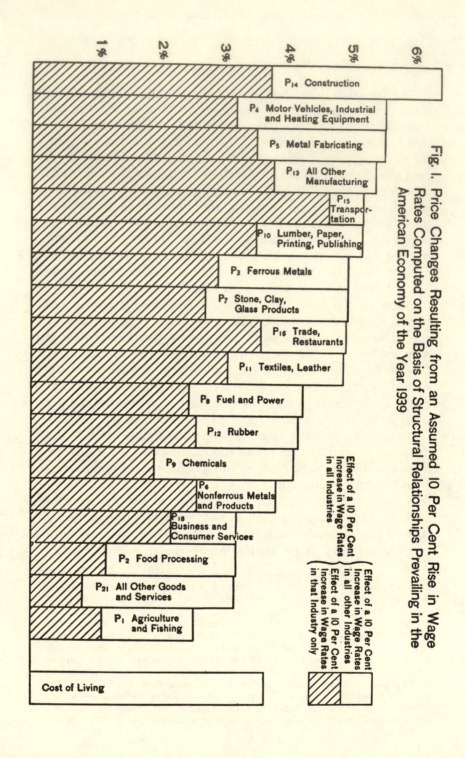

Fig. 1. Price Changes Resulting from an Assumed 10 Per Cent Rise in Wage Rates Computed on the Basis of Structural Relationships Prevailing in the American Economy of the Year 1939

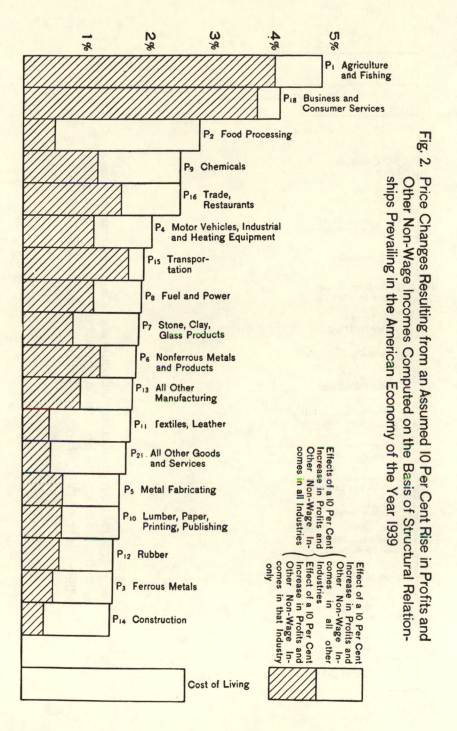

Fig. 2. Price Changes Resulting from an Assumed 10 Per Cent Rise in Profits and Other Non-Wage Incomes Computed on the Basis of Structural Relationships Prevailing in the American Economy of the Year 1939

P₁ Agriculture and Fishing

P₁₈ Business and Consumer Services

P₂ Food Processing

P₉ Chemicals

P₁₆ Trade, Restaurants

P₄ Motor Vehicles, Industrial and Heating Equipment

P₁₅ Transportation

P₈ Fuel and Power

P₇ Stone, Clay, Glass Products

P₆ Nonferrous Metals and Products

P₁₃ All Other Manufacturing

P₁₁ Textiles, Leather

P₂₁ All Other Goods and Services

P₅ Metal Fabricating

P₁₀ Lumber, Paper, Printing, Publishing

P₁₂ Rubber

P₃ Ferrous Metals

P₁₄ Construction

Cost of Living

Effects of a 10 Per Cent Increase in Profits and Other Non-Wage Incomes in all Industries

Effect of a 10 Per Cent Increase in Profits and Other Non-Wage Incomes in all other Industries
Effect of a 10 Per Cent Increase in Profits and Other Non-Wage Incomes in that Industry only

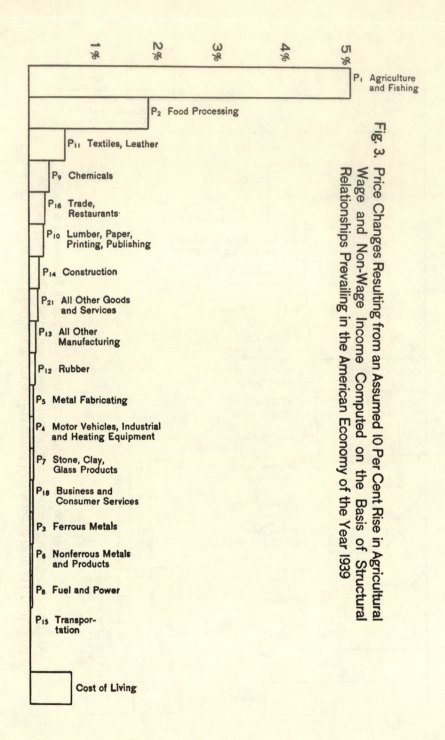

Fig. 3. Price Changes Resulting from an Assumed 10 Per Cent Rise in Agricultural Wage and Non-Wage Income Computed on the Basis of Structural Relationships Prevailing in the American Economy of the Year 1939

the costs of living in the same ratio. The assumed constancy of the depreciation costs, of the tax burden, as well as all the other non-income elements of the values added, is responsible for the fact that the assumed increases of wage and of non-wage incomes add in their combined effect 6.3, rather than 10 per cent, to the average costs of living.

3. CONSTANCY OF TECHNICAL COEFFICIENTS

The assumption of fixed technical coefficients, which constitutes the basis of the foregoing empirical analysis, can be questioned from the point of view of general theory of production. Insofar as the proportions in which the separate factors can be combined within the same production function (i.e. at any given state of engineering information) are variable, these proportions will most probably vary with every change in their relative prices. This theoretical proposition so clearly stated by Pareto in his criticism of Walrasian fixed coefficients of production is beyond dispute. It is, however, not the fundamental validity of the principle of substitution but its quantitative significance which is important from the point of view of empirical analysis. The smaller the variation in production coefficients induced by any given range of changes in factor prices, the smaller obviously will be the empirical error introduced in our computations by the assumption of invariable input ratios. Lack of detailed statistical data covering sufficiently wide sectors of the national economy makes it impossible to determine the actual magnitude of errors introduced in our quantitative findings. An indirect test presented elsewhere [5] seems to indicate that, within the range of price changes which actually have taken place between 1929 and 1939, these errors lie within relatively narrow limits. So far as the direction of these errors is concerned, on general theoretical grounds one can state that neglecting the principle of substitution we arrived at computed price changes somewhat in excess of those which actually would have resulted from the assumed income variations.

For purposes of prognostication the possibility of large spontaneous changes in the magnitude of technical input coefficients would, of course, be as damaging as any secondary change of comparable magnitude induced through price variations. Here again the indirect test referred to above seems to justify ex-

[5] See A and B in Part IV.

pectation of a considerable degree of stability in the general pattern of price relationships. The results of a more detailed statistical investigation into the nature of technological changes since 1919 will be presently available. Without conclusive factual evidence, the reader's judgment on this controversial problem is certainly as good as the author's, and for obvious reasons it might even be less prejudiced.

D. Recent Developments in the Study of Inter-industrial Relationships

1. APPLICATION OF GENERAL EQUILIBRIUM THEORY TO EMPIRICAL ANALYSIS OF THE ECONOMY

The only excuse that I can give for speaking on the subject of the recent developments of input-output techniques is that this title is not of my own making. I realize perfectly well that before embarking upon the elaboration of any of its finer points I must give you an account of the general outlines of the method and describe its conceptual background. These outlines are very simple — all too simple indeed in the eyes of some of the more skeptical critics.

We are dealing here essentially with attempted application of the economic theory of general equilibrium to empirical quantitative analysis of the concrete national economy. The economy is visualized as a combination of a large number of interdependent activities; that is, of various branches of production, distribution, transportation, consumption, etc. Each one of these activities involves absorption of commodities and services originating in some other branches of the economy, on the one hand, and production of commodities and services which in their turn are transferred to and absorbed in its other sectors, on the other. The commodity and service flows (transfers) taking place between the separate branches of the economy within some specified period of time, say a year, can be conveniently described by a rectangular input-output table. The main body of the table contains as many rows and columns as there are separate sections of the economy, and every row and the corresponding column are labeled accordingly. The allocation of the total output of any one industry among all the others is shown by the series of figures entered along its particular output row. The distribution of all the inputs absorbed by any one industry by origin is at the same time represented by the sequence of figures entered in the appropriate input column. Since everybody's output constitutes somebody's input, the figure entered, say, in the intersection of the "Lumber and Timber" row and the "Cotton Yarn and Cloth" column, shows the amount of lumber and timber products absorbed by the Cotton Yarn and Cloth industry. ("Double entry" bookkeeping!) The figures along any particular distribution row added together will naturally give the total output of the corresponding industry.

All entries in the input-output table must in this context be considered as representing physical quantities measured in terms of strictly physical units, a different one for each ·type of commodity and service. That is why one can add them row by row to get the corresponding total outputs of the separate industries while it makes no sense to combine them column by column, since such an operation would involve adding yards of cotton goods with, say, tons of steel and man-hours of labor. Actually the contrast between the two cases of addition is somewhat less sharp than it appears to be from the foregoing argument. Depending upon the degree of differentiation achieved by the underlying industrial classification, even the entries along any one row are not entirely homogeneous and have to be treated as indices of physical quantities rather than purely physical quantities themselves.

i. The Input-Output Technique versus Partial Equilibrium Analysis

Having given an empirical description of the system of interindustrial relationships, we can turn now to the theoretical problem of its explanation. To explain means in this case, as in any other, to reduce to a set of, in some sense, more fundamental relationships. Following the traditional outlines of the general equilibrium theory, these fundamental relationships can be conveniently subdivided into two sets. The first describes the balance — the external relationships — between all the various sectors of the national economy in terms of the outputs (supply) of and the inputs (demand) for each and every kind of goods and services. These supply-and-demand equations are simple in form and noncontroversial in content.

The second set of relationships reflects what one might call the internal structure of each individual sector of the economy. By structure I mean the interdependence between the quantities of the inputs absorbed and the amounts of the product or products turned out in a given process. The relationships of that second type are anything but simple.

The partial equilibrium theories explaining the behavior of a firm on the one hand and the consumer's behavior on the other are essentially engaged in elucidation of this type of structural relationships. So are also the numerous empirical studies of industrial cost and supply curves as well as various statistical investigations of consumer demand and savings schedules. One almost suspects that whoever coined the definition of a specialist as one who finds out more and more about less and less had in mind the development of these particular fields of empirical economic analysis during the last two decades.

The input-output analysis represents an attempt to straighten out our line of advance by bringing up the other wing — the study of interindustrial relationships. The typical partial equilibrium analysis concerned with the study of the operation of one particular sector of the economy, say a single industry or even an individual enterprise, leans heavily on the simplifying *ceteris paribus* assumption, according to which the external setting of that particular unit in its relationships to the rest of the economy are considered as given. The input-output analysis being, on the contrary, a study of the mutual interdependence of the different sections of the economy focuses its attention precisely on these external relationships. Insofar as — and this mainly for lack of sufficient empirical information — some simplifying assumptions have to be made, they should better be made in regard to the internal cost-output structure of the individual industries. In particular the controversial assumption of constant input ratios (fixed "production coefficients") enables us to engage in a factual study of interindustrial relationships and to apply to it the powerful tools of the general equilibrium theory without waiting for a complete and definitive solution of all the theoretical and factual aspects of the partial equilibrium analysis.

ii. Derivation of Technical Coefficients

The technical coefficients of all the separate inputs in all the individual industries can be derived directly from the information entered in the input-output table. By dividing all the entries in each input column by the total output of the industry the cost structure of which that particular column represents, we find how much of every particular kind of inputs had been absorbed per unit of the finished output.

This method of deriving the input ratios from total input and output figures is of course not the only one which can be used to determine the quantities of each cost element absorbed in a given industry per unit of its total product. An alternative and more direct way of determining, for example, the amount of coke required to produce a ton of pig iron or the amount of corn feed required per hundredweight of live hogs is that of asking the ironmaster in the first and a specialist in animal husbandry in the second case. As a matter of fact one can easily visualize the possibility of assembling a complete set of input coefficients describing the structural characteristics of all branches of the national economy entirely on the basis of such direct information without recourse to any actual statistical input or output figures. Such a complete table of technical coefficients combined with the corresponding set of theoretical balance equations would in principle enable us to reconstruct all the actual input-output figures without recourse to any additional factual information. This statement, however, must be supplemented by the following qualifying observation. So long as the structural characteristics of the system are described in terms of various input-output ratios, the actual input and output quantities can be reconstructed also only in relative terms; we could obtain, so to say, only a scale model of the real system without being able to say anything about the absolute magnitudes involved.

iii. The National Economy as an Open System

Such considerations, however, become important only if one makes an attempt to reconstruct the economic system in its entirety. For many purposes, such, for example, as the evaluation of the quantitative implications of alternative policies in respect to allocation of primary resources or, say, various patterns of public works or governmental purchases, it is necessary to treat the national economy as an open rather than as a closed system. A closed system becomes open as soon as one disregards (that is, considers as being pliable at will or even entirely unknown) one or more of the basic structural relationships of which it has been made. Thus reduced, the number of available equations becomes insufficient to determine uniquely the magnitude of all the unknown variables. That means that an analytical economist is free to prescribe arbitrary magnitudes to some of these variables and then determine the corresponding magnitude of all the other variables on the basis of the still available equations. Translated in the pragmatic language of active policy making, this says that in an open system it is possible to "fix" a certain number of variables by deliberate choice while the remaining will fall in line in accordance with the existing necessities of the still inviolate structural relationships. The general logic of this procedure is essentially identical with that followed in somewhat less articulate form in different models of Keynesian multiplier analysis.

All the practical applications of the input-output technique as developed in the course of the last five years followed precisely this open pattern. One omits from the theoretically complete set of structural coefficients some of those which connect, for example, the consumers' and governmental purchases with the other parts of the system. Then one fixes the actual magnitude of these particular kinds of inputs by prescribing a specific "bill of goods" constituting what in this context might be called the final demand; and then one determines through theoretical computations — which amount to the solution of a large system of simultaneous linear equations — the structurally necessary magnitudes of all the remaining inputs and outputs.

Cutting a piece out of a closed band results in appearance of two loose ends. So does the cutting of a closed general equilibrium system. The "final bill of goods" is the loose end which adjoins the cut out stretch on the demand side. The labor inputs and the inputs of all the other services produced by the household, government, and other sectors of the economy which were eliminated mark the other end or rather the beginning of the new open economy. They must be treated now as original, primary inputs. In a closed system, for example, the level of the labor supply would have been directly connected with the level of real income; that is, the quantities of consumers' goods absorbed by the households. Now such direct connection between the two is disregarded. But the numerical computation described above will give us the total amounts of labor and other primary inputs directly and indirectly required to produce commodities and services included in the final bill of goods.

The actual volume of numerical operations involved in such

a computation is very large compared with that to which we were hitherto accustomed in economic and statistical studies, or even in the natural sciences. It can be said, however, that with the spectacular advance in the field of large-scale computers, the numerical solution of such sets of equations represents the least bothersome of the practical and theoretical problems involved in the empirical application of the general equilibrium theory.

An analogous approach can be used also in the study of the price system. Consider an economy in which the profit earned in each industry per unit of its output and all wage rates were arbitrarily fixed. It is clear that only one particular set of prices could simultaneously balance the revenue and outlay accounts of all individual industries. The actual numerical magnitude of each price will depend upon the structural characteristics; that is, the technical coefficients, of all the industries. In the same way as it is possible to compute the direct and indirect effects of a given change in the final demand for one particular commodity upon the total outputs of all the sectors of the economy, one can also determine the effect which an increase or decrease in any given profit or wage rate would have on the prices of all the goods and services. In short, the input-output structure of an open system defines a unique relationship between (a) the set of all prices, (b) the set of all wage rates, and (c) the set of all unit profit rates. Given any two of these, the third can be computed indirectly.

2. PROBLEMS OF AGGREGATION

It would be hardly an exaggeration to say that up to now the practical difficulties of efficient utilization and interpretation of large amounts of detailed quantitative information constituted one of the principal obstacles in the path of the development of empirical general equilibrium analysis. The only possible way of overcoming the resulting impasse seemed to point toward the detour via aggregative analysis — a very unsatisfactory detour indeed. Many of those who followed it have bogged down in the morass of index numbers difficulties. Others ended up in the trackless field of oversimplified economic models, while those who succeeded in the end in regaining the original thoroughfare found that the double transfer from particulars to aggregates and then back from the aggregates to the particulars all but destroyed the empirical significance of their final factual conclusions. The input-output technique, on the other hand, enables us to study the national economy as a whole directly in terms of its separate components; that is, taking account of the peculiar characteristics of its individual sectors.

Having thus sharpened the issue, I must now take off its brittle edge. As already mentioned before, the practical choice is not between aggregation and non-aggregation but rather between a higher and lower degree of aggregation. The immediate factual observations are always particular, not general, although in putting them down on paper we often are already consciously, and more often unconsciously, introducing a certain amount of implicit aggregation. The final results of the analysis, insofar as it is at all operational, that is comparable with the observable course of events, must again be expressed in or at least translatable into particular statements about particular industries, households, etc. Aggregation represents essentially an intermediate step. As such it must be judged on the basis of purely operational criteria. As the following observations will show, the question of aggregation represents essentially a special aspect of the more general problem of the classification of industries and of relevant distinction between different sectors of the national economy in general.

For argument's sake, let us visualize a very simple (!) economic system consisting of households and of one hundred closely delineated and thus sharply distinguishable industries. Let us furthermore assume that the internal structure of each one of these one hundred individual industries can be accurately described in terms of a set of (at most) one hundred constant technical input coefficients and finally that the numerical magnitudes of all these coefficients are actually known and available in the form of a 100 × 100 table. Having this information, let us proceed now to determine the effect of an increased *final* demand for the products of, say, the Automobile industry upon the *total* output of the Paper industry. Following the previously described procedure, we form a system of one hundred linear equations and solve it for the total output of the Paper industry in terms of the final demand for automobiles. It hardly needs to be explained that the numerical results of this computation will depend not only upon the technical structure of the two industries immediately involved but also upon the magnitudes of the input coefficients of each one of the other ninety-eight industries.

Under the given assumptions the answer thus obtained will obviously be entirely correct. That is, if after having finished theoretical computations we had performed the difficult but still possible controlled experiment of increasing the final demand for automobiles and observed what happens to the paper output, the latter will have changed exactly by the amount predicted by the previous theoretical computation.

What would we do, however, if our computers refused (as they would have a very good reason to if not equipped with large-scale calculators) to solve any system of more than fifty linear equations? The number of individual industries would have to be reduced in this case by a process of reclassification which in this particular instance would actually mean also partial consolidation. The definition, i.e., the identity, of the Automobile and Paper industries immediately involved in the formulation of our original problem and of the final answer could of course be left unchanged. But the remaining ninety-eight of the original industries would have then to be combined in forty-eight groups some of which at least would now contain two or more of the original industries.

A new set of structural coefficients, some of them aggregative, that is, hybrid, will now fit into a smaller 50×50 table, which in its turn can be transformed into a new system of only fifty simultaneous equations. Our computers will now go to work and arrive at a new answer showing the effect of increased final demand for automobiles upon the paper output.

This new result can be compared with the true answer obtained on the basis of undistorted original data (and also checked by subsequent controlled experiment). If the two turn out to be identical, one could rejoice and note down the whole procedure as a case in which labor pressure results in introduction of technological improvement. More probably, however, the new answer will differ by a larger or smaller amount from the correct one.

There are many alternative ways of aggregating the ninety-eight original industries under some forty-eight broader headings. Each reclassification will lead to a different system of fifty simultaneous equations and most likely also to a different solution. By comparing these alternative short-cut answers with the known correct solution of our problem, on the one hand, and with each other, on the other, it is possible to measure the comparative "goodness," i.e., operational efficiency, of alternative aggregative classifications of the ninety-eight basic industries. Considerable theoretical as well as experimental work on the problem of industrial classification is being done now along these lines.

Even this simplified analysis shows that the decision whether some two or more industries and their products should be consolidated and treated in aggregative terms or not cannot be based upon consideration of only their own technical characteristics. The structural properties of all the other sectors of the economy must also be taken in account. Moreover, a system of aggregation which can serve as an acceptable basis for the analysis of the interdependence between the Paper and the Automobile industries might prove to be completely inefficient if one tried to use it in estimating the indirect effects of housing construction upon, say, rubber imports.

The progress of empirical general equilibrium (or if you wish, general disequilibrium) analysis will to a large extent depend upon our ability to eliminate highly aggregative procedures which have dominated this field since the middle thirties; to be more precise, since the emergence of various attempts at the empirical verification and numerical application of different Keynesian models. Hand in hand with the nearly exclusive reliance on global aggregate such as GNP, "total consumption," etc., one notes the widespread use of various methods of indirect statistical inference exemplified by multiple regression (correlation) techniques applied to economic time series. It is easy to understand why aggregation and correlation go together. Direct observation can have only very limited use in discovery and explanation of quantitative interdependence of highly aggregative quantities. The very process of aggregation obscures the sharp outlines of the underlying structural relationships to such an extent that one is naturally forced to give up the simpler methods of direct induction and take recourse to "blind flying" by the complicated but hardly foolproof instruments of indirect statistical inference. Multiple correlation analysis as applied to typical general equilibrium problems at the same time has the tendency to become ineffectual whenever the number of simultaneously considered variables exceeds half a dozen or so. Thus the habitual reliance on such techniques promotes in its turn continued use of highly aggregative models.

The radically different methods of input-output analysis as described above, being much better suited to manipulation of very large sets of simultaneous relationships, make it possible to conduct the empirical analysis of the national economy as a whole in terms of the peculiar structural characteristics of its many individual parts, thus combining the virtues of general equilibrium analysis with the obvious but all-too-often neglected advantages of direct detailed observation.

3. INTRODUCTION OF DYNAMIC ELEMENTS

The conceptual framework of the system of interindustrial relationships as I have presented it to you up to now contained no elements which carried in them any explicit indication, not to say explanation, of necessary change. Most of the original empirical elaboration and application of the input-output method have up to now been essentially static. Comparative statics is really the most appropriate term to be used in this connection. For some time now, theoretical work has been done and factual quantitative information collected which should make it possible to apply the input-output technique also to empirical study of at least some of the more important aspects of economic dynamics.

i. Capital Stock and Capital Coefficients

The static description of interindustrial relationships is formulated entirely in terms of flows of commodities and services. The structural input coefficients are after all nothing but characteristic ratios between certain rates of output and the corresponding rates of input. The bills of goods used in connection with the open general equilibrium systems describe a static final demand in terms of so many tons of steel per year or so many "ton miles of railroad transportation" per year.

The actual economic process — and this is why a separate theory of capital is needed — involves not only flows but also *stocks* of commodities — inventories of raw materials, "goods in process" and finished products, also stocks of machinery and buildings usually identified as fixed capital, and, last but not least, residential dwellings and household stocks of durable consumer goods.

The former tabulation scheme used to summarize the relevant information on the direction and magnitude of interindustrial commodities and service flows can be also used to describe the distribution of all kinds of stocks among the same different sectors of the national economy. The cell which in the original input-output table contained a figure showing, for example, the amount of the products of the Copper industry absorbed in the course of a year by the Electrical Appliances industry will show in the new additional table the stock of copper products held by the Electrical Appliances industry on some given date, say January 1, 1949. Similarly the figures entered along the Machine Tools industry row will indicate amounts, i.e. stocks, of machine tools held on that particular date by each of the tool-using industries.

The previously described set of structural input coefficients can now be supplemented by a parallel set of corresponding stock/output ratios, the underlying theoretical assumption being that technological, in the widest sense of the word, conditions determine the amount of each type of stock which each particular industry must have at its disposal per unit of its output (or, rather, of its rate of output). This of course implies that an increased output would require proportionately larger stocks and that diminished output would lead to a proportionately reduced stock requirement.

Each of the original set of balance equations must be expanded accordingly. If an industry increases its output, its demand for the products of the other sectors of the economy goes up, not only on account of the increased current input requirements governed by the regular technical flow coefficients; it will absorb additional inputs so as to be able to increase its necessary stock holdings in accordance with the previously defined technical stock coefficients. We are facing here an application of the well-known acceleration principle.

ii. Inventories

In the opposite case of diminished output, it is necessary to distinguish between inventory holdings in the narrow sense of the word, on the one hand, and investments of the more fixed kind, on the other. The first can be used up, that is, reduced, through transformation into inputs on current account, which is an automatic reversal of the process by which they have originally been built up. Fixed stocks on the contrary cannot be adjusted downward through the same simple process of absorption on current account. When the stock requirements of an industry go down in proportion to its diminished output, the previously accumulated amounts of fixed equipment, buildings, etc., are not diminished accordingly. Instead, the difference between the technically necessary and the actually available stocks results in the appearance of unused, idle capacity.

In case of a subsequent upturn, the current input requirements of the industry will naturally at once begin to grow in proportion to its increased output. To these will also be added inputs required to replenish — in accordance with the magnitude of their respective stock coefficients — the (previously reduced) inventories of raw materials, goods in process, and finished commodities. The call for addition to its stock of fixed investment, however, will be absent so long as the previously reached (or maybe somewhat depleted) capacity had not yet been fully absorbed.

Inserting the two sets — one containing the current input ratios and the other the corresponding stock coefficients — of structural constants in the expanded balance equations, we obtain a set of linear first order differential equations; that is, equations which contain not only rates of flow of various commodities and services but also the rates of changes of these rates of flow. It is a dyamic system; i.e., if solved, it determines all the rates of outputs and inputs over the whole stretch of time, provided the magnitude of various stocks and outputs at any one point of time is given.

This complete dynamic system can be transformed into an open one by elimination of one or more of the underlying basic equations; those, for example, which reflect the input-output structure of the households, government, and, say, the foreign trade (the "terms of trade"). The remaining part of the system will reflect now only the dynamic characteristics of what roughly can be referred to as the productive sectors of the national economy.

The freely chosen hypothetical bill of goods must in this case also be described in dynamic terms. Instead of asking the static question of what the annual rates of output of all the individual industries would have been if the annual rates of *final* demand for their products were such and such, we must postulate a (possibly changing) pattern of final demand over a period of, say, five or ten years, and then — starting with a given initial distribution of stocks of all kinds — determine the necessary (possibly also changing) pattern of total outputs of individual commodities and services over the same five- or ten-year period. The corresponding picture of increasing and decreasing stocks, investments, disinvestments, and idle capacities would constitute a part of an answer thus obtained.

iii. General Dynamic Solution

The general dynamic solution of the open system described above would enable us to answer also the following more pragmatic kind of question: Given the distribution of all available inventories and capacities at some initial point of time, at what particular constant (or variable) annual rate can the final consumption of various commodities be maintained during, say, the next ten years, if at the end of that period the production capacities of all the individual branches of the economy had to reach such and such specified level? In describing the final position of our economy in terms of the *total outputs* (capacities) rather than specific rates of *final consumption*, I emphasize here the fact that in an open system the reallocation of available total outputs between consumption and additional investment at the end of this ten-year period is not subject to any internal constraint.

Preliminary statistical information on magnitudes of the stock coefficients of the ninety-eight industries of our basic classification have been collected for the year 1939, and experimental work on the actual numerical solution of the corresponding empirical dynamic system will be undertaken shortly.

4. CONSTANT INPUT AND STOCK RATIOS

Now let me turn to the subject which I am sure will occupy, and rightly so, a prominent place in the discussion following the conclusion of my formal presentation — the subject of constant input and stock ratios. To begin with, the question is not whether these ratios are constant or not — they certainly cannot be expected to be constant in the strict sense of the word. The real questions are: How does the actual range of their variations affect the empirical validity of the analytical computations based on the assumption of fixed coefficients; and to what extent and on the basis of what theoretical and empirical procedures can their variability effectively be taken into account?

Considered from the point of view of a particular industry,

a change in the input ratios of its various cost elements can reflect an adjustment — within the same technological horizon — occasioned by a change in the supply conditions of the factors or the demand conditions in the finished product market. It can also be directly caused by change in the available technological possibilities. In case of a discovery of a new process, the change in the observable input ratios represents the result of a deliberate choice between the old and the — previously unknown — new input combinations. One can, however, also cite instances of realignment resulting from an actual deterioration; that is, from a narrowing down of technological possibilities. Think, for example, of soil erosion or exhaustion of mineral resources.

Whether caused by new price conditions or a widening (but not narrowing) of the technological horizon, an introduction of new input ratios, since the old ratios were technically still possible, must necessarily signify increased efficiency. That means that an empirical computation based on the original rather than the new set of input coefficients will in general somewhat overstate the effect of a given change in the final demand upon the demand for various original resources.

After the previous comment on the problem of industrial classification it hardly needs to be explained why any concrete instances of changed input ratios would fall within one or another of the possible theoretical types described above depending upon the precise manner in which the line of definitional distinction between various kinds of economic activities has been drawn in the particular area under consideration. The shift of consumer demand from large to smaller cars (incomes and prices remaining the same as before) must be interpreted as an elemental change in basic tastes, if pleasure driving falls within the broadly defined domain of the household sector of the economy. With introduction of a finer distinction between technical household operations on the one hand and ultimate consumers' demand on the other, the same change in input ratios must be described as factor substitution caused by specific consideration of cost economy.

To measure the over-all effects of a specific structural change which has taken place in one particular sector of the national economy, I have found it interesting to perform "bill of goods" computations based on artificial, "hybrid" systems of input coefficients. Thus we have replaced, for example, the steel column in the complete 1939 set of structural coefficients by the corresponding input ratios for the year 1929 and then computed the total labor requirements of the whole economy from it on the basis of the actual 1939 final demand. These labor requirements naturally turned out to be larger than the actual 1939 employment. The difference between the two reflects the over-all labor-saving resulting from the change which took place in the input structure of the steel industry between the years 1929 and 1939.

One of the new and, from the point of view of its possible application to the study of technological relationships, most promising developments in pure theory of production is the study of maximizing and minimizing choices between discontinuous, discretely defined, alternative sets of linear input ratios. Since a special session of the Econometric Society has been devoted to the subject of "Linear Programming," I will not discuss it here.

5. EMPIRICAL TEST OF CONSTANCY OF INPUT-OUTPUT RATIOS

So much for the theory of variable input ratios, but how about the facts? The empirical evidence available at the present time consists of the tables of interindustrial relationships for the years 1919, 1929, and 1939. The first two, results of single-handed purely exploratory efforts, are very rough indeed, and even the last, although much more comprehensive in its scope, can hardly be considered as representing more than a first approximation to a thorough statistical job that could be done under the present-day conditions. The large size of the "Undistributed" outputs (approximately 25-30 per cent of the totals even in 1939) gives a fair measure of the deficiencies of the empirical data now available for testing purposes. Due to disparity in the basic industrial classification (the 1919 and 1929 figures are much less detailed), the three tables can be made comparable only in terms of thirteen grossly consolidated industrial groups. This implies a degree of aggregation far in excess of that which would be considered desirable for purposes of the following empirical test.

This test has been designed to compare the magnitude of error resulting from a purely mechanical application of the input-output technique, with assumption of constant input coefficients, to "prediction" of unknown *total outputs* of individual industries from a known bill of *final demand* with the error resulting from a similarly mechanical application to the same data of the more conventional methods of prediction currently in use.

The total output of each of the individual industries has been "predicted" for the years 1929 and 1919 by application of the input-output technique on the basis of constant 1939 input coefficients. The actual computation consisted of the following steps:

1. The original 1919, 1929, and 1939 tables were reduced so far as possible to a comparable basis through: (a) consolidation into a 13 × 13 grid; (b) deflation of the 1919 and 1929 figures by specially compiled thirteen separate price indices with a 1939 base.

2. The theoretical system of thirteen linear equations based on the 1939 input coefficients was solved for each of the thirteen total outputs in terms of the final demands "per dollar worth" of each of the thirteen kinds of output.

3. The total 1929 output of each of the thirteen industries was indirectly computed (i.e., predicted) through insertion of the actual 1929 final demand figures into the previously obtained solution of the 1939 equations. The same method was used to predict the 1919 total outputs.

To reproduce the application of conventional statistical methods to the solution of the same problem of predicting the 1919 and 1929 total outputs of each of the thirteen industries from the given 1919 and 1929 final bill of goods on the basis of the 1939 experience, two additional computations have been performed; one is based on the assumption that the 1919 and 1929 total output of each industry bears the same relation to the aggregate final demand of that year as in 1939. This is essentially the prediction of the total output of individual industries on the basis of their relationship to the Gross National Product. The third computation is based on a somewhat different assumption according to which the output of each industry bears a constant ratio not to the aggregate final demand but rather to the final demand for the products of that particular industry.

The comparison of the discrepancy between the actual 1919 and 1929 outputs and the outputs "predicted" for these years from 1939 data on the basis of the three alternative methods is summarized in the table below. It seems to point toward unmistakable superiority of the input-output technique at least in this particular case.

STANDARD ERRORS OF "PREDICTION" OF THIRTEEN INDUSTRY OUTPUTS IN 1919 AND 1929 FROM 1939 DATA

(in millions of dollars)

	1919	1929
Method I*	380	237
Method II†	1363	1744
Method III‡	2021	1539

* Input-Output Method.

† Method based on 1939 proportion of each industry's total output to the Aggregate Bill of Goods.

‡ Method based on 1939 ratio of each industry's total output to that particular industry's contribution to the final Bill of Goods.

Even if the assumption of fixed coefficients were proved to be tolerably acceptable for pragmatic purposes of short-run analysis, there can be no doubt that an intensive and relentless study of structural changes which mark the development of every national economy constitutes an important, maybe the most important, task of empirical research. If such study is to lead to something more than high-sounding generalities, it must be ruthlessly concrete; it must be specialized in detail and diversified in coverage. In analyzing the changing structure of the steel industry, we must get our information from the technical literature, from ironmasters and from rolling mill managers. To study the changing pattern of consumer behavior, we have to develop practical co-operation with psychologists and sociologists.

This call for detailed empirical analysis does not sound new. Gustav Schmoller and his German Historical School filled volumes, shelves, and libraries with their monographs. In more recent times, the essentially similar empiricist school of statistical economists has — using figures instead of words as its method of description — provided us with a very large amount of quantitative information.

Why is it that despite such prodigious accumulation of building materials the edifice which we are supposed to be erecting still seems to be in the stage of preliminary excavations? Some tell us that all we have to do is to haul in some more brick and mortar. Is it not possible that what is needed even more is a workable building procedure? Without having given them any detailed specifications, how can one expect our suppliers to deliver materials which will actually fit together?

APPENDICES

APPENDIX I

SIMPLIFIED EXAMPLE OF A CLOSED ECONOMIC SYSTEM

IN THIS appendix, the application of some of our general formulae is demonstrated by means of a simple algebraic example. For this purpose, it is interesting to analyze the frequently used, or rather abused, model of an economic system consisting of only three sub-divisions:

Industry 1. Households
Industry 2. Consumption Goods Industry
Industry 3. Production Goods Industry

The following technical relations are usually assumed to exist among these three industries: households use only products of the consumption goods industry; the consumption goods industry absorbs part of the households' services and the total output of the production goods industry; the production goods industry absorbs (from the outside) only households' services. The system is stationary, i.e., all investment coefficients — $B_1\beta$, $B_2\beta$, and $B_3\beta$ — equal 1.

Thus the two fundamental determinants are:

$$\begin{vmatrix} -A_1 & a_{12} & 0 \\ a_{21} & -A_2 & a_{23} \\ a_{31} & 0 & -A_3 \end{vmatrix} \equiv \Delta \text{ and } \begin{vmatrix} -A_1 & a_{21} & a_{31} \\ a_{12} & -A_2 & 0 \\ 0 & a_{23} & -A_2 \end{vmatrix} \equiv D$$

The corresponding three sets of fundamental equations are:

(I)
$$-X_1 + x_{21} + x_{31} = 0$$
$$x_{12} - X_2 \qquad\quad = 0$$
$$\qquad\quad x_{23} - X_3 = 0$$

(II)
$$-X_1 P_1 + x_{12}P_2 \qquad\qquad = 0$$
$$x_{21}P_1 - X_2\ P_2 + x_{23}P_3 = 0$$
$$x_{31}P_1 \qquad\qquad - X_3\ P_3 = 0$$

(III)
$$x_{12} = \frac{a_{12}X_1}{A_2}$$

$$x_{21} = \frac{a_{21}X_2}{A_2} \qquad\qquad x_{23} = \frac{a_{23}X_2}{A_2}$$

$$x_{31} = \frac{a_{31}X_3}{A_3}$$

In addition, we have the two identical (see p. 51) consistency conditions:

(IV) $\qquad \Delta = D = -A_1A_2A_3 + a_{12}a_{23}a_{31} + A_3a_{12}a_{21} = 0$

Assuming that physical commodity and service outputs are defined so that each of the initial output values X_1^0, X_2^0, X_3^0 equals 1, and having at the same time $A_1^0 = A_2^0 = A_3^0 = 1$, we find from the preceding equations that

(V) $\qquad\qquad a_{31} + a_{21} = a_{12} = a_{23} = 1$

Substituting successively 1, 2, and 3 for i and k computing the values of the resulting minors from matrices Δ and D, and substituting those in formulae XVII b and XXI b, we arrive at the following results:

Quantity reactions, $\dfrac{dX_{t10}}{dA_k} \cdot \dfrac{1}{X_{t10}}$

i \ k	2	3
1	0	0
2	1	a_{31}
3	0	a_{31}

Price reactions, $\dfrac{dP_{t10}}{dA_k} \cdot \dfrac{1}{P_{t10}}$

i \ k	2	3
1	0	0
2	−1	$-a_{31}$
3	−2	$-a_{31}$

Although only the general type of the hypothetical interindustrial relations has been postulated, and notwithstanding the absence of any separate assumptions concerning the magnitude of different production coefficients, the results obtained are quite definite. As all technical coefficients must naturally be positive, equations v, above, show that $0 < a_{31} < 1$. On the basis of these two tables, two distribution graphs similar to Charts 2 and 3 can be constructed.

The study of this example might facilitate acquaintance with certain formal features of our theoretical system. The oversimplified setup, with its usual distinction between aggregate consumption and production goods industries has, however, hardly any empirical significance. No material meaning whatsoever should be attached to the numerical results obtained.

APPENDIX II

THE fundamental framework of our statistical analysis, as well as the main outlines of its practical application, is developed in Part I. Lack of space precludes the possibility of a complete reproduction of the preliminary calculations, on which Tables 5 and 6 are actually based.

Detailed description of the distribution of agricultural outputs and of the steel works and rolling mills products are given below. The last nine rows of the general tables — covering wages and capital services, undistributed items, and gross and net total outlays — are also analyzed in detail.

No attempt is being made to acquaint the reader with all the details of individual computations or to present the series of alternative estimates which in many instances are used for checking purposes.

A similar description of all the rest of the statistical material is available in mimeographed form and can be obtained on request from the Harvard University Committee on Research in the Social Sciences, Harvard University, Cambridge, Massachusetts.

The primary statistical information relating to 1919 is in general somewhat less complete than that available for 1929. Thus in many instances different sources and different methods of indirect estimate had to be used. For this reason the distribution for each year is described separately. Except in the few specifically mentioned cases the final figures are comparable, however, for both years.

Preliminary Comments

a. Unless otherwise stated, the values of the total outputs of all the separate industries are based on the Census of Manufactures.

b. Whenever total production or total consumption data are used as a basis of distribution, adjustments for exports or imports are carried through. These adjustments are not commented upon separately in each particular instance.

c. References to production indicate that the particular items are based on production statistics; references to cost or consumption data show that cost statistics of the industry which uses the particular product have been utilized.

d. Whenever the output of an industry is distributed on the basis of production values, transportation costs (if any) are added separately on the basis of a fixed proportion of the total value of the output. In all the cases where the distribution is based on cost data of the industries which use the particular product, no such adjustment is necessary.

e. Abbreviations: *Mfr.* and *Min.* indicate the Census of Manufactures and the Census of Mines and Quarries, respectively. The abbreviation "n. e. s." stands for "not elsewhere specified." For brevity, the term "transportation (steam railroads)" is usually written "transportation (railroads)."

f. All original calculations are made in thousands of dollars. The rounding off is carried out in such a way as to avoid any discrepancy between the sum totals and their respective parts.

g. The following comments are arranged by distribution rows and within each row for each year according to the order of the items, reading from left to right, in Tables 5 and 6. The italicized main headings refer to the rows of the table, while reference to the items within each row is introduced by the word "*To.*"

1: Agriculture

Agriculture is basically defined as farming, and, in accordance with the Census, includes the entire field of crop production, fruits and vegetables, livestock products, animals for sale or slaughter, forest products cut on farms, and products of nurseries and greenhouses. The value of the total output at farm is taken from the Census of Agriculture, and increased by the amounts of railroad transportation costs of agricultural products. In 1929, however, the Census of Agriculture does not give a value figure for animals for sale or slaughter. The value used by us for these products is an estimate by the Bureau of Agriculture of the value at farm of these products and is from the *Statistical Abstract of the United States, 1932,* p. 602.

1919. *To* Agriculture: determined on the basis of the average percentage of products sold from the farm in 1924–28 (*Farm Value, Gross Income and Cash Income from Farm Products 1924–1929,* Part V, Bureau of Agricultural Economics, United States Department of Agriculture, Washington, October 1930). *To* Flour and Grist Mills: quantity milled (*Mfr.,* at farm prices). *To* Canning and Preserving: estimated on basis of *Mfr.,* 1929. *To* Bread and Bakery Products: milk, eggs, nuts, and fruits (estimated). *To* Sugar, Glucose, and Starch: production and cost data, Census of Agriculture and *Mfr. To* Liquors and Beverages: data taken from Senate Hearings (S. 436 and S. 2473, 72d Congress, 1st session). *To* Tobacco Manufactures: U. S. production. *To* Slaughter and Meat Packing: data from Census of Agriculture, *Mfr.,* and Department of Agriculture. *To* Butter, Cheese, etc.: data from *Mfr. To* Other Food Products: dairy products, fruits, and nuts (estimated on the basis of *Mfr.,* 1923–29). *To* Chemicals: cottonseed, flaxseed, etc. (Production [Census of Agriculture], sold at farm

[See Agriculture: *To* Agriculture, above]). *To* Paper and Wood Pulp: straw (costs, *Mfr.*). *To* Yarn and Cloth: quantities consumed (*Mfr.*) at farm prices. *To* Leather, Tanning: estimated; difference between total consumption of hides and skins and supply from meat packing and imports. *To* Consumption: edible products not distributed to other industries plus part of nursery and greenhouse products. *To* Undistributed: includes increase in cotton, wheat, and corn stocks, undistributed part of forest products.

1929. To Agriculture: total production of firewood and fenceposts, mixed grains, miscellaneous seeds, and feed crops (production data, Census of Agriculture); all corn not elsewhere distributed (see below); 90 per cent of the farm value of horses and mules (*Statistical Abstract of the United States, 1932*, p. 602); farm value of animals for slaughter less cash income from them (includes cattle and calves, hogs, sheep, and lambs; *Statistical Abstract of the United States, 1932*, p. 602); butter made on farms less butter sold (*Abstract of the Census of 1930*, p. 626; no other dairy products are distributed to Agriculture, since butter is the only product retained on the farm for which total value of products is given; all other products are given as for sale); eggs produced less eggs sold, and chickens raised less chickens sold (*Abstract of the Census of 1930*, p. 626); geese, ducks, and turkeys (the proportion of farm consumption of chickens to total production of chickens is used for distributing these products to Agriculture); honey and peanuts (farm value less cash income; *Statistical Abstract of the United States, 1932*, p. 602); the other products (cottonseed, wheat, oats, barley, rye, miscellaneous cereals, miscellaneous grains, crops for sugar, other nuts, flaxseed, and fruits and vegetables) are distributed on the basis of the percentage of products sold from the farm in 1929 (the ratio of farm value less cash income to farm value). These data are from the *Yearbook of Agriculture, 1931*, p. 978. In addition, the value of farm gardens is distributed to Agriculture. *To* Flour and Grist Mill Products: corn, wheat, oats, barley, rye, buckwheat, and mixed grains ground or milled in the flour and other grain-mill products industry (quantity consumed, *Mfr.*, p. 141, at farm prices plus transport. In the case of wheat, the amount consumed as given in *Mfr.* is reduced by a large amount because of substantial imports); corn and oats for the cereal preparations industry (quantity consumed estimated from the weight of finished breakfast foods made from corn and oats, *Mfr.*, p. 99; this estimated quantity is multiplied by farm prices and augmented by transport costs); rough rice for rice cleaning and polishing industry (total less share attributed to Agriculture). *To* Canning and Preserving: corn and fruits and vegetables (cost data, *Mfr.*, p. 95, stepped up). *To* Bread and Bakery Products: fluid milk (cost data, *Mfr.*, p. 60, stepped up); eggs (cost data, *Mfr.*, pp. 59 and 158; this adjusted total is reduced to allow for the consumption of processed eggs, which are included in the Census cost data). *To* Sugar, Glucose, and Starch: sugar beets and sugar cane for sugar (production data from the Census of Agriculture, with consumption data in *Mfr.*, pp. 208 and 211). *To* Liquors and Beverages: hops (amount consumed, *Mfr.*, at farm prices); barley (quantity consumed estimated from quantity of barley malt produced, *Mfr.*, p. 171, at farm prices). *To* Tobacco Manufactures: total production from Census of Agriculture, less a small amount to Undistributed (stocks). *To* Slaughtering and Meat Packing: *Mfg.*, p. 183, gives the cost of cattle, calves, sheep and lambs, and hogs consumed by this industry. However, these cost figures include items, such as distribution costs, which cannot be legitimately credited to Agriculture. Therefore, the total cost as given in *Mfr.* is stepped down. For each type of animal, a ratio is computed between its farm price and its Chicago price, and this percentage applied to the *Mfr.* cost data. The price data are from the *Statistical Abstract of the United States, 1932*, p. 613. (For example, the procedure for beef cattle:

$$\frac{\text{Price of beef cattle at farm}}{\text{Price of beef cattle at Chicago}} = \frac{9.20}{13.43} = 68.5\%$$

The costs of cattle to the meat packing industry amount to 937.8 million dollars; 68.5 per cent of this makes 642.4 million dollars, which is the estimated farm cost.) To these estimated farm costs, 2013 million dollars, are added 89 million dollars of Railroad Transport for the above enumerated animals, making a total of 2102 millions; poultry (the Census, *Materials used in Manufactures, 1929*, p. 45, gives a total of 100 million dollars of domestic live poultry consumed in the Food Industries. This total is stepped down to 90 million dollars to allow for distributive, etc., costs. The total cost of materials and containers for the poultry industry as given in *Mfr.* is 106 million dollars).

To Butter, Cheese, etc.: the Census, *Materials used in Manufactures, 1929*, p. 45, gives 911 million dollars, as consumption of domestic dairy products (milk and cream) in the Food Industries. Distributed independently to other industries of this group are 109 millions (see below). The residual of 802 millions is assigned to the Butter, Cheese, etc., industry. This total compares favorably with the cost of materials and containers for this industry given in *Mfr.*, p. 67 (880 millions). *To* Other Food Industries: corn (for corn syrup, etc. The quantity consumed is estimated from the weight of corn products of this industry, *Mfg.*, p. 122; multiplied by farm prices); hops (amount consumed from *Mfr.*, at farm prices); fruits and vegetables (for confectionery and flavoring extracts industries; cost data, *Mfr.*, stepped up to include all industry); sugar cane for syrup (50 per cent of total produced, as a rough estimate); peanuts and other nuts (total produced less share to exports and farm consumption); milk and cream (for chocolate and cocoa, confectionery and ice cream; cost data, *Mfr.*, stepped up to include all industry); eggs (estimated on the basis of value of eggs consumed in the Food Industries as given in Census, *Materials used in Manufactures, 1929*, p. 45; 50 per cent of eggs not distributed in other branches of the Food and Kindred Products Industry are distributed to Other Food Industries). *To* Chemicals: cottonseed and flaxseed (for the cottonseed and linseed oil industries; total produced from Census of Agriculture less farm consumption. The amount of cottonseed distributed to this industry is almost equal to the amount of cottonseed crushed as given in *Mfr.*, p. 711). *To* Lumber and Timber Products: saw logs and veneer logs (production data, Census of Agriculture). *To* Other Wood Products: broomcorn (production data, Census of Agriculture. Compare with Census, *Materials used in Manufactures, 1929*, p. 55). *To* Paper and Wood Pulp: straw (cost data, *Mfr.*, p. 550); pulpwood (production data, Census of Agriculture). *To* Yarn and Cloth: total farm value (plus transport) of lint cotton less value of exports; total farm value of wool and mohair (production data, Census of Agriculture; the quantity consumed in various branches of the textile industry as given in *Mfr.* is approximately equal to the quantity distributed here but the dollar values are much greater owing to intermediate costs). *To* Leather Tanning: hides and skins sold (quantity, Census of Agriculture, IV, 705) at prices estimated from value of uncured hides of each type as given in *Mfr.*). *To* Consumption: edible beans, fruits and vegetables, dairy products, honey, eggs, and poultry not distributed to other industries; maple syrup and sugar (production data, Census of Agriculture); 90 per cent of animals for slaughter not elsewhere distributed (consisting mainly of non-federally inspected slaughter); and 90 per cent of nursery and greenhouse products. *To* Undistributed: all products not elsewhere distributed, consisting mainly of undistributed wheat, oats, barley, rye, miscellaneous cereals and grains, forest products, and animals for slaughter (increase in stocks of crops is included in Undistributed).

13: Steel Works and Rolling Mills

1919. To Agriculture: staples, barbed and woven wire, horseshoes (calculated on basis of *Mfr.*). *To* Iron Mining: This, as well as a number of subsequent items, is calculated on the basis of the statistics of distribution of rolled steel products compiled by the *Iron Age* for 1922 and later years. These distributions show certain relatively stable proportions, on the basis of which a corresponding table for 1919 has been constructed. In the *Iron Age* distribution, all mining industries are treated as a single industry. The final distribution to individual mining industries is made on the basis of the total cost of materials as given in the Census. *To* Blast Furnaces: mill cinder, scale, slag, etc. (cost data, *Mfr.*). *To* Steel Works and Rolling Mills: cost of materials (*Mfr.*). *To* Automobiles: estimates based on the *Iron Age* distribution (see Steel Works and Rolling Mills: *To* Iron Mining). *To* Other Iron and Steel: this item is the result of a detailed analysis of census data. It is the difference between the total outputs of products of the types and qualities used by "Other Iron and Steel" and the amount of these materials distributed to other industries. *To* Non-Ferrous Metal Mining: estimated (see Steel Works and Rolling Mills: *To* Iron Mining). *To* Petroleum and Natural Gas: estimated (see Steel Works and Rolling Mills: *To* Iron and Steel). *To* Coal: estimated (see Steel Works and Rolling Mills: *To* Iron Mining). *To* Rubber: estimate of wire used in tire production. *To* Construction: estimated on basis of *Mfr.* *To* Transportation (Railroads): railway track materials and cars. *To* Undistributed: residual item consisting partly of rolled products and partly of advanced products such as nails, bolts, wire manufactures, etc., made in rolling mills.

1929. To Agriculture: horse and mule shoes and calks, iron and steel barbed wire, poultry netting, woven wire fence, and bale ties (production data, *Mfr.*; this distribution is in addition to the same products made in Other Iron and Steel Industries, below). *To* Iron Mining: miscellaneous products. The distribution of a considerable portion of the products of Steel Works and Rolling Mills is based on the statistics of the distribution of rolled steel products (by consumer and type of product) for 1929, published by the *Iron Age*. In many cases, however, it is necessary to make various adjustments so as to bring the *Iron Age* classification in line with the corresponding census classification of the same products. Furthermore, it is necessary to bring the *Iron Age* classification of consumers into line with our classification of industries.

In the *Iron Age* distribution, all mining industries are treated as a single industry. The final distribution to individual mining industries (Iron Mining, Non-Ferrous Metal Mining, Non-Metal Minerals, and Coal) is made on the basis of expenditures for development by each of these industries in 1929, as given in *Min.*, 1929, p. 45. The *Iron Age* class "Oil, gas, and water companies" is split between Petroleum and Natural Gas and Undistributed (for water). The *Iron Age* class "furniture and stove makers" is split between Other Iron and Steel Industries and Other Wood Products; the total cost of iron and steel to the census industries, stoves, ranges, steam fittings, etc., as given in *Mfr.*, page 998 (adjusted to include all firms in industry) is deducted from the total cost found on the basis of the *Iron Age* distribution; the difference is distributed to Other Wood Products (furniture makers). The *Iron Age* class "miscellaneous" is divided between Other Iron and Steel Industries

(60 per cent) and Undistributed (40 per cent). The remaining *Iron Age* classes fall clearly into Transportation (Steam Railroad), Other Iron and Steel Industries, Construction, and Automobiles. In all cases, the *Iron Age* class "jobbers and warehouses" is divided among the other users in proportion to their consumption. In addition to using the *Iron Age* distribution as a basis, many products are distributed on the basis of production data in *Mfr.* For example, the distribution to Steel Works and Rolling Mills is the result of a detailed analysis of census cost and production data.

In the description of the distribution below, if any industry has received a share on the basis of the *Iron Age* distribution, it is referred to as such without further comment. Any additional distribution is described separately.

To Blast Furnaces: cinder and scale for sale and transfer (*Mfr.*). *To* Steel Works and Rolling Mills: scrap iron and steel, ingots, blooms billets and slabs, sheet and tin-plate bars and scrap bar, hot rolled strips for cold rolling (all of these are classified "for sale and interplant transfer"); direct steel castings and rolled and forged iron and steel products, n. e. s., transferred for consumption in other plants of same company; steel and iron rolls for rolling mills (all of preceding are from production data, *Mfr.*). (Compare this distribution with census comments on duplication in this industry, *Mfr.*, page 950). *To* Other Iron and Steel Industries: forgings, structural shapes, not assembled or fabricated; crucible plate steel and saw plate; armor plate and ordnance; grey-iron, malleable iron, and non-ferrous metal castings, pressed, stamped, and other shapes; rolled or forged, axles and car and locomotive wheels; plain wire; and springs for internal-combustion engines (all from production data, *Mfr.*); direct steel castings (total less share to Steel Works and Rolling Mills, above); skelp, wire rods and bolts, etc. (total less amounts distributed on *Iron Age* basis); cold rolled strip steel and cold-finished steel bars (total less the share distributed to Automobiles on basis of *Iron Age* data); tin plate and terneplate (cost data, *Mfr.*); and a miscellaneous number of semi-fabricated products such as bars, wire rods, plates and sheets, pipes and tubes, etc., which are distributed on the basis of data in the *Iron Age* (see above). *To* Automobiles: auto body sheets for sale and transfer (production data, *Mfr.*); miscellaneous products such as bars, plates and sheets, hooks and bands, etc. (based on the *Iron Age* distribution). *To* Non-Ferrous Metal Mining: products estimated on basis of *Iron Age* distribution (see *To* Iron Mining, above). *To* Non-Metal Minerals: products estimated on basis of *Iron Age* distribution (see *To* Iron Mining, above). *To* Petroleum and Natural Gas: miscellaneous products, mainly pipes and tubes, estimated on basis of *Iron Age* distribution (see *To* Iron Mining, above). *To* Coal: products estimated on basis of *Iron Age* distribution (see

To Iron Mining, above). *To* Other Wood Products: wire springs for furniture (estimated at 50 per cent of production as given in *Mfr.*); miscellaneous products estimated on basis of *Iron Age* distribution (see *To* Iron Mining, above). *To* Industries, n. e. s.: wire springs for furniture (for bedsprings, etc., estimated at 50 per cent of production as given in *Mfr.*). *To* Construction: concrete-reinforcing bars (estimated from production data in *Mfr.* and from *Iron Age* distribution); fabricated structural steel (production data, *Mfr.*); nails, brads, and spikes (estimated at 80 per cent of production as given in *Mfr.*); and a small value of miscellaneous products estimated on basis of *Iron Age* distribution. *To* Transportation (Steam Railroads): rails, and rail joints and fastenings (distributed on basis of *Iron Age* data; most of these products are absorbed by Railroads); switches, frogs and crossings (production data, *Mfr.*); and miscellaneous products estimated on basis of *Iron Age* distribution. (Products used for cars and locomotives are distributed to Other Iron and Steel Products; the share going to Railroads is used for track, buildings and bridges). *To* Consumption: iron and steel fly screening and auto skid chains (production data, *Mfr.*; these products are also made in Other Iron and Steel Industries; the distribution from various producers in this and similar cases is proportional to total value of wire products produced). *To* Undistributed: all products not elsewhere distributed, consisting partly of rolled products and partly of advanced products made in rolling mills.

43a: Wages and Salaries

1919. To Agriculture: total of money wages paid to farm laborers (Census of Agriculture). *To* Manufacturing and Mining Industries (all industries from Flour and Grist Mills to Industries Not Elsewhere Specified, with the exception of Electric Utilities): calculated on the basis of *Mfr.* and *Min. To* Electric Utilities: calculated on the basis of the Census of Electric Utilities. *To* Construction: rough estimate. The percentage relation of wages and salaries and cost of materials to the value of product of the industry in the year 1929 was calculated on the basis of the Census of Construction. These ratios were corrected for the change in wage level and variation in the cost of materials between 1919 and 1929 and then applied to the total value of output in 1919. *To* Transportation (Railroads): total wages and salaries (*Statistics of Railways, 1919*) diminished by the amount of wages and salaries paid out by steam railroad repair shops. (The latter are included in the Other Iron and Steel Industries.) *To* Consumption: estimate; the total of direct services (intangibles) absorbed by households amounted, according to W. H. Lough (*High Level Consumption*, New York, 1935), to 6546 million dollars. It is assumed that the material costs connected with the direct services are negligible and that consequently the total amount is distributed among wages, salaries, and capital and entrepreneurial services. The ratio between the two shares is obtained on the basis of the income distribution within the "Unclassified Industries" as given by W. I. King (*The National Income and Its Purchasing Power*, 1930). *To* Undistributed: includes wages and salaries paid out in banking, mercantile industry, Pullman and express industry, shipping, undistributed unclassified (W. I. King: *The National Income . . .*). The last amount represents the difference between the total wages and salaries paid out in unclassified industries and the amount of wages and salaries assigned to Consumption (see Wages and Salaries: *To* Consumption).

1929. To Agriculture: total cash expenditures on farm labor exclusive of housework (data from *Census of Agriculture*, 1930, IV, 504). *To* Manufacturing and Mining Industries (all industries from Flour and Grist Mills to Industries Not Elsewhere Specified, with the exception of Petroleum and Natural Gas and Electric Utilities. (1) Wages and salaries for the manufacturing industries are totaled from data in the 1929 *Census of Manufactures*, II, 20–33. The Census industries are totaled by groups in accordance with our classification. Salaries include "principal salaried officers of corporations" and "other salaried officers and employees." Wages include "wage earners." (Cf. Census of Manufactures, I, 5, and II, 310 ff.) Omitted from wages and salaries of manufacturing industries in 1929 (but not in 1919) are employees of central-administrative offices. (Cf. *Census of Manufactures*, 1929, II, 33, Footnote 1. Although an aggregate figure is given for 1929, the Census does not apportion it among the various industries, and no attempt is made here to do so.) (2) Since electric-furnace ferroalloys are transferred in the present set-up from the Chemicals to the Blast Furnaces Industry, a corresponding adjustment is made for wages and salaries (estimated from Census data on value of product and wages and salaries in the Chemical Industry). (3) Data for the Iron Mining, the Non-Ferrous Metal Mining, and the Coal Industries are from the *Census of Mines and Quarries, 1929*, pp. 44 and 23. For these industries, salaries of central-administrative-offices employees are included, since they are classified by industries. (4) The Non-Metal Minerals Industry includes both manufacturing and mining industries. Wages and salaries from manufacture were derived as under (1) above; wages and salaries from mining were derived as under (3) above.

To Petroleum and Natural Gas: S. Kuznets, *National Income, 1929–32* (Government Printing Office, Washington, 1934, p. 60, table 46. To this total is added compensation to pipe line employees, I.C.C., *Statistics of Railways*, 1929, p. cxi). *To* Electric Utilities: Salaries and Wages to motor busses were estimated by us from Census data. Salaries and wages (including labor income other than salaries and wages) for electric light and power, street railways, telephone, and telegraph are from Kuznets (p. 65, table 53; p. 94, table 84; p. 105, table 112; p. 105, table 113). *To* Construction: Salaries and wages are from Kuznets, p. 84, table 74 (labor income other than salaries and wages is also included by us). *To* Transportation (Steam Railroads): Salaries and wages are from Kuznets, p. 97, table 90 (labor income other than salaries and wages is also included). This total is diminished by the amount of wages and salaries paid out by steam railroad repair shops (these are included in the Other Iron and Steel Industries).

To Consumption: Direct services (intangibles) absorbed by households were taken from W. H. Lough, *High-Level Consumption*, pp. 236–47. Only those intangibles are selected which fit the present classification. On the assumption that the material costs connected with these direct services are negligible, the total amount is divided between wages and salaries and capital and entrepreneurial services on the basis of free estimates. *To* Undistributed: includes all wages and salaries not distributed otherwise: in particular water transport (Kuznets, p. 94), motor transport (p. 94), air transport (p. 94), railway express (p. 98), the Pullman Company (p. 99), wholesale and retail trade (p. 114), finance (p. 121ff), government (p. 130), service (p. 141), and miscellaneous industries (p. 157). To these are added the undistributed salaries and wages of central-administrative offices in the manufacturing industries (Census of Manufactures, 1929, II, p. 33, footnote 1); and "other labor income" from mines and quarries (Kuznets, p. 58), manufacturing (Kuznets, p. 75), and manufactured gas (Kuznets, p. 66). Deducted from this grand total are Wages and Salaries: *To* Consumption (see Wages and Salaries: *To* Consumption).

43b: Capital and Entrepreneurial Services [1]

1919. To Agriculture: see p. 27. *To* Manufacturing Industries and Mining: calculated on the basis of the corporate income tax data in *Statistics of Income, 1919* (published by the Bureau of Internal Revenue). For each industry, the amount of the net corporate income, earned by "corporations reporting net income" less tax, is augmented by the estimated amount of interest paid. In the *Statistics of Income* for 1919, the industrial classification used in the distribution of interest charges is somewhat less detailed than that which is given in our table. The necessary subdivision is obtained through a very rough estimate: the interest charges within each industrial group are distributed in proportion to the value of product. The results obtained thus for corporate enterprises only are stepped up so as to cover each industry as a whole (see "Gross Total Outlays" for manufacturing, below).

[1] For definition and general discussion see pp. 24 ff.

1929. *To* Agriculture: all undistributed costs with the exception of taxes are considered capital and entrepreneurial services and are shifted to this box from the undistributed box (see above, p. 28). *To* Manufacturing and Mining Industries: calculated on the basis of the corporate income tax data in *Statistics of Income, 1929* (published by the Bureau of Internal Revenue). For each industry, the amount of the net corporate income, earned by "corporations reporting net income," less tax, is augmented by the amount of interest paid by all corporations (including those corporations showing deficits). (Note that net income does not include dividends received from other corporations and tax-exempt interest. These are omitted in order to avoid double counting.) In the *Statistics of Income, 1929,* interest paid is given only by major industrial groups; and although net income figures are available also for smaller subdivisions this classification differs from ours in many cases. Thus, for both net income and interest paid, it is necessary to resort to estimates in order to break down the official statistics to a subdivision corresponding to ours. The main lines of these estimates are given below. The results thus obtained for corporate enterprises only are stepped up so as to cover each industry as a whole (see "Gross Total Outlays" for manufacturing, below).

(1) The *Statistics of Income* major classification "Food products, beverages, and tobacco" is divided among Flour and Grist Mill Products, Canning and Preserving, Bread and Bakery Products, Sugar, Glucose, and Starch, Liquors and Beverages, Tobacco Manufactures, Slaughtering and Meat Packing, Butter, Cheese, etc., Other Food Industries, and Industries Not Elsewhere Specified (a small share from manufactured ice). The total interest paid is divided among our industries in proportion to the value of products (using our classification which is based on the Census of Manufactures). Net income is given for various subdivisions (see *Statistics of Income, 1929,* pp. 288–289), and these are the basis of the following distribution of net income after tax: (*a*) Flour and Grist Mill Products: this consists of "Mill products — Bran, flour, feed, etc." (*Statistics of Income,* serial no. 11) plus an estimated (on basis of value) amount for cereals (included in "Other food products," serial no. 16). (*b*) Canning and Preserving: this consists of "Canned products — Fish, fruit, vegetables, etc. (serial no. 10). (*c*) Bread and Bakery Products: "Bakery and confectionery products" (serial no. 9) is divided between bakery and confectionery products on the basis of value of product. From this an estimated (on basis of value) amount for macaroni is added to the Bread and Bakery Products Industry's share (included in "Other food products," serial no. 16). (*d*) Sugar, Glucose, and Starch: consists of "Sugar-beet, cane, maple and products" (serial no. 13). (*e*) Liquors and Beverages: consists of "Beverages — Soft drinks, cereal beverages, etc." (serial

no. 14). (*f*) Tobacco Manufactures: consists of "Tobacco, cigarettes, cigars, snuff, etc." (serial no. 15). (*g*) Slaughtering and Meat Packing: consists of "Packinghouse products — Fresh meats, ham, lard, etc." (serial no. 12). (*h*) Butter, Cheese, etc., estimated (on basis of value) for "dairy products" (included in "Other food products," serial no. 16). (*i*) Other food products: estimated amount, for confectionery (see Bread and Bakery Products, above) (from value of products) and for miscellaneous food products (included in "Other food products," serial no. 16). (*j*) Industries Not Elsewhere Specified: receives a share for an estimated (on basis of value of product) amount for manufactured ice (included in "Other food products," serial no. 16).

(2) The *Statistics of Income* major classification "Metal products and processes" is divided among Blast Furnaces, Steel Works and Rolling Mills, Other Iron and Steel Industries, Automobiles, Smelting and Refining, Brass, Bronze, and Copper Manufactures, Coke, and Industries Not Elsewhere Specified (a share from "Precious metal products and processes, jewelry, etc."). The total interest paid is subdivided on the basis of value added by manufacture (using our classification which is based on the Census of Manufactures). Interest figures thus computed for Other Iron and Steel Industries is augmented by an estimated amount from Other Iron and Steel Products included in the *Statistics of Income* "Miscellaneous manufacturing" classification (see below). Net income is given for various subdivisions (see *Statistics of Income, 1929*, pp. 290–91), and these are the basis of the following distribution of net income after tax: (*a*) Automobiles: consists of "Motor vehicles, complete or parts" (serial no. 40). (*b*) Industries Not Elsewhere Specified: consists of "Precious metal products and processes; jewelry, etc." (serial no. 50). (*c*) The remaining net income after tax (serial nos. 38–49, excepting 40), plus the net income after tax of "Radios" (serial no. 51), and "Airplanes, etc." (serial no. 53), both of which are included in the *Statistics of Income* "Miscellaneous manufacturing" classification, is divided among our remaining industries partaking of this classification (see above, under 2) on the basis of value added by manufacture.

(3) The *Statistics of Income* major classification "Chemicals and allied substances" is split between Refined Petroleum and Chemicals. Interest paid is divided on the basis of value of product. Net income is given for various subdivisions (*Statistics of Income, 1929*, p. 290): (*a*) Refined Petroleum: consists of "Petroleum and other mineral oil refining" (serial no. 33). (*b*) Chemicals: consists of all other net income after tax of this major classification (serial nos. 34–36).

(4) The *Statistics of Income* major classification "Lumber and timber products" is divided between Lumber and Timber Products and Other Wood Products. Both interest paid and net income after

tax are split between these two industries on the basis of value of product. The share of Other Wood Products is augmented by an estimated amount of these products made in the "Miscellaneous manufacturing" classification (see below).

(5) The *Statistics of Income* major classification "Paper, pulp, and products" is divided between Paper and Wood Pulp and Other Paper Products. Both interest paid and net income after tax is split on the basis of value of product.

(6) The *Statistics of Income* major classification "Printing and publishing" corresponds to our Printing and Publishing Industry. Both the interest paid and the net income after tax figures are taken as given.

(7) The *Statistics of Income* major classification "Textiles and textile products" is divided among Yarn and Cloth, Clothing, and Other Textile Products. Interest paid is split on the basis of value of product. Net income is given for various subdivisions (*Statistics of Income, 1929*, p. 289): (*a*) Clothing: consists of "Clothing, etc." (serial no. 22) plus an estimated (on basis of value) amount for furs (included in "Textiles n. e. s., etc.," serial no. 21). (*b*) The remaining net income (after tax) of this group is apportioned to Yarn and Cloth and Other Textile Products on the basis of value of product.

(8) The *Statistics of Income* major classification "Leather and leather products" is divided among Leather Tanning, Leather Shoes, and Other Leather Products. Interest paid is split on the basis of value of product. Net income is given for two subdivisions (*Statistics of Income, 1929*, p. 289): (*a*) Leather Shoes: consists of "Boots, shoes, slippers, etc." (serial no. 24). (*b*) The remaining net income after tax ("Other leather products, gloves, saddlery, etc.," serial no. 25) is divided between Leather, Tanning, and Other Leather Products on the basis of the value of product of each of these industries.

(9) The *Statistics of Income* major classification "Rubber and related products" corresponds to our Rubber Manufactures Industry, and both the interest paid and the net income after tax figures are used as given.

(10) The *Statistics of Income* major classification "All other manufacturing industries" is included mainly with Industries Not Elsewhere Specified. Interest paid is split among Industries Not Elsewhere Specified, Other Wood Products, and Other Iron and Steel Industries on the basis of value of product (to the latter two industries, only that share of value of product is assigned which is included in the classification "All other manufacturing industries" — a very small share in each case). Net income is given for various subdivisions separately (*Statistics of Income, 1929*, p. 291): (*a*) Industries Not Elsewhere Specified: consists of "Musical instruments, optical goods, canoes, etc." (serial no. 52) less an estimated (on basis

of value of product) amount assigned to Other Wood Products (for musical instruments, brooms, and brushes). To this is added (to get the total amount) the share to Industries Not Elsewhere Specified from other groups (see above) for manufactured ice and precious metals, etc.

(11) The mining industries: S. Kuznets, *National Income, 1929–32*, p. 214, gives data on interest paid by the mining industries which is better subdivided for our purposes than the *Statistics of Income* data (although Kuznets' data comes from the Bureau of Internal Revenue). (*a*) Coal: interest paid — from Kuznets; plus net income after tax — from *Statistics of Income, 1929*, p. 288, "Anthracite coal" (serial no. 4) and "Bituminous coal, lignite, and peat" (serial no. 5). (*b*) Petroleum and Natural Gas: interest paid from Kuznets; plus net income after tax from *Statistics of Income, 1929*, p. 288, "Oil and gas" (serial no. 6), plus an estimated (on basis of value) amount from the *Statistics of Income* subgroup "Gas companies, natural and artificial" (serial no. 64). (*c*) Iron Mining and Non-Ferrous Metal Mining: grouped together under "Metal mining" both in Kuznets and in *Statistics of Income* (serial no. 3). The share of "Metal mining" going to each is estimated both for interest paid (from Kuznets) and for net earnings after tax (from *Statistics of Income*) on the basis of value of product.

(12) Our group Non-Metal Minerals includes both manufacturing and mining and quarrying operation. For manufacturing, the *Statistics of Income* major classification "Stone, clay, and glass products" corresponds to our group, and both the interest paid and the net income after tax figures are used as given. For mining and quarrying, interest paid is taken from Kuznets ("Non-metallic and others"; see 11 above); net earnings after tax from *Statistics of Income, 1929*, p. 288, including "Other minerals — Asbestos, etc." (serial no. 7) and "Mining and quarrying n. e. s., etc." (serial no. 8). (These two groups are identical with the corresponding Kuznets group.)

(13) For the Manufactured Gas Industry, interest paid is used as computed by Kuznets, p. 220 ("Gas companies, artificial and natural") and net earnings after tax from *Statistics of Income, 1929*, p. 292, for the same subgroup (serial no. 64). A small deduction is made for natural gas included (see above, 11-b).

(14) Electric Utilities: Data for interest paid for electric light and power companies, telephone and telegraph companies, and electric railways and motor busses are from Kuznets, pp. 217 and 220. Data for net earnings after tax for the above component industries are from *Statistics of Income, 1929*, pp. 291 and 292 (serial nos. 58, 63, and 65). Since "Electric railways" (serial no. 58) includes some activities not included in our group Electric Utilities (such as Pullman cars, etc.), only that portion of this subgroup is included (both

for interest paid and net earnings) which pertains to electric railways. This amount is estimated on the basis of the value of product of electric railways and motor bus operation (as computed by us for our own group) and the gross income of the *Statistics of Income* subgroup as a whole (serial no. 58).

. *To* Construction: Interest paid and net earnings after tax from *Statistics of Income, 1929.* The *Statistics of Income* major group "Construction" differs from ours because of the inclusion of "Shipbuilding and repairing." Both interest paid (amount estimated on basis of value) and net earnings (p. 291, serial no. 56) for shipbuilding are subtracted (the deduction is small compared with the total amount involved). Finally, as in the case of manufacturing and mining, the results thus obtained for corporate enterprises only are stepped up so as to cover the construction industry as a whole (see "Gross Total Outlays" below). *To* Transportation (Steam Railroads): Interest paid by all corporations (from S. Kuznets, *National Income 1929–1932*, p. 217) plus net earnings after tax for corporations reporting net income (from *Statistics of Income, 1929*, p. 291, serial no. 57). *To* Consumption: comprises rentals paid for leased non-farm homes (W. H. Lough, *High-Level Consumption*, Appendix A), plus capital and entrepreneurial income derived from personal services (see Wages and Salaries: *To* Consumption). *To* Undistributed: includes (*a*) dividends and interest paid by water transport, motor transport, air transport, railway express, Pullman Company, wholesale trade, retail trade, and miscellaneous industries; dividends paid by commercial banking, life and other insurance, and real estate; interest on individuals' mortgages, interest paid on government service (federal, state, county, and city); net rentals of individuals; property income originated in the service industries; withdrawals by individual entrepreneurs from retail trade, wholesale trade, service, and miscellaneous industries; and business savings of individuals in wholesale trade, retail trade, recreation and amusement, professional services, and business services. (All of above data are from S. Kuznets, *National Income, 1929–1932*), *plus* (*b*) undistributed corporate savings (note that undistributed individual savings have been included under (*a*) above). Undistributed corporate savings are estimated from data in *Statistics of Income, 1929*, as follows: Compiled net profits after deducting tax for *all* corporations reporting net income with the exception of "Agriculture and related industries"; *minus* cash dividends paid by these corporations (p. 273, line 1). From this figure (which gives estimated corporate savings for all industry except agriculture), those corporation savings already distributed by us to industries 2–41 (see Gross Total Outlays, below) are subtracted (this final figure gives undistributed corporate savings); *minus* (*c*) capital and entrepreneurial services charged to consumption (see above: an adjustment was made here, because (*a*) above does not include *all* these services charged to consumption). Although the theory and the results are the same as in the 1919 distribution, the procedure is somewhat different, due to a change in the data used. In 1929, it is not necessary to add back the aggregate corporate deficit of undistributed industries (as was done in 1919), since all our previous data are free from deductions on account of firms reporting deficits (e.g. our corporate savings estimate is based only on corporations reporting net income).

44a: Taxes

Taxes paid are listed separately in the Census of *Mfr.* for 1919, but not for 1929. Thus, for 1929, the Undistributed values are not subdivided into Taxes and Others.

1919. Taxes Paid by Agriculture: estimate made by W. I. King (*The National Income . . .*). Taxes paid by manufacturing industries and mining (from Flour and Grist Mills to Industries Not Elsewhere Specified, excluding Electric Utilities); federal, state, county, and local, including excises, as reported in *Mfr.* and *Min.* Taxes paid by the Electric Utilities: comprise corporate income, war profit, excess profit, and other domestic taxes as listed in *Statistics of Income* (Bureau of Internal Revenue). Taxes paid by Construction: include the same items as taxes paid by Electric Utilities. Taxes paid by consumers: comprise income taxes, direct personal property taxes, poll taxes, licenses, and fees for personal activities. Estimate taken from W. H. Lough, *High-Level Consumption*.

44b: Other Undistributed

1919 and 1929. Each item represents the difference between the Gross Total Outlays and the total of all other items included in each column.

45: Gross Total Outlays

The definition of the concept of Gross Total Outlays, as well as the general outlines of its statistical derivation, is given on pp. 28ff above. The following comments are limited to description of actual statistical calculations.

1919. To Agriculture: this item is obtained by adding the value of the total product (22,147 million dollars) as given in row 1 to the estimated net increase in agricultural indebtedness between the beginning and the end of the year 1919.

According to data presented in the *Federal Reserve Bulletin* (April 1936) the increase in agricultural mortgage indebtedness amounted in 1919 to four or five hundred million dollars. Agricultural loans by commercial banks expanded between July 31, 1918, and December 31, 1920, from 3517 million dollars to 5317 million dollars, which gives an average annual increase of 720 million dollars. Augmenting this sum by the 400 million dollars of new mortgage credits, we have 1120 million dollars as the total of additional agricultural credits. To obtain a net figure, it will be necessary to subtract from this amount that part of the mortgage credit which originated in financing sales of agricultural land by non-farmers. Furthermore, the increase in bank savings and other non-agricultural financial investments by the farm population has also to be taken into consideration. Neither of these items can be determined with any degree of accuracy. Thus the gross total of 1120 million dollars is simply reduced to 900 million dollars, 220 million dollars being allowed for the two items mentioned above.

To Manufacturing Industries and Mining (from Flour and Grist Mills: *To* Industries Not Elsewhere Specified, with exception of Electric Utilities): the aggregate additional corporate investment is obtained by combining the data on corporate savings as estimated by W. I. King (*The National Income . . .*) with the statistics of new capital issues (stock and bond, excluding refunding) compiled by the *Commercial and Financial Chronicle.* The distribution of this total among the separate industries is based upon the analysis of the financial statistics of approximately 2000 corporations covered in the *Source Book for the Study of Industrial Profits,* compiled by Ralph C. Epstein and published by the Department of Commerce.

The increment in the total capital investment between 1919 and 1920 is calculated for each particular industrial group as represented among these 2000 corporations. In order to make the industrial groups of the sample representative, the relative size of each of them is brought into accord with the relative size of the respective total industries. This was accomplished in two steps: first, the capital increase within each sample industrial group was related to the value of product (sales) as given for the identical sample; i.e., the capital increase per dollar of output (sales) was calculated. Next, the ratios thus obtained are weighted by the total corporate product of each particular industry as given in the Census, and each of these weighted ratios was expressed as a proportion of the sum of such weighted ratios. Finally, after these two steps were taken, the estimate of the *relative* corporate capital increase within the different industrial groups is applied to the sum total of new investment.

The capital increase as calculated for each industry must be further augmented by the total of the deficits for the corresponding industry (as given in *Statistics of Income,* published by the Bureau of Internal Revenue). According to conventional accounting principles, these are charged against the net income of profitable corporations but in our set-up (see p. 26) the offsetting influence of deficits has to be eliminated, which means that they have to be "added back."

The last stage in these calculations consists in stepping up the results which apply only to the corporate part of the industry so as to include all producers covered in the Census. The ratio between the total output of each separate industry and that part of it which was produced by corporations is used as a multiplier in each case.

The "Gross Total Outlays" were obtained by adding the new capital investment in each industry as derived above to the value of its total product.

To Electric Utilities: the total is obtained by adding to the total value of product new stock and bond issues (estimate taken from W. I. King, *The National Income . . .*) and additional corporate surplus, roughly estimated at 15 million dollars. *To* Construction: no attempt is made to estimate additional stock and bond issues or additions to undistributed surplus. Thus this item represents the total output of the industry increased by the total deficits of corporate construction enterprises (*Statistics of Income*, Bureau of Internal Revenue). *To* Railroads: total of new issues, additions to undistributed surplus (W. I. King, *The National Income . . .*), augmented by total corporate deficit (*Statistics of Income*, Bureau of Internal Revenue), added to the total value of product. *To* Exports: total exports of domestic products augmented by domestic transportation costs charged to imported goods (see Transportation: *To* Exports). *To* Consumption: total consumption expenditures, i.e., total consumers' spendings and withholdings (received income), less savings as estimated in *High-Level Consumption* by Lough. *To* Undistributed: total of undistributed products and services listed in column 44.

1929. *To* Agriculture: this item is obtained by deducting the estimated net decrease in agricultural indebtedness (266.6 million dollars) between the beginning and the end of the year 1929 from the total value of product (15,487.7 million dollars) as given in row 1. Three credit elements are considered in obtaining the decrease in agricultural indebtedness: (*a*) the *Federal Reserve Bulletin*, April 1936, p. 224, states that personal and collateral loans to farmers by commercial banks declined from 2943.8 million dollars as of December 31, 1923, to 1936.4 million dollars as of June 30, 1931, making an average annual decrease of 134.3 million dollars, which is assumed to be the decrease during 1929. (Note that loans of commercial banks secured by farm real estate are *not* included in these totals.) (*b*) the *Agricultural Finance Review* (Department of Agriculture), May 1939, vol. 1, no. 1, p. 76, states that the total farm-mortgage debt declined from 9468.5 million dollars as of January 1, 1928 to 9214.3 million dollars as of January 1, 1930, making an average annual decrease of 127.1 million dollars, which is assumed to be the decrease during 1929. (*c*) According to data in the *Farm Credit Quarterly* (Farm Credit Administration), March 31, 1936, p. 16, loans to coöperatives and short term credit outstanding by institutions under the supervision of the Farm Credit Administration decreased 5.2 million dollars from December 31, 1928 to December 31, 1929. (Note that farm mortgage loans are *not* included in this total.) The total of these three items (266.6 million dollars) is taken as representing the net decrease in agricultural indebtedness. No allowance is made for changes in the amount of bank savings and other non-agricultural financial investments by the farm population.

To all industries from Flour and Grist Mill Products to Transportation (Steam Railroads), inclusive: for each industry, total new corporate investment is obtained by adding corporate savings and new outside corporate investment. This total capital increase for corporations is stepped up so as to include all producers covered in the Census. Ratios between the total output of each separate industry and that part of it which was produced by corporations are used for this purpose. Finally, the "Gross Total Outlays" are obtained by adding the new capital investment in each industry (corporate and non-corporate) as derived above to the value of its total product ("Gross Total Output" in Tables 5 and 6).

Corporate savings are obtained as follows: (1) For Electric Utilities: cash dividends are deducted from compiled net profit less total tax for electric railways (S. Kuznets, *National Income, 1929–1932*, p. 218), electric light and power companies (Kuznets, p. 220), and telephone and telegraph companies (Kuznets, p. 221). The net total for these industries is equivalent to net corporate savings. To these are added the deficits of the corresponding industries (*Statistics of Income, 1929*, pp. 291–292, lines 58, 63, and 65). Even after the addition of deficits, the electric railways industry shows negative corporate savings, which are disregarded in computation of total corporate savings. (2) For Manufactured Gas: no corporate savings are distributed to this industry, because cash dividends exceed compiled net profits less total tax (Kuznets, p. 220). If this negative figure is diminished by adding deficits (*Statistics of Income, 1929*, p. 292, line 64), the result is still negative. These negative savings are disregarded, and corporate savings for this industry are taken as zero. (3) For Transportation (Steam Railroads): see "For Electric Utilities" above. Net profits less tax and cash dividends are from Kuznets, p. 218; the deficit which is added back is from *Statistics of Income, 1929*, p. 291, line 57. (4) For all remaining industries mentioned above: for these industries, data are from *Statistics of Income, 1929*. Cash dividends are subtracted from compiled net profits less tax. It is not necessary to add back deficits here, since we use cash dividends and net profits less tax data *only* for those corporations reporting net income. (In the case of the industries previously described, Electric Utilities, Manufactured Gas, and Transportation, it is necessary to add back deficits, because the net profit less tax less cash dividends taken from Kuznets *includes* firms reporting deficits. This is also true of the data used in the 1919 distribution, wherefore deficits are added back. Although the procedure differs for most industries in the 1929 distribution because of this difference in the basic data used, the theoretical setup and the results are the same for both years. This applies also to our distribution of Capital and Entrepreneurial Services — see p. 156 above.) Since the *Statistics of Income* classification of industries differs from ours in many respects, it is often necessary to resort to estimates in order to break down the official statistics to subdivisions corresponding to ours. This breakdown is described above in connection with the distribution of net income (after tax) to Capital and Entrepreneurial Services. Since *Statistics of Income* does not contain data on cash dividends for the individual industries included in each of the major classes, it is necessary to estimate corporate savings for each of our industries (cash dividends being the unknown factor). This is accomplished by dividing corporate savings for each major *Statistics of Income* class (i.e., net profits less tax less cash dividends for corporations reporting net income) among the industries in our classification in proportion to our distribution to them of net earnings after tax. (For Rubber, Printing and Publishing, and Non-Metal Mineral Manufactures, no adjustment is necessary, because the *Statistics of Income* major classes coincide in entirety with ours.)

New corporate investment is obtained as follows: the basic data are from "Security Issues and Real Investment in 1929," by George A. Eddy (*Review of Economic Statistics*, May 1937, vol. XIX, no. 2, pp. 79–91), particularly Table 3, p. 85, labeled "Real investment issues" which is based on an exhaustive analysis of new capital issues data published by the *Commercial and Financial Chronicle*. The purpose of Eddy's revision of these data is to classify as "real investment issues" only those issues which can with reasonable certainty be classed as used for new investment. (1) For Transportation (Steam Railroads): 160.5 million dollars, as specified by Eddy for this purpose. (2) For Automobiles: 30.0 million dollars as specified by Eddy for "motors and accessories." (3) For Rubber: 48.3 million dollars specified for "rubber manufactures." (4) For Electric Utilities and Manufactured Gas: Eddy indicates that the total real investment in Public Utilities was 594.2 million dollars in 1929. This is divided between Electric Utilities and Manufactured Gas in proportion to our distribution to them of Capital and Entrepreneurial Services. Computed on this basis, the share to Electric Utilities is 552.2 million dollars and to Manufactured Gas, 42.0 million dollars. In addition, the share to Electric Utilities is increased by 153.4 million dollars, which, according to Eddy (p. 89) is the amount of securities sold by electric light and power companies directly to consumers. (These results are found to correspond closely to data on p. 82 of Eddy's article, where the larger real investment issues are given by companies.) (5) For Petroleum and Natural Gas and Refined Petroleum: Eddy states that the total real investment in "oil" amounted to 124.9 million dollars in 1929. This total is divided between Petroleum and Natural Gas (25.9 million dollars) and Refined Petroleum (99.0 million dollars) in proportion to our distribution to them of Capital and Entrepreneurial Services. (Because of the great amount of vertical integration in the "oil" industry, even if data were available for all individual borrowing corporations, it would be almost impossible to split the aggregate real investment exactly between these two industries. Furthermore, an indeterminable part of this new investment went probably for wholesale and retail distribution outlets.) (6) For Iron Mining, Blast Furnaces, Steel Works and Rolling Mills, Non-Ferrous Metal Mining, Smelting and Refining, Non-Metal Minerals (mining only), Coal, and Coke: Eddy states that the total real investment in 1929 for "iron, steel, coal, copper, etc." was 55.4 million dollars. The share to coal is 12.0 million dollars, which is a bond issue of the Pittsburgh Coal Co. (Eddy, p. 82, Table 2). The remaining real investment of this group is divided among the other industries cited above in proportion to our distribution to them of Capital and Entrepreneurial Services. (7) For industries from Flour and Grist Mill Products to Other Food Industries, inclusive; for Other Iron and Steel Industries, Brass, Bronze, Copper, etc., and Non-Metal Minerals (Manufacture); and for Lumber and Timber Products to Other Leather Products, inclusive: Eddy states that real investment for "equipment manufactures," "other industrial and manufacturing" and "miscellaneous" was equal to 472.0 million dollars in 1929. For distribution to these industries, the share to "miscellaneous" is halved, leaving a total of 418.4 to be distributed. A stock issue of 13.8 million dollars by the American Tobacco Co. (Eddy, p. 82, Table 2) is distributed to Tobacco. A 50.0 million dollar stock issue by the Union Carbide and Carbon Corporation and a 36.3 million dollar issue by the American Cyanide Company (Eddy, p. 83, Table 2) are assigned to Chemicals. A 25.8 million dollar stock issue by the Eastman Kodak Company (Eddy, p. 82, Table 2) — to Industries, n.e.s. The remaining undistributed 292.4 million dollars are divided among the other industries listed above in proportion to our distribution to them of Capital and Entrepreneurial Services. (These results correspond closely to data on p. 82 of Eddy's article, where the large real investment issues are given by companies. From this check it may be concluded that at least 60 per cent of our distribution is fairly accurate; lack of information makes it impossible to check the remaining 40 per cent).

To Exports: total exports of domestic products augmented by domestic transportation costs charged to imported goods (see Transportation: *To* Exports). *To* Consumption: consumers' savings and imputed net rental values are deducted from total consumers' outgo (data are from Lough, *High-Level Consumption*, pp. 236, 243, and 246). *To* Undistributed: total of undistributed products and services listed in column 44.

APPENDIX III
BASIC TABLES

TABLE 1. — $\dfrac{\Delta_{10i.kk}}{\Delta_{10i}}$ 1919.

k \ i	1	2	3	4	5	6	7	8	9	10
1		+ .989	+1.009	+1.010	+ .793	+1.022	+ .460	+ .962	+ .972	+1.049
2	+ .974		+ .933	+ .998	+1.001	+ .992	+ .962	+ .938	+ .981	+1.030
3	+ .987	+ .937		+ .895	+ .957	+ .786	+ .771	+ .932	+ .872	+1.132
4	+1.025	+ .874	+ .977		+ .979	+ .929	+ .914	+ .989	+ .985	+1.045
5	+ .997	+1.014	+1.008	+1.017		+1.025	+ .896	+1.024	+ .866	+1.044
6	+ .942	+ .893	+ .978	+ .887	+ .988		+ .934	+ .980	+ .969	+1.041
7	+ .972	+1.003	+1.034	+1.044	+ .884	+1.056		+ .967	+1.037	+1.070
8	+ .994	+ .961	+ .969	+ .963	+ .912	+ .993	+ .775		+ .891	+1.054
9	+2.568	+ .627	+ .600	+ .613	+ .990	+ .793	+1.493	+ .989		+2.406
$\dfrac{\Delta_{ki}}{\Delta_{10.10}}$	+ .378	+ .049	+ .267	+ .120	+ .207	+ .107	+ .078	+ .245	+ .072	+1.000

TABLE 2. — $\dfrac{\Delta_{104.kk}}{\Delta_{104}}$ 1929. First Classification of Industries

k \ i	1	2	3	4	5	6	7	8	9	10
1		0.998	1.007	1.012	0.887	1.019	0.687	0.990	1.003	1.031
2	0.990	0.941	0.930	0.992	0.990	0.985	0.924	0.930	0.989	1.029
3	0.953	0.887		0.907	0.933	0.794	0.654	0.903	0.928	1.098
4	0.988	0.887	0.976		0.971	0.954	0.851	0.979	0.959	1.048
5	1.005	1.005	0.995	0.993		1.011	0.948	1.016	0.996	1.020
6	0.945	0.889	0.965	0.892	0.986		0.936	0.969	0.974	1.038
7	0.982	0.985	1.023	1.032	0.883	1.039		1.000	1.024	1.052
8	0.969	0.975	0.975	0.978	0.949	1.001	0.869		0.889	1.105
9	0.783	1.431	0.678	0.765	0.673	1.169	0.717	0.691		1.197
$\dfrac{\Delta_{kk}}{\Delta_{10.10}}$	0.274	0.061	0.245	0.159	0.147	0.100	0.079	0.282	0.743	1.000

TABLE 3.— $\dfrac{D_{104.kk}}{D_{104}}$ 1919. FIRST CLASSIFICATION OF INDUSTRIES

k \ i	1	2	3	4	5	6	7	8	9	10
1		0.932	0.911	0.995	1.092	0.833	0.779	0.960	0.948	1.179
2	1.223		1.156	1.100	1.202	1.085	1.150	1.173	1.150	1.224
3	1.235	0.695		1.052	1.192	0.878	1.161	1.100	0.980	1.298
4	1.266	1.113	1.129		1.251	0.979	1.233	1.182	1.131	1.289
5	0.942	0.947	0.947	0.999		0.999	0.622	0.999	0.955	1.152
6	1.104	1.017	0.952	0.985	1.100		1.090	1.062	1.039	1.117
7	1.664	1.670	1.758	1.841	1.938	1.833		1.867	1.927	2.158
8	1.116	0.763	0.946	1.012	1.130	0.977	1.000		0.944	1.204
9	1.233	0.625	0.597	0.911	1.169	0.817	1.078	0.669		1.380
$\dfrac{D_{kk}}{D_{10.10}}$	.444	.092	.348	.170	.257	.131	.341	.295	.802	1.000

k \ i	1	2	3	4	5	6	7	8	9	10
1		0.863	0.872	0.959	1.000	0.766	0.737	0.889	0.886	1.043
2	1.069		1.042	1.013	1.069	0.990	1.033	1.050	1.038	1.080
3	1.216	0.675		1.070	1.172	1.007	1.109	1.088	1.024	1.247
4	1.179	1.070	1.034		1.171	0.866	1.029	1.102	1.083	1.194
5	0.984	0.960	0.962	0.978		0.971	0.740	0.973	0.958	1.066
6	1.158	1.060	0.996	1.074	1.130		1.120	1.096	1.086	1.146
7	1.006	0.956	0.961	1.004	1.064	1.009		1.039	1.054	1.117
8	1.135	0.626	0.922	1.021	1.130	0.939	0.941		0.966	1.202
9	1.262	0.644	0.680	0.841	1.170	0.733	0.994	0.640		1.368
$\dfrac{D_{44}}{D_{10.10}}$	0.313	0.086	0.369	0.238	0.187	0.148	0.113	0.381	1.036	1.000

TABLE 5. $\dfrac{dP_{t10}}{dA_k} \cdot \dfrac{1}{P_{t10}}$ 1919. FIRST CLASSIFICATION OF INDUSTRIES

i \ k	1	2	3	4	5	6	7	8	9	10
1	−1.049	−0.060	−0.040	−0.039	−0.256	−0.027	−0.589	−0.087	−0.077	0.000
2	−0.056	−1.030	−0.097	−0.032	−0.029	−0.038	−0.068	−0.092	−0.049	0.000
3	−0.145	−0.195	−1.132	−0.237	−0.175	−0.346	−0.361	−0.200	−0.260	0.000
4	−0.020	−0.171	−0.068	−1.045	−0.066	−0.116	−0.131	−0.056	−0.060	0.000
5	−0.047	−0.030	−0.036	−0.027	−1.044	−0.019	−0.148	−0.020	+0.178	0.000
6	−0.099	−0.148	−0.063	−0.154	−0.053	−1.041	−0.107	−0.061	−0.072	0.000
7	−0.098	−0.067	−0.036	−0.026	−0.186	−0.014	−1.070	−0.103	−0.033	0.000
8	−0.060	−0.093	−0.085	−0.091	−0.142	−0.061	−0.279	−1.054	−0.163	0.000
9	+0.162	−1.779	−1.806	−1.793	−1.416	−1.614	−0.913	−1.417	−2.406	0.000
10										

k \ i	1	2	3	4	5	6	7	8	9	10
1	−1.031	−0.033	−0.024	−0.019	−0.144	−0.012	−0.344	−0.041	−0.028	0.000
2	−0.039	−1.029	−0.099	−0.037	−0.039	−0.044	−0.105	−0.099	−0.040	0.000
3	−0.145	−0.157	−1.098	−0.191	−0.165	−0.304	−0.444	−0.195	−0.170	0.000
4	−0.060	−0.161	−0.072	−1.048	−0.077	−0.094	−0.197	−0.069	−0.089	0.000
5	−0.015	−0.015	−0.025	−0.027	−1.020	−0.009	−0.072	−0.004	−0.024	0.000
6	−0.093	−0.149	−0.073	−0.146	−0.052	−1.038	−0.102	−0.069	−0.064	0.000
7	−0.070	−0.067	−0.029	−0.020	−0.169	−0.013	−1.052	−0.052	−0.028	0.000
8	−0.136	−0.130	−0.130	−0.127	−0.156	−0.104	−0.236	−1.105	−0.216	0.000
9	−0.414	+0.234	−0.519	−0.432	−0.524	−0.028	−0.480	−0.506	−1.197	0.000
10										

TABLE 7. $\dfrac{dX_{i10}}{dA_k} \cdot \dfrac{1}{X_{i10}}$. 1919. FIRST CLASSIFICATION OF INDUSTRIES

k \ i	1	2	3	4	5	6	7	8	9	10
1	+0.2926	+0.1873	+0.1619	+0.2340	+0.3147	+0.0893	+0.0333	+0.2025	+0.1899	0.0000
2	+0.0647	+0.0299	+0.0196	−0.0343	+0.0453	−0.0411	+0.0098	+0.0291	+0.0087	0.0000
3	+0.2371	−0.2331	+0.1207	+0.0806	+0.1946	−0.0709	+0.1824	+0.1252	+0.0134	0.0000
4	+0.1022	−0.0040	+0.0061	+0.0638	+0.0982	−0.1188	+0.0895	+0.0471	+0.0048	0.0000
5	+0.0289	+0.0489	+0.0466	+0.0887	+0.1513	−0.0939	−0.2612	+0.0891	+0.0477	0.0000
6	+0.1044	+0.0303	−0.0341	−0.0048	+0.0995	+0.0630	+0.0948	+0.0684	+0.0462	0.0000
7	−0.1306	−0.0759	−0.0429	−0.0145	+0.0104	−0.0020	+0.0090	+0.0008	+0.0313	0.0000
8	+0.1808	−0.1384	+0.0318	+0.0884	+0.1920	+0.0611	+0.0786	+0.1268	+0.0243	0.0000
9	+0.2959	+0.0684	−0.0518	+0.1401	+0.2019	+0.1611	+0.3203	−0.0792	−0.7184	0.0000
10										

TABLE 8. $\dfrac{dX_{i10}}{dA_k} \cdot \dfrac{1}{X_{i10}}$ 1929. FIRST CLASSIFICATION OF INDUSTRIES

k \ i	1	2	3	4	5	6	7	8	9	10
1	+0.232	+0.088	+0.098	+0.185	+0.228	−0.008	−0.036	+0.116	+0.114	0.000
2	+0.054	+0.038	+0.033	+0.004	+0.054	−0.016	+0.024	+0.039	+0.027	0.000
3	+0.237	−0.237	+0.129	+0.115	+0.197	+0.066	+0.156	+0.133	+0.071	0.000
4	+0.156	+0.072	+0.036	+0.115	+0.149	−0.111	+0.111	+0.094	+0.075	0.000
5	+0.071	+0.052	+0.053	+0.067	+0.120	+0.061	−0.163	+0.062	+0.047	0.000
6	+0.082	+0.071	−0.024	+0.045	+0.092	+0.064	+0.089	+0.066	+0.056	0.000
7	−0.021	−0.062	−0.059	−0.020	+0.034	−0.012	+0.022	+0.014	+0.028	0.000
8	+0.230	−0.237	+0.039	+0.129	+0.226	+0.057	+0.056	+0.163	+0.076	0.000
9	+0.673	+0.148	+0.172	+0.308	+0.591	+0.223	+0.452	+0.130	+0.547	0.000
10										

TABLE 9. $\dfrac{dX_{i10}}{dB_k} \cdot \dfrac{1}{X_{i10}}$ 1919. FIRST CLASSIFICATION OF INDUSTRIES

k＼i	1	2	3	4	5	6	7	8	9	10
1	+0.127	+0.213	+0.132	+0.146	+0.123	+0.054	−0.050	+0.121	+0.099	0.000
2	+0.049	+0.039	+0.012	−0.054	+0.018	−0.059	−0.004	+0.019	−0.004	0.000
3	+0.117	−0.243	+0.099	+0.014	+0.064	−0.110	+0.133	+0.062	−0.058	0.000
4	+0.067	+0.004	−0.010	+0.043	+0.042	−0.160	+0.074	+0.023	−0.028	0.000
5	−0.070	+0.065	+0.027	+0.037	+0.044	+0.077	−0.330	+0.047	−0.007	0.000
6	+0.057	+0.040	−0.045	−0.032	+0.043	+0.057	+0.073	+0.045	+0.022	0.000
7	−0.314	−0.138	−0.100	−0.067	−0.060	−0.015	−0.020	−0.031	+0.019	0.000
8	+0.072	−0.141	+0.002	+0.028	+0.066	+0.043	+0.026	+0.067	−0.040	0.000
9	+0.283	+0.075	−0.063	+0.131	+0.179	+0.167	+0.328	−0.101	+0.283	0.000
10	−0.365	+0.025	−0.075	−0.195	−0.405	−0.075	−0.175	−0.185	−0.205	0.000

TABLE 10. $\dfrac{dX_{i10}}{dB_k} \cdot \dfrac{1}{X_{i10}}$ 1929. FIRST CLASSIFICATION OF INDUSTRIES

i \ k	1	2	3	4	5	6	7	8	9	10
1	+0.078	+0.090	+ .057	+ .103	+ .079	− .036	− .092	+ .044	+ .022	0.000
2	+0.020	+0.038	+ .023	− .017	+ .022	− .025	+ .011	+ .023	+ .005	0.000
3	+0.106	−0.256	+ .097	+ .042	+ .068	+ .043	+ .113	+ .073	− .014	0.000
4	+0.073	+0.080	+ .012	+ .073	+ .069	− .146	+ .088	+ .058	+ .024	0.000
5	−0.012	+0.055	+ .032	+ .024	+ .042	+ .049	− .198	+ .025	− .001	0.000
6	+0.068	+0.142	− .042	+ .017	+ .042	+ .060	+ .076	+ .044	+ .025	0.000
7	−0.070	−0.065	− .075	− .047	− .010	− .023	+ .006	− .008	+ .000	0.000
8	+0.074	−0.250	− .005	+ .045	+ .075	+ .028	− .002	+ .093	− .020	0.000
9	+0.279	+0.166	+ .062	+ .088	+ .203	+ .160	+ .332	− .075	+ .328	0.000
10	−0.488	−0.006	− .139	− .268	− .472	− .096	− .181	− .232	− .311	0.000

TABLE 11.

k	$\dfrac{d\beta}{dA_k}$		$\dfrac{d\beta}{dB_k}$		$\dfrac{d}{dA_k}\left(\dfrac{1}{A_n}\right)\left(=\dfrac{\Delta_{k,k}}{\Delta_{n,n}}\right)$	
	1919	1929	1919	1929	1919	1929
1	− .011	+ .002	− .126	− .082	+ .378	+ .274
2	− .009	− .003	− .026	− .022	+ .049	+ .061
3	− .015	− .015	− .098	− .096	+ .267	+ .245
4	− .006	− .007	− .048	− .062	+ .120	+ .159
5	− .009	− .002	− .073	− .049	+ .207	+ .147
6	− .005	− .005	− .037	− .039	+ .107	+ .100
7	− .029	− .004	− .096	− .029	+ .078	+ .079
8	− .010	− .008	− .083	− .099	+ .245	+ .282
9	− .193	− .018	− .227	− .270	+ .072	+ .743
10			− .222	− .258	+1.000	+1.000

TABLE 12. $\dfrac{dX_{t10}}{dA_k} \cdot \dfrac{1}{X_{t10}}$ 1929. THIRD CLASSIFICATION OF INDUSTRIES

k \ i	1	2 + 3a	3b	4	5	6	7	8	9	10
1	+.2276	+.0722	+.2143	+.2857	+.2205	−.0100	−.0169	+.1168	+.1060	.000
2 + 3a	+.2047	+.1116	+.1714	+.0646	+.1910	+.0160	+.0518	+.1094	+.0550	.000
3b	−.0634·	−.1435	−.0623	−.0861	−.0952	−.1032	−.0799	−.0865	−.1095	.000
4	+.1589	+.0202	+.1588	+.1125	+.1620	−.1203	+.1403	+.0808	+.0670	.000
5	+.0639	+.0342	+.0838	+.0595	+.1160	+.0717	−.1917	+.0578	+.0440	.000
6	+.1155	−.0246	+.0991	+.0402	+.1105	+.0617	+.0854	+.0676	+.0460	.000
7	−.0688	−.0941	−.1212	−.0589	−.0127	−.0505	−.0215	−.0319	−.0135	.000
8	+.2245	−.0492	+.2183	+.1550	+.2388	+.0771	+.0467	+.1620	+.0725	.000
9	+.6575	+.1161	+.5537	+.3312	+.5661	+.2249	+.4777	+.1327	+.5280	.000
10										

TABLE 13. $\dfrac{dP_{i10}}{dA_k} \cdot \dfrac{1}{P_{i10}}$. 1929. THIRD CLASSIFICATION OF INDUSTRIES

i \ k	1	2+3a	3b	4	5	6	7	8	9	10
1	−1.070	−.064	−.070	−.058	−.192	−.046	−.393	−.086	−.129	.000
2+3a	−.162	−1.113	−.373	−.207	−.177	−.324	−.435	−.271	−.191	.000
3b	−.013	−.010	−1.009	−.008	−.024	−.113	−.105	−.014	−.017	.000
4	−.062	−.090	.069	−1.047	.081	.093	.195	.071	.078	.000
5	−.013	−.024	.077	.013	−1.024	.007	.084	.016	.025	.000
6	−.091	−.077	.088	.146	.054	−1.037	.104	.067	.064	.000
7	−.071	−.039	.029	.022	.176	.015	−1.059	.059	.035	.000
8	−.146	.134	.145	.137	.185	.111	.245	−1.110	.219	.000
9	−.462	.545	.570	.480	.575	.380	.527	.557	−1.245	.000
10										

TABLE 14. $\dfrac{dX_{i10}}{da_{nk}} \cdot \dfrac{a_{nk}}{X_{i10}}$ 1929. FIRST CLASSIFICATION OF INDUSTRIES

k \ i	1	2	3	4	5	6	7	8	9	10
1	+ .619	− .096	− .099	− .141	− .192	− .020	+ .001	− .106	− .103	.000
2	− .002	+ .039	− .001	+ .000	− .002	+ .002	− .000	− .001	− .001	.000
3	− .091	+ .067	+ .211	− .027	− .049	− .010	+ .033	− .028	− .017	.000
4	− .068	− .022	− .006	+ .416	− .065	+ .062	− .043	− .031	− .023	.000
5	− .047	− .023	− .033	− .046	+ .718	− .041	+ .049	− .044	− .030	.000
6	− .014	− .003	+ .004	− .005	− .013	+ .144	− .012	− .008	− .007	.000
7	+ .006	+ .014	+ .011	+ .006	− .004	+ .003	+ .179	− .000	− .004	.000
8	− .086	+ .083	− .018	− .048	− .087	− .020	− .013	+ .288	− .029	.000
9	− .336	− .066	− .099	− .148	− .291	− .099	− .225	− .055	+ .223	.000
10										

INDEX

Acceleration principle, application in dynamic input-output system, 212

Aggregation, and correlation, 210; in input-output technique, 208–211. *See also* Industries

Bill of goods, determination of 1929, 153; direct and indirect contributions to, 141; effect on employment, 159–160; in statistical computation of outputs and employment, 143f.

Business conditions, 10

Capital and entrepreneurial services, distribution, 24, 232–238; estimates, 27. *See also* Deficits, Investment, Saving, Industry: *Households*

Capital stock, use in dynamic input-output model, 211–214

Coefficients, constancy of, 150–152, 158–159, 177–178, 201–202, 204, 214f.; derivation of technical, 204–205; labor input coefficients, 144–152; technical coefficients in analysis of interrelationship of profits, prices, and taxes, 188–195

Consolidation of accounts, 14, 69, 124, 125–132

Consumption, adjustment, 47; bill of goods, 154; coefficients, 42, 132–136

Cost-of-living, index and changes in, 197f. *See also* Prices

Costs, accounts, 11f.; computed variations compared with actual, 118; statistical determination of total, 156–161; structure affecting output reactions, 89, 97f.; structure affecting price reactions, 87; total, measuring the size of an industry, 86; variations, 58; variations theoretically computed, 115–118

Deficits, accounting, 20, 26. *See also* Capital and entrepreneurial services

Demand, final, definition of, 206; in dynamic input-output system, 213–214; treatment of exports and domestic demand in, 169–172. *See also* Bill of goods

Demand and supply analysis, versus general equilibrium analysis, 5

Dynamics, basic data, 42; open system, 213–214; use of stocks in input-output system, 211f.; versus statistics, 33

Efficiency, *see* Productivity

Employment, effects of foreign trade on, 163f., mathematical formulation, 173f., variation in results, 178–186; primary and secondary effects of, 178–186; relationship with output and national income, 141–142; statistical computation of, 143–152; total and direct coefficients, 159–160

Equilibrium, application of general equilibrium theory to empirical analysis of economy, 202f.; external and internal relationships, 203–204; general, homogeneity of equations, 46, 49; general versus partial, 33; partial versus input-output technique, 204; stationary, 35; theory, 33–51

Exports, *see* Industry: *Foreign trade*

Households, *see* Industry: *Households*

Imports, *see* Industry: *Foreign trade*

Income, influence of flow on output, employment, and national income, 142, 147. *See also* National income

Industries, classification, 14, 20f., 23, 42, 69f., 99, 126–132, 162–163, 187–188; change in classification, 195n.; consumers and producers goods, 99; effect in prediction analysis, 156–157, 159; effect of relative size, 86, 88, 92–93, 97

Industry: *Agriculture,* computed change in the investment coefficient, 115; as consumption goods industry, 99, 102; computed productivity change, 113; distribution of products, 142–145; effect of changed investment coefficient, 93; effects of productivity changes, 84, 87, 94, 96f., 104–105, 129; labor and capital services, 27; output